The Curse of History

The Curse of History

Jeremy Black

THE
SOCIAL
AFFAIRS
UNIT

British Library Cataloguing in Publication Data
A catalogue record of this book is available from the British Library

Printed and bound in the United Kingdom

ISBN-13: 978-1-904863-29-8

Social Affairs Unit
314 322 Regent Street
London W1B 5SA
www.socialaffairsunit.org.uk

For
Peter Lilley

CONTENTS

BIOGRAPHICAL NOTE

Jeremy Black is Professor of History at the University of Exeter. Graduating from Cambridge with a Starred First, he did postgraduate work at Oxford and then taught at Durham, eventually as Professor, before moving to Exeter in 1996. He has lectured extensively in Australia, Canada, Denmark, France, Germany, Italy, Japan, the Netherlands, New Zealand and the USA, where he has held visiting chairs at West Point, Texas Christian University and Stillman College. A past council member of the Royal Historical Society, Black is a fellow of the Royal Society for the Encouragement of Arts, Manufactures and Commerce, a senior fellow of the Foreign Policy Research Institute and a trustee of Agora. He was appointed to the Order of Membership of the British Empire for services to stamp design.

He is, or has been, on a number of editorial boards, including the *Journal of Military History*, the journal of the Royal United Services Institute, *Media History* and *History Today*, and was editor of *Archives*.

His books include *War and the World, 1450–2000* (Yale), *The British Seaborne Empire* (Yale), *Maps and History* (Yale) and *European Warfare in a Global Context, 1600–1815* (Routledge).

PREFACE

> History is full of examples where people who had right on
> their side fought against tremendous odds and were victo-
> rious. And it is also full of examples of people passively
> hoping to wait it out, only to get swallowed up by a horror
> beyond what they ever imagined. The future is unwritten.

The advertisement cited above for The World Can't Wait movement's 5 October march, published in the mass-circulation *USA
Today* on 20 September 2006, and directed against the Bush
government and the American commitment in Iraq, is certainly
instructive for historians. It offers yet another instance of the
commonplace tendency to seek validation in the arms of Clio,
the muse of history. This search for validation and quest for justification in the past is of particular note at the present. It joins such
unlikely bedfellows as Tony Blair and Osama bin Laden and is
widespread across the political spectrum and around the world.

The significance of this tendency to look to the past is less
clear. It can be seen as a product of a lack of confidence in the
future and one that contrasts markedly with the situation in the
1960s, or, alternatively, as a construction of the future in terms of
a continuity with the past. The latter can be linked to the marked
assertion of religious identities that has attracted greater attention
since the end of the Cold War, for religions tend to be heavily
historicist in character. More generally, a sensible desire to learn
lessons from the past, and, in doing so, to appreciate the difficulties of learning lessons, is not prominent in the quest for historical
justification.

In the following study, I seek to focus on some of the aspects
of what is, at once, the kaleidoscopic variety of readings of the
past and yet also the tension between those readings that unite

people and those that divide. The weight of the past in framing senses of identity and, at the same time, in fuelling the politics of grievance, is the theme of this book. It will offer a wide-ranging and up-to-date account, and the emphasis will very much be on these characteristics, as there will be an attempt to link the analysis to current issues and disputes, in short to make the book relevant, which is a key characteristic of the public history under discussion.

Should collective grief become public policy? The central thesis of the book is that there is a politics of grievance that runs through the political uses of history around the world and that, overall, this is a bad thing because, politically, it splits communities rather than drawing them together, while, historically, it leads to distorted and monolithic interpretations. The emphasis on the past for identity and grievance creates serious problems for academic historians, as their quizzical and critical stance is not suited to the assertiveness about the past that is central to these stances. This will doubtless cause difficulties at the individual level in the classroom, with committed and intolerant students complaining about being asked to read or listen to different views. More serious is the extent to which competing views of the past will also make any public account of it necessarily divisive. As a result, the presentation of history is a potential threat to public order, and thus safety. If this is also true of tensions at the international level, competing views of the past also threaten to undermine culturally federative schemes such as the European Union (EU). The challenge there is far greater than that posed in the United States of America (USA) by rival interpretations of the past, although the nature of federation is also controversial in the USA.

As a result of competing views of the past, British politicians can expect to be under steady pressure, both domestic and international, to apologise for Britain's history. Aside, however, from the questionable character of such apologies, they also will feed empowerment through grievance, aggressive victimhood, and the divisiveness of the past. For the Conservatives, this process of apology is a particular challenge as they have traditionally claimed a role as guardian of national identity, not least as an aspect of their stress on patriotism, unionism (between England

and Wales, Scotland and Ireland) and continuity. Moreover, politicians and others can expect to be ambushed by interviewers asking about historical questions that may seem irrelevant but that will be overly important to sections of the electorate. Kashmir's recent history may not feature as an issue in Bournemouth, but it does in Birmingham due to the number of concerned immigrant households there.

For me, this is a strange book to write, indeed a troubling one. A sense of the past as a living force has always been important to my work, and, at times, the sub-Burkean note has been markedly in the ascendant. In my Eurosceptical *Convergence or Divergence? Britain and the Continent* (1994), I claimed that 'a sense of place and continuity is crucial to the harmony of individuals and societies' and closed 'In defending the configuration and continuity of British practices, politicians are fighting not for selfish national interests but for the sense of the living past that is such a vital component of a people's understanding, acceptance and appreciation of their own society and identity.'[1]

From this perspective, to argue the case for the curse of history must appear peculiar, not to say perverse. I hope, however, that the following makes clear that my target is not the Burkean notion of a bond and trust between the generations, one that has been so important to the moral dimension of Conservatism, and a concept that the Left has yet to match, but, rather, the idea of empowerment through grievance and, in particular, the locating of both grievance and empowerment in a misleading, as well as destructive, historical context.

Linked to this is my concern about the prevalence of 'history wars', which can be seen as the heavily historicised equivalent of what the Americans call 'culture wars'. If cultures take on meaning in terms of time passing, and if memories of the past are crucial in fixing and framing thought, this meaning and thought are all too often destructive. History in these cases serves not only as the metaphor of causes but also as their substance.

Thus, there is a confusion in this book that reflects the Janus-faced character of the past, at once the solace of continuity and the sore of grievance. Moreover, as an additional source of complexity, memory and history vie as interpreters of the past, each able to take either approach; continuity and grievance. In society at large, memory is generally dominant. To add to the complexity, memory and history are not necessarily different. Instead, there are histories in which memory is the key component and means of exposition.

The curse of history is an ambiguous phrase. It is, at once, the remembered past as a curse for today, and yet also history as a necessary, indeed benign, process that, however, has to bear the curse not so much of contrasting accounts of the past as of malign and hostile readings of it. Although it is easy to separate the two conceptually, there is no such ready separation in practice. What to one commentator is a malign reading is necessary to another. It is easy to take one's own history, indeed national myth, as benign, as well as a source of strength and social cohesion, and, instead, to be more critical of those of others. Conversely, it is possible to be hypercritical of one's own history and not to show comparable, or any, criticism of the history of other countries. Both tendencies are seen in Britain, in the press, in public opinion and in the establishment.

Yet, accepting that relative views exist does not mean that judgement should be discarded. Instead, it opens up a richer field for discussion. Not least, the role of historical myths, and related 'history wars', in nationalism leads to the question whether such myths are a necessary basis for identity. This study probes aspects of nationalism, not least the tension between civic and ethnic nationalism.

It is also appropriate to ask whether these historical myths are more important for authoritarian states that have to allege a destiny through time, past, present and future, because they cannot readily rest on the present consent that is crucial to the democratic process. Yet, democracies themselves require an identity and a sense of value that is greater than that of elections; which are only episodic referenda. This can also be seen with political parties. They can find legitimacy in heritage, as with Conservatives vying for who succeeds to the mantle of Thatcherism.

A focus on identity also raises the issue of what is a nation, a question that is particularly pressing in a world affected by very high rates of migration. Does a nation amount to more than whoever lives in a state at a particular moment? Whether the answer is yes or no, how does the use of the past serve to define and integrate the resulting population, both at that moment and in the future?

I would very much welcome the response of readers to this discussion of the historical spectrum we all share.

After an introduction, a historical chapter about nationalism, and a chapter on some prominent 'history wars', presented as different case studies, the book is divided into chapters on a geographical basis. These chapters can be read in a different order to that offered, but the organisation rests on a plan. The issues and problems of creating a new history for countries freed from imperial control and, in the case of eastern Europe, a totalitarian ideology, link Chapters 4 and 5. Chapter 6 then directs attention to western Europe, before Chapter 7 assesses transoceanic states of primarily European antecedents, principally the USA but also Australia, New Zealand and Canada.

The typescript was commented on by Ian Bickerton, John France, Maria Fusaro, John Gascoigne, Bill Gibson, Ken Hendrickson, Nicholas Henshall, Malcolm McKinnon, Peter Mandler, Rana Mitter, Thomas Otte, Murray Pittock, Keith Robbins and Keith Windschuttle, while sections of it were read by Gabor Agoston, Michael Bregnsbo, Roger Burt, Erhard Busek, Harald Kleinschmidt, Stewart Lone, Geoff Rice and Mark Stocker. I have benefited from advice from, or from discussing 'history wars' with, Kenneth Baker, Simon Barton, Daniel Branch, Alexander Evans, Brenda Laclair, Timothy May, Anna-Maria Misra, Tim Rees, Karin Sidén, Tim Simmons and Adair Turner. None is responsible for any errors in what follows. Liz O'Donnell proved a most helpful copy-editor.

I would also like to thank the Social Affairs Unit and the *New Criterion* for inviting me to speak at their conferences in Winchester (2006) and New York (2007), the Historical Society and the Templeton Foundation for a similar invitation for London (2007), the European Leadership Centre for inviting me to speak at a conference in Bled (2007), Burgh House and Hampstead Museum for inviting me to speak on the slave trade (2007), and Jimmy Carter for sending a copy of *The Hornet's Nest*. I also benefited in 2007 while working on this book from visiting Denmark, Estonia, Finland, Germany, Greece, the Netherlands, Norway, Russia, Slovenia, Sweden, Switzerland, Turkey and the USA. This book takes forward some of the arguments in *Maps and History: Constructing Images of the Past* (1997) and *Using History* (2005) and profits from the opportunity to lecture to the history foundation course at the University of Exeter.

It is a great pleasure to dedicate this book to Peter Lilley, a fascinating and considerate conversationalist, a quick and incisive intellect and a stalwart and eloquent defender of Conservative truths of freedom and opportunity.

CHAPTER 1

INTRODUCTION
ACADEMIC AND PUBLIC HISTORIES

IRISH OPENINGS

In May 2007, soon after becoming First Minister of Northern Ireland, the normally splenetic Ian Paisley, the most prominent exponent of Protestant Ulster Unionism, paid his first official visit to the Republic of Ireland. The trip was richly symbolic but also indicated how events could be differently interpreted. Paisley visited the site near the river Boyne where William III, William of Orange, the new Protestant ruler of Britain, defeated his Catholic predecessor James II in 1690, a battle that settled the fate of Ireland for over two centuries. This visit appeared to echo the annual celebrations of the battle by Protestant Orangemen in Northern Ireland, celebrations that, at once, underline Protestant unity, present it in an aggressive, indeed bellicose, fashion and offend Catholics. Previous anniversaries had led some Catholics in Northern Ireland to resort to violence, and even terrorism, in order to block the celebratory marches.

At the same time, the presence, as Paisley's host, of the Irish Prime Minister Bertie Ahern provides a very different assessment of Paisley's visit. Ahern claimed the battle of the Boyne as an aspect of 'a shared and complex history' and located it in terms of the international conflict of the period, the Nine Years' War (1688–97). This was an accurate contextualisation[1] but not one often advanced, still less understood, in the sectarian dissension of Northern Ireland. Moreover, Ahern correctly pointed out that Catholics and Protestants had fought on both sides of the war. He also sensibly pressed the need to acknowledge history in its complexity, arguing that this was owed to the future, adding 'We cannot change what went before, on this ground or across these islands, but history can take many turns'.

The Republic's willingness to engage with the long period of Protestant Ascendancy in Ireland, an age of oppression in the traditional historical account of Irish Catholic nationalism, was further exemplified by the Irish government's conversion of nearby Oldbridge House into a world heritage centre intended to strengthen new relations between Northern Ireland and the Republic. The Boyne was no longer seen as extraneous to this process but, instead, as something that had to be part of it, an occasion and memory that had to be accepted before a united history could be offered. This episode captured an ambiguity in the use of history as, at the same time, the divisive reiteration of past episodes and the opportunity to offer a less divisive interpretation. More generally, of late, Irish governmental and cultural institutions have gone out of their way to present a complex, multifaceted history. Indeed, in 1999, Orange marches resumed in Dublin, and the Lady Mayoress donned the 'white horse' badge of King Billy (William III).

Also in May 2007, on the 15th, references to history were much in evidence when Ahern, then engaged in a bitter, and eventually successful, re-election campaign, became the first Irish Prime Minister to address both Houses of Parliament in London. Ahern described his visit with Paisley as 'an act full of the symbolism of new days of hope and promise in Ireland'. More generally, he called for history to be made, not repeated, a Blairite theme: 'Now let us consign arguments over the past as we make history, instead of being doomed to repeat it. Violence is part of our shared past that lasted too long. Now we close the chapter, we move on, and it will remain there as it was written'.

History was also presented by Ahern as offering a guide to the future for the whole world: 'Reconciliation has brought us closer [. . .] This is the great lesson and the great gift of Irish history. This is what Ireland can give to the world'. Ahern and Tony Blair, then still British Prime Minister, coated each other with flattery – and understandably so given the welcome cessation of violence and the hard work that had gone into it. Ahern said that Blair had a place 'in Irish hearts and in Irish history', while Blair, in contrast, in his cloying mateyness, proved more ready to present the past as disposable:

In a curious way, Bertie and I symbolise the past – him from a staunch Irish republican background, me whose maternal grandfather was an Orangeman living in Donegal. Yet today we are friends and partners and close neighbours.

Suddenly, in a few short years, our countries have shuffled off all the old and disagreeable sentiments and replaced them with affection founded on a modern and shared vision of these islands. At long last, both nations seem to have found comfort in a shared future.

History as difficult legacy, history as the process of change, history as progenitor of the future: all were present in what were deliberately presented as symbolic acts. They represented a worthwhile aspiration for change but one that is possibly belied by the continued strength of sectarianism, encapsulated in the faith-based schooling that Blair, ironically, more generally promoted. Given that neither Blair nor Ahern could know the future, however much they might want to predict it, their statement about the historic lacked what would have been an accurate tentative note, but, to be realistic, that note is rarely the sound of politics.

PUBLIC HISTORY

The public use of history has indeed become more widespread and urgent in recent decades. Since 1945, over 120 new states have been created, each of which has had to define a new public history, while earlier states have been transformed, in part thanks to indigenous developments but, to a large extent, due to the pressures of often unwelcome outside pressure: invasions, wars and aggressive diplomacy all playing a major role in the collapse or transformation of the older states. National history is, in part, the record of this pressure and transformation and an attempt to come to terms with it. This transformation can be seen with new constitutional and political systems, as in Germany, Japan, Italy, France, eastern Europe, Russia and South Africa between 1945 and 1994.

At the same time, public histories, in both old and new states, have been, and are, contested due to different public voices, and this process is encouraged by the growth of public education and by the related democratisation of culture. Far from there being any 'Death of the Past' (J.H. Plumb, 1969) or 'End of History' (Francis Fukuyama, 1989), this process continues to be active and important, albeit at very different levels.

The past, indeed, can be presented, even conceptualised, as a living presence in order to deal with the travails and challenges of the present. Time travel offers a potent fictional form that has a power to grip the imagination. It can also be employed for didactic purposes as in a 2007 visit by Doctor Who to Shakespeare's London in which the Doctor informs his black companion that Africans then lived in London, thus helping to ground an idea of national identity that is of relevance today.

The theme of the past as a living presence was humorously probed in the film *Good Bye Lenin!* (dir. Wolfgang Becker, 2003), with its idea that it could be pretended that East Germany had really not ceased to exist. However, the reluctance to confront change satirised in that film is both widespread and, also, often a central aspect of an atavistic and dark identification in terms of the past.

In 1804–8, Francisco Goya painted *Truth, Time and History*, an allegorical canvas with symbolic figures representing each. Hanging prominently in the National Museum in Sweden,[2] the painting offers a benign and harmonious account of the relationship between these factors. Ironically, it also indicates the way in which interpretations can shift. First mentioned as *Truth, Time and History*, the painting was also known in the nineteenth century as *Spain, Truth and History*. In 1979, Eleanor Sayre related this painting to the adoption of the Spanish constitution in 1812 seeing the standing female form as 'Liberty'. For a while, the painting was called *Spain, Time and History*, the present, in this case, dictating the naming of the past. Sayre's interpretation has been since rejected, and the painting is now seen as an allegory of Truth, Time and History, with Time protecting Truth.

The relationship between truth, time and history, however, has been very different to that suggested by Goya, and this is not simply a matter of key episodes nor of major countries. Indeed, it is useful to begin not with one of those episodes and countries, but, instead, with a lesser episode. It indicates that controversies over the past do not have to lead to violence or sustained contention, but, nevertheless, also reveals their insistent presence and role. In 2005, indeed, the discussion of nineteenth-century rural social changes created a public furore in Scotland. The argument, advanced by Michael Fry, a prominent popular historian, that these social changes were not as harsh and disastrous as was once commonly believed, was bitterly criticised by those who grounded Scottish national identity on a sense of loss, suffering and victimhood, of 'foreign' (i.e., English) exploitation and domestic betrayal. Such a grounding is a frequent theme around the world and one that is useful to Scottish nationalists concerned to assert that being linked to England as part of Britain had been disastrous. One politician compared Fry to David Irving, a notorious Holocaust denier, while twenty-three members of the Scottish Parliament backed a motion criticising him for 'Clearances denial'.

This was not only a ludicrous comparison that reflected a paranoid failure to contextualise events and arguments but also a response to the extent to which grievance plays a major role in the culture and politics of Scottish nationalism and, indeed, of the sense of separate Scottish identity, a topic over which Labour politicians as well as their Scottish National Party (SNP) counter-parts are frequently active. SNP grievances frequently focus on the origins of Union with England, although the terms of griev-ance are historically flawed.[3] Victimhood is an important aspect and concept because it implies an absolution, explanation and blame for national 'failings'.

Looked at differently, and from a critical scholarly perspec-tive, there are extreme and jingoist views on the Clearances from a Scottish perspective, but Fry's book caused annoyance in part because it was intended to contradict almost all existing scholarly opinion without, in practice, refuting it. Indeed, far from being jingoist, the critical scholarly account of the Clear-ances is hardly the simplistic voice of Mel Gibson seen in the film *Braveheart* (1995), which deals with the far earlier war of independence. The continued role of the Clearances was shown in July 2007 when Scotland's First Minister, the Scottish Nation-alist leader, Alex Salmond, unveiled a statue to commemorate the victims. Erected in Helmsdale, Sutherland, it was matched by an

identical statue erected near Winnipeg, the Canadian city created by Scottish emigrants.

A far more significant aspect of contested public memory occurs in China, as a growing academic stress in the outside world on the iniquities and harshness of Mao Zedong's rule and regime clashes with the state orthodoxy. The latter was willing to admit to Mao's mistakes but not to the reality of what had been a very bloody, cruel and inefficient tyranny. This type of tension is widespread. In the case of China, public criticism eventually followed Mao's death in 1976. The Cultural Revolution that started in 1966 and formally ended under Hua Guofeng in 1976 (the crucial Red Guard phase ended in 1969), was officially condemned in 1981. The Gang of Four trial of radicals in 1980 and the official efforts to create a simulacrum of cathartic memory marked this breach.

Despite this, there is only limited discussion of the Cultural Revolution within China because the Communist Party does not like to see reference to its past mistakes. This is an Orwellian non-history that cries out for the light of Clio. When, in September 2006, a new history textbook for the senior secondary schools made little mention of Mao, or, indeed, of the mistreatment of pre-Communist China by foreign imperialists, this led to a furore that resulted in the book's recall the following year. The problem is that the current system of governance in China grounds its legitimacy totally on the Communist Revolution of the 1940s under Mao. Without recourse to this Revolution, the current Chinese state must be disclosed (as what it actually is) as a military dictatorship. Thus, the lack of willingness to address Mao's brutalities throughout his period of control is due to a core political dilemma and is not a contingent aspect of the sense of the past.

Discussion of the brutality and failure of the Cultural Revolution might lead to the expression of grievances, which could be seen as destabilising, but it would also provide a welcome airing of the faults of a totalitarian ideology that, in the shape of the Communist Party, remains all too potent in China. Thus, individual examples of the treatment of the past look in different directions, inviting contrasting judgements, and this introduces a powerful theme of subjectivity, one that is a major issue for this study. One observer's 'unnecessary indulgence of mistaken grievance' becomes another's 'appropriate aspect of public education'. Sometimes, this reflects a confusion that is at once conceptual, methodological and historiographical.

More generally, however, the complexity of judgement about the past that is part of the historian's lexicon is also relevant for the public treatment of the past. This is a very positive development: the complexity of judgement in part reflects the degree to which history is more open than it is presented in authoritarian societies. Moreover, this complexity is a product of the extent to which history, both the past and its presentation, was, and is, contested by different forces.

Charges of subjectivity are applied to historians when they work on the past, and they are trained to respond to the issue. These charges should not prevent them from employing their insights when considering the present, including, in this case, the current state of public histories. A similar courage and intelligent professionalism is called for from readers. An awareness of subjectivity, and also of the different conclusions that will be drawn, should not banish the willingness to apply critical judgement.

The situation is made more complex because it is inherently dynamic, with changes in the public use of history proving crucial to the general understanding of the past. These developments stem largely from current political shifts and pressures, the past being created by the present, rather than from academic activity, a point not appreciated by most academics. Thus, for example, the recent collapse of Communism across much of Eurasia was followed by a reorganisation of Communist parties, as in Poland, but, more obviously, by a recovery of non- and anti-Communist themes, topics and approaches. In Estonia, for example, it became possible, indeed appropriate, to emphasise the destructiveness of Soviet conquests in 1940 and 1944 and of the subsequent occupations and to discuss the many victims, as well as those who resisted. Although the historical legacy is different, not least with no foreign occupation, it will be instructive to see how far a process of re-presenting history occurs in post-Castro Cuba.

The role of public history in politics is significant, not least because it is central to, or regarded as central to, issues of national identity and political legitimation. The contexts, or, at least, frames of reference, for the two overlap but are also different. The context is often a long-term one, as in England with references to Magna Carta (1215) by critics of Charles I (r. 1625–49). Such a long-term frame of reference now seems anachronistic to most of the English public but when, for example, members of the Polish Parliament from two populist parties occupied the Chamber in 2002, they were criticised for reviving what were seen as the anarchic traditions of the old Polish Commonwealth. This was a very charged comparison. Anarchic impulses were seen as a significant factor in the weakness of this Commonwealth that led to, and made possible, the partitions of Poland by Austria, Prussia and Russia in 1772–95, partitions that removed Poland as a state from the political map of Europe until 1918. Thus, the description of these political parties was an accusation of selfish behaviour that amounted to national destruction.

TIME, EXPERIENCE AND HISTORY

Turning to a broader scenario, different societies, of course, have interpreted time in varied ways,[4] not least as a consequence of the diverse nature of creation and revival myths, and of ecclesiological accounts of time and of divine intervention. Religious accounts were of cultural weight (and remain so), and in societies that looked to the past for example and validation, societies that were indeed reverential of and referential to history, this weight was of great significance.[5]

Issues of divine intervention and religious purpose remain central in some societies. Indeed, in traditional East Asian Buddhist cultures, it is impossible to separate past from present. Hence, a non-partisan, neutral, academic approach to the past as practised by many historians, for example in Japan, is an aspect of the Westernisation project that has been going on for about 150 years. It is unclear, however, that the cultural and ideological impact of this project is as powerful as a Western perspective might suggest.

Public history today across most of the world, especially in the West, however, is less defined by, and expressed in, religious accounts than in the nineteenth century and before. Instead, public history is, in large part, a product of broader patterns of experience, such as shifts in collective memory, and of social change – for example, the rise of literacy (although in Muslim countries this is linked with a religious resurgence), as well as of the specific experience of conflict and survival. These patterns of social experience and change create narratives and analyses (and related issues and problems) that are somewhat different from those that predominate in Western academic circles.

In part, this is a matter of method, which itself is of wider significance. There is a particular tension between popular and academic approaches over the role of contingency and of human agency. Popular narratives generally rely upon the drama of human agency: people make history. For a long time, there was an emphasis on exceptional 'persons' making history, a theme celebrated in the influential European genre of history painting,[6] as well as in fictional and supposedly factual accounts of the hero, such as Thomas Carlyle's *On Heroes, Hero-Worship, and the Heroic in History* (1841). This emphasis continued into the twentieth century,[7] but has since become less prominent in a Western society that, in part, has become uneasy with martial values, although the hero does not have to be martial, as Gandhi, Mandela and Havel all show. In 2007, Ken Livingstone, the Mayor of London, suggested that a statue of Gandhi be erected in Trafalgar Square.

Instead of focusing on the historical hero, ordinary people constitute history in the case of the most popular form of historical research and private recollection, genealogy and family history. Thus, the definition of the curse of history offered me by one academic friend – that the bulk of people do not signify and, indeed, are actively ignored by those who determine or mould historical processes – is, to an extent, counteracted by the popular interest in themselves and their ancestors reflected in family history.

ACADEMIC AND POPULAR HISTORIES

Progress and salvation through liberal and Christian activism were key languages of history as it developed as an intellectual discipline in the nineteenth-century West. They are both outmoded discourses now, the first decried as Whig history, the second overthrown with the collapse of the Christian meta-narrative,[8] but, partly as a result, there is a major tension between academic and popular approaches to the past. In contrast to popular accounts, academic historians, now drawing frequently on the social sciences, often emphasise the structural aspects of situations. However, the resulting focus on determinism, on the apparently necessary consequences of these structures, can be purchased at the expense of a role for the choice and contingency that much of the public, instead, see as more pertinent.

The popularity of contrasting approaches to the past is more generally an issue, as seen in the very differing responses to developments in academic historiography. For example, although the French *Annales* approach to history, with its emphasis on social structures and economic pressures, was highly influential in the academy after 1945, it has had very little impact on popular views other than, indirectly, through encouraging 'bottom-up' perspectives of history, which provide an emphasis on particular individuals and communities. Similarly, the public has often shown limited appetite for the more fractured, complex discussions of the past produced by Western scholars.

Instead, a crude and unilinear approach is frequently taken by those explicitly writing for the public. For example, an article by the British journalist Gerard Baker in *The Times* on 25 May 2007 included the passages 'In the broader Middle East the war that was supposed to turn history in America's direction seems to have done the opposite [. . .] All we've really learnt in the past five years is that even the US is probably not powerful enough to remake 700 years of history in five years'. The latter is a curious remark, as it implies that the past is an undifferentiated force, and is also self-serving in that it overlooks the extent to which American policies may have been responsible for the problems being experienced. In short, like many who emphasise structural factors, Baker underplays agency and mistakes its relationship with structure, a feature also apparently shared, judging only by the sample of their works I have read, by Muslim fundamentalists. A unilinear approach is also conducive to those who wish the past to provide lessons and to be exemplary, which is what religious-inspired writers seek.

In contrast to those who offer certainty, academics seek to provide the best explanation of present evidence, a course that offers probably true knowledge but not knowledge that is true in an absolute sense outside of time, certainly as far as explanation is concerned. Thus, research can only offer increasing plausibility and, while scholars can counter bad history, they cannot provide more than a partial grasp of the past. This is a situation that is unsatisfactory from a populist perspective and, also, that is not sought by those who offer apparently definitive answers in their books and lectures.[9]

A related divide between public interest and academic fashion focuses on objectivity. Popular history is meant to be 'ours', which means that it cannot by definition be objective, but it assumes the possibility of objectivity or, at the minimum, detachment. Academic historians used to share these ideas, and many still do. Others, however, influenced by the 'linguistic turn' in historiography, consider the possibility of objectivity in a world in flux to be epistemologically naïve.[10] Moreover, the contrasting use of oral-history sources exemplify tensions between popular and academic history, with popular history proving less critical in the employment of such material, as it seeks to provide a 'bottom-up' history focused on individual experience, or on collective practice understood in these terms.

This is an aspect of the degree to which history operates as a form of cultural reconstruction, both producing and disseminating cultural memory, so that communities 'develop an understanding of who they are and where they come from',[11] and what they think. Identity, therefore, is an aspect of history and traditions, and the latter two, in turn, become an aspect of identity. Thus, for example, the concept of Zeitgeist (spirit of the age), which is much employed, explicitly or implicitly and in both academic and public history, to describe the supposedly dominant set of ideas (for example, Thatcherism) is, in practice, subjective. Like the public, historians indeed interpret the concept in their own ways and reflecting their own preoccupations.

At the same time, national identity, like the Zeitgeist, cannot only be charged with myth but can also arise from political and propaganda struggles that entail the development and sustaining of enmities in order to create and emphasise identity. Dissolution, however, can overlap with construction, for, underlining the extent to which historical identity is intertwined with contention, both academe (the academic world) and the public can also challenge state-sponsored historical fictions.

Public history is a topic rich in intellectual and pedagogic possibilities but academics' teaching and writing about history tends, in contrast, frequently to reflect a self-referencing fascination with the technical aspects of research and, even more, the epistemologies of history. Academics are accustomed to seeing themselves as the drivers of historical assessments and trends – for example, the rise of comparative or 'transnational' history. They are mistaken. The academic approach is becoming less prominent, not only due to the nature of public history but also with the rise of media (so-called secondary intellectuals) in which it plays little role. Each of these changes are aspects of the degree to which history is a social activity and one in which this social dimension relates not solely to the reception or consumption of historical ideas, works and notions but also to their production. The academic may like to feel separate from this process but is mistaken to do so. This social dimension contributes powerfully to the preference for what appears to be a single, clear, historical truth.[12]

A limited role for the academic approach is certainly the case with the Internet. Whereas academic publishing and presentation were, and are, a section of the worlds of book and (albeit to a lesser extent) television history, and, in part, helped to validate them, the Internet is different. The contrast is also apparent with archives, with official archival systems now supplemented (and thus, in part, challenged) by online archives, such as the digital community archives developed in Britain from 1994, as well as the Nations' Memorybank, which went public in Britain in May 2007, and the Canadian Letters and Images Project.[13]

Such online activity 'from below' has been joined by an increased habit, 'from above', of consulting the public in ranking national events and icons. For example, in 2006, the Department for Culture, Media and Sport asked the public, in the project 'Icons: A Portrait of England', to choose and vote on their favourite symbols of English culture. These are aspects of a democratisation of history that very much reflect present concerns,[14] while, at the same time, repeating the extent to which, in a democratic country, the resulting understanding of history varies. In the USA, popular 'icon' polls put Ronald Reagan at the top of the twentieth-century presidents, but academic political history does just the opposite.

Democratisation is not the sole factor. There is also a downplaying, if not denial, of history as a linear process, and its replacement, instead, by a focus on memory. Memory offers a punctuated past in which time does not take a linear form. Such a punctuated past can be seen as a 'presentist' history that is deliberately framed in terms of individual memory, with memory, moreover, serving as intuition and impression and not as precise record. More generally, presentism, the construction of the past in terms of the present, is a process in which the implications of democratisation as a social dimension are joined by the governmental direction of the depiction of the past. The latter is most obviously seen in totalitarian states, where folk and intuitional history are both manipulated.

Currently, as a result of the emphasis in the West on the value of popular memory, the past loses authority to the present, a key point, as it is the present-day individuals who are remembering who define the memory. Memory also collapses any role supposedly presented, by teleology, for the future, or reinterprets it in terms of individuals and their families – for example, in terms of narratives of betterment or resettlement, each of which is very important, and notably in the USA, where they are also significant in fiction.

Whether this shift towards a focus on present attitudes and concerns is primarily social in character (the rise of individualism), or cultural (a different attitude to time), or political (the decline of the nation-state and of collective narratives of race and class), is open to speculation. Memory also provides a linkage in terms of family groupings, with the key stages being parents and grandparents. The major boom in genealogy extends this process, not least by helping create memory.[15] Memory is also influenced by the mass media. For example, in Britain, the role of women in the Home Guard during the Second World War was 'forgotten' by those involved through watching the popular series *Dad's Army* on the television. In that sense, popular meant influential.

The desire for memory says something distinctive about humanity in general. In some respects, memory is a return to the earlier quality of identity and history as mythic and myth, and at the level of individuals and families as well as at that of society as a whole. The electronic media, for example, played a crucial role in creating at once an individual and a collective experience of the death of Diana, Princess of Wales in 1997: individuals watched television and thus participated.

The scrutiny of many individual and family accounts, however, indicates that there is a high level of myth-making in the shaping of the relationship to the past, not least in providing consistency and in demonstrating fortitude, heroism, victimhood and prescience. Study, as a call for detail and an introduction of qualifications and ambiguities, is generally not welcome in this process.

At the collective scale, the tension over myth-making is greater as there is the need to reconcile clashing myths. In November 2007, Ricardo Blásquez Pérez, the President of the Spanish Bishops Conference, pressed the right of all social and political groups 'to recall' their history, claiming that this would contribute to a true social cohesion: 'Collective memory cannot be selective. It is quite possible for different evaluations of the same event to exist side by side. If a genuine desire to discover what happened exists, these accounts will be reconciled.'

In the public domain, myths are more exposed to scrutiny. It would be difficult to go to a pit village in Yorkshire and tell families there which were torn apart by the strike that Britain had been making a dash for North Sea gas, that the trade unions had to be weakened for economic and political reasons, and that the National Union of Miners was poorly and destructively led. Historically, there is much to this argument. Possibly the miners' own narrative of their strike cannot be expected to accommodate this, but if they are to avoid living in a past of grievance they need to do so. At the same time, it is valuable to integrate popular folklore into the historical account in order both to appreciate the current resonances of past events and to capture aspects of the past.[16]

In short, this book is, in part, a call for maturity and a commitment worthy of a democratic society. People need to listen to alternative views and to seek historical objectivity and nuances in circumstances where history is, like rhetoric, used for essentially ideological purposes or, indeed, to deal with personal traumas. The aspiration may be naïve, but the alternative is one of closed minds, of communities trapped in atavistic hatreds based on remembered grievances.

This brings forward the more general question of the reputation of academic historians outside the profession. In recent decades, the idea of the intellectual, the practice of free speech, and the institutional autonomy of universities, combined to give Western academic historians a measure of independence within the wider context of the triumph of liberalism in the West in the aftermath of the Second World War. But, apart from the position further afield, which is considered in the next section, this situation is now under challenge in the West. Political and governmental pressures are serious. Both are in evidence in Britain, with the conflation of the different drives of political correctness and of the institutional funding, oversight and direction of research and the focus of research support on what is deemed appropriate and relevant. Political correctness usually comes today from the left, although in Australia, at least in part, it recently appeared to come from the right, with mainstream projects on gender and race being turned down for research grants by the Howard government after passing peer review. Like pressure elsewhere from the left, this highlights issues of accountability and permission in state-funded systems.

There are also those pressures that stem directly from popular interests and from the nature of public interest. Thus, if a branch of history is seen as less relevant, it can lose students and funding, the fate that has threatened ancient history in Britain. More generally, public interest can also challenge the contours of subjects. This is readily apparent in the case of religious history, where academic discussion of key aspects of Christian history was swamped in the mid-2000s by the outpourings stemming from Dan Brown's novel *The Da Vinci Code* (2004).

Conversely, academics today benefit from better funding and technology than a generation ago. The Internet, easy photocopying, digital resources and cheap air travel have all helped. Moreover, the past was always the golden age of academic conversation, but, at the institutional level, academic independence often meant in practice a lack of concern by universities about nurturing research.

THE SITUATION AROUND THE WORLD

Irrespective of this, and in contrast to the self-image of the modern Western academic, the role of the academic as the servant of the state is more important across much of the world, not least because free speech is limited, if not constrained, in many countries. It is likely that this role will become more significant in the future, especially if economic and political power, or a significant model of such power, increasingly focus in East and South Asia. Their academics depend on public funding and operate under the threat of censorship within a context in which the goal and content of most historical research and teaching are very sensitive: history is a crucial aspect of nationalism, and the problems arising from this are a key aspect of the curse of the past.

Recent controversies in China and Japan provide ample evidence of this process (see pp. 67–74). Advance word that the 2005 edition of *The New History Textbook*, created by the nationalist Japanese Society for History Textbook Reform, would remove 'any reference to matters associated with [. . .] "dark history" [issues such as the 'comfort women' or the rape of Nanjing in 1937] that might make Japanese schoolchildren uncomfortable' prompted demonstrations across China including angry Chinese stoning the Japanese Consulate in Shanghai. There was also anger about Japan's quest for a permanent seat on the United Nations' Security Council.

Outrage, not equivalence, was the issue. In Japan, issues such as textbooks are actively debated as well as mediated by the courts, with the Japanese Society for History Textbook Reform opposed by the Center for Research and Documentation on Japan's War Responsibility. Political partisanship played and plays a major role in bitter disputes over how to present the imperial period and, in particular, the Second World War. In the shape of the left-wing Japan Teachers' Union, created in 1947, there is a powerful educational lobby for a particular interpretation, that directed against nationalist revisionists.

The Chinese government, in contrast, of course washes propaganda through its schoolbooks and passes off the product as history; not that this invalidates Chinese perspectives, but it does draw attention to their moulding by government. Partly as a consequence of this moulding, recent polls have shown that China's young are more anti-Japanese than the generation that lived through the war.

Without eulogising the West, there is the question of whether the relationship between academic and public history in the West (also valid for Japan) is typical for the rest of the world – indeed, whether there can be global criteria for historiography, not least the free enquiry that is precious and is held up as a Western norm. Before continuing on this theme, it is important to underline that the Western approach itself faces serious problems. The teleological self-congratulation of Whig history is one, but another difficulty is posed by the self-image of the USA as the stadial[17] apotheosis of Europe and the only Enlightenment society. There are also more specific problems such as the Atlanticist myth of the Second World War.

The issue posed by the applicability of the Western model can be clearly seen in debates over the relationship between nationalism and objectivity. Scholars in the West divide over the possibility of recovering the past, but they generally subscribe to a desire to avoid nationalist partisanship and, as a related feature, there is considerable sensitivity about the dangers of portraying the national past in jingoistic terms or in what, however unfairly, could be seen thus. In Britain, for example, this led the Blair government to deny financial support to the Museum of the British Empire and Commonwealth, which, nevertheless, finally opened in Bristol in 2002. Looked at differently, this was (and is) a scholarly and balanced museum that was denied appropriate support because of misplaced sensitivity about Britain's role as an imperial power – an aspect of political correctness that remains all too powerful.

A determination to shun nationalist partisanship, however, means little in many states across the world, where partisanship and national identity are intertwined. This is a key theme of this book and yet also a difficulty as it is all too easy to neglect the value of national identities (which draw heavily on views of the past) and, conversely, to underplay the problems of other, and possibly alternative, levels and forms of identity, for example transnational or regional levels and racial or religious forms.

CONTENTION

It would be woefully mistaken to imagine that these are only issues in the developing world. In the USA, the controversy over the National History Standards, and, indeed, within academic circles, the unease that lay behind the establishment of the Historical Society in 1998 as a conservative alternative to the politically correct American Historical Association,[18] reflected the contentiousness of historical content and methods in *both* popular and academic circles (see p. 181). Yet, the very possibility of free debate over these issues contrasts with the situation in much of the world.

In Europe, there is considerable contention over the historical nature of its identity and culture (see pp. 140–1). Far from this being of only academic interest, the issue is very much to the forefront as Turkish accession to the EU is debated. This directly relates to such questions as the role of Christianity in European identity (an issue in the response to large-scale Muslim immigration) and also the nature of Turkish development in the twentieth century. The latter has been especially contentious in the case of persistent Turkish unwillingness to confront the Armenian Massacres, while there has also been European criticism of the nature of Atatürk's regime and legacy, which are crucial to the identity of the Turkish state (see pp. 63–7). This is balefully apparent in Istanbul, a once cosmopolitan city but one from which much of the non-Turkish population has left, in large part in response to discrimination which, in 1955, extended to riots with which the government connived.

In European settlement societies, particularly Australia, Canada and New Zealand and, to a lesser extent, the Andean States and the USA, there is also the question of how 'First Peoples' were treated. This was very much an issue in the New Zealand General Election of 2005, with the centre-right opposition

National Party criticising what its leader, Winston Peters, then termed the 'grievance industry' centred on Māori land claims. He promised an end to the numerous claims and the reversal of any legislation granting special privileges to Māoris (see pp. 201–5).

What is termed 'black armband' history with reference to the treatment of the Aborigines has also proved very contentious and divisive in Australia, and this contention has become more pronounced in recent years, linking to issues of national identity that have become politicised (see pp. 197–201).[19] Conversely, the 'grievance industry' can be regarded as an aspect of truth and reconciliation processes that often have been seen as fruitful, particularly in South Africa (see pp. 92–4).

More generally, history, as a record of achievement, real or alleged, plays a major role in political applause and abuse. Thus, in May 2007, Jimmy Carter claimed that George W. Bush's presidency was 'as far as the adverse impact on the [American] nation around the world the worst in history'. Such remarks are very frequent.

The use of history to make political points is frequently ahistorical, in that past episodes are taken out of their context and used as false analogies. Yet, this reflects the extent to which legacy is a complex area of memory, with politicians presenting stories that are different to those which historians wrote. Moreover, however ahistorical the use of history may be in the making of political points, the role of historical legacy in this form is also potent. This can be seen, for example, in the discussion of the use of the atomic bombs in 1945 on the subsequent attitude to nuclear weaponry. This discussion is particularly marked in Japan, where, on 6 August 2007, Shinzo Abe, the Prime Minister, used the anniversary of the attack on Hiroshima to make a speech underlining the country's commitment to a non-nuclear policy: 'The tragedies of Hiroshima and Nagasaki should never be repeated on any place on Earth'.

Moving away from this example, if what can be seen as ahistorical comments and conclusions reflect a tension over the values that historical writing is supposed to pursue, with accuracy often pulling in a different direction to relevance and accessibility, there is also a related problem about the use of the historical record. In recent decades, there has been a widespread trend to greater accessibility to government archives, and this has reflected a major shift in the relationship between state and public. The restrictive ownership of the past by government was limited by such steps as the French legislation of 1979 that provided for free access to most government archival material after thirty years. The American Freedom of Information Act of 1974 allows American citizens to request a review of classified material (many of the requests were related to UFO sightings), while in 1995, with effect from 2000,[20] automatic declassification after twenty-five years was introduced. Freedom of Information material released in the USA also came to throw much light on the policies of other states such as Britain. The focus of attention and contention shifted in many states to the material that was still not released, but the discussion about accessibility was now from a different background.

This, however, was largely a Western process. The situation was less benign elsewhere. Nevertheless, wherever it occurred, there was a threat that greater accessibility to historical material would lead to a wariness in documenting actions and views, lest subsequently they be judged both ahistorically and critically.[21]

Global demographics will affect public history around the world. Ninety-five per cent of the world's population increase is taking place in the developing world, and it is there that the pressures to provide a readily comprehensible public history will seem most acute, although it is also acute in countries with rapid population decline such as Russia. It is interesting to note, for example, how Indian politicians in the mid-2000s, both from the Congress government and the BJP (Bharatiya Janata Party) opposition, faced criticism as they addressed traditional suppositions about the unhelpful nature of British imperial rule (Nehru, the first Prime Minister from 1947 to 1964, had described it as overwhelmingly destructive), as well as the role of Pakistan. The welcome willingness of the current Congress Prime Minister Manmohan Singh to offer a good-and-bad account of British rule, rather than simple criticism, caused controversy.

In another former British colony, Kenya, there has proved an even greater willingness to express a sense of grievance based on alleged colonial mistreatment during the suppression of the Mau-Mau Rising of 1952–7. Far from this grievance abating, with the possibility of holding a mature debate, not least over the respective merits of those who cooperated with or opposed British rule, as indeed seemed possible at the time of the 2002 election, over-blown talk of British genocidal policies led to a raising of tension, and, in 2007, a legal case against the British government on the grounds of alleged negligence was pursued. This was intertwined with politics, with a corrupt and unpopular Kenyan government able to use the issue in order to seek nationalist endorsement and also to divert attention from British charges of corruption. The case was, in part, designed to help in electioneering.

CONCLUSIONS

Aside from the situation in other states, governments in developing countries feel a need to develop unifying national myths, especially as the liberation myths used in the immediate post-colonial period become less potent. A variety of factors make this more urgent: the volatility of societies in the developing world, with the relatively large percentage of their populations under the age of twenty-five; the disruptive impact of urbanisation and industrialisation; the breakdown of patterns of deference and social control; and pressures on established networks, identities and systems of explanation. There is also the challenge posed by particular constructions of ethnicity and religion within these states and, also, how they interact with historicised notions of national identity and development.

We need to devote more attention in historiography to the process of forging new public histories in the developing world on which, see Chapter 4. It will be both interesting and important to see how dynamic societies come to grips with their recent, and more distant, past. And this will probably be the most significant aspect of historiography over the next century. Unfortunately, as this book suggests, the past may well be defined in terms of hostilities, a practice that helps make sense of 'history wars' within and between countries. Indeed, to extend Winston Churchill's remark about the Balkans, the world may have more history than it can consume. This history is striking back.

CHAPTER 2

NATIONALISM AND THE CURSE OF HISTORY

NATIONALISM AND HISTORY

Identity requires assertion and differentiation. It is an active pulse, for, without feeling and expression, there is no identity. Furthermore, among the range of possible feelings and expressions on offer, there is competition; and the presentation of identity is a key aspect of this competition. Indeed, any account of nationalism in terms of the encapsulation and presentation of cultural myths and symbols[1] necessarily leads to an emphasis on the role of history.

The assertion of nationalism can be compatible with other, for example sub-national or international, identities, but they can also compete and, indeed, even be part of a zero-sum situation. Whatever the rhetoric, identity, nevertheless, is neither singular, nor exclusive, nor constant: a sense of collective self-awareness can include a number of levels or aspects of identification. These often develop or are expressed in opposition to other groups and their real or imagined aims and attributes, and these groups are frequently ones with which relations are close – for example, Britain and France, Canada and America, Australia and Japan.

At the same time, senses of identity are more amorphous, and also changeable, than the secular positivism implied by any stress on constitutions and laws might suggest. Thus, the antipathies just mentioned can be qualified or altered. What about, at the sub- or problematic-national level, Scotland and England, complementary or competing, rather than Britain – or Québec separate to Canada?

The chronological dimension also forms part of the equation, as time alters the meaning of identity. A long-established national identity, such as that of Sweden, has had the time to establish roots and become normative in a way that more recent nationalisms, for example that of Congo, will lack, and thus the latter will seem new, maybe weak, and possibly disruptive, if not destructive, even if their genesis is similar. This was very much a problem in the nineteenth century and post-1919 and has been again as new states were created in the post-1945 world, not that such new states and nationalisms were restricted to these periods.

From this perspective, nationalism is, in part, an aspect of revisionism, specifically a challenge to imperial hegemonies, and indeed this was important to the development of European nationalisms, as well as that of Japan in response to China. In the European Middle Ages, whatever the weakness of nationalism, not least as opposed to regionalisms such as Burgundian and Norman, what would later be seen as national ideas served in part as the language of difference when rejecting rule that could be stigmatised as outside and illegitimate. This was seen between 1290 and 1350 in Scottish, Flemish and Swiss resistance, respectively to the kings of England and France and to the Habsburgs.[2] Care, however, is needed on this point. For example, it is difficult to see 'Flemish' resistance as being mounted by 'the Flemish' as a would-be nation. Instead, resistance was mounted by local communities for diverse reasons throughout the period. Subsequently, this resistance would be presented in nationalist terms. For example, in what became Switzerland, the eulogisation of William Tell as a thirteenth- or fourteenth-century national hero opposing Habsburg rule belongs to the eighteenth century.

This idiom of identity politics and power was not restricted to what can be seen as 'small countries' resisting larger neighbours. Instead, these stronger rulers also found the language of nationalism necessary and valuable in opposing the equivalents of modern super- or hyper-powers, namely medieval claimants to universal empire. Such claims to sovereignty drew on a tradition that looked back to the authority and power of Imperial Rome and one that had been strengthened by the pretensions of the papacy to head the one, true, church. This Caesaro-papalism fused in the cooperation of Holy Roman Empire and papacy, and it was largely in opposition to this that arguments of national independence were advanced. Similarly, they were asserted by lay rulers, including the Holy Roman Emperors on behalf of a proto-Germany, against the jurisdictional, ecclesiastical and political pretensions of the papacy. In the nineteenth century, as academic and public national history became more prominent, criticisms of the overblown medieval papacy were common.

The pretensions of the papacy were contested in the Middle Ages, not in terms of a presentist legitimacy born of consent, but, instead, for example by Emperors Henry IV and Frederick Barbarossa, with reference to ideas of competing rights and privileges that were located with regard to the authority of the past. This was an authority that brought together both secular and ecclesiastical legitimacy, and, thus, to defy the claims of papacy and/or of Caesaro-papalism, it was necessary to search for alternative historical pathways to contemporary legitimacy.

If this is a functional account of the relationship between history and Western nationalism, and one that omits, or underplays, the groundswell of popular national sentiment, that indeed appears appropriate. This is particularly so for the Middle Ages and can also be seen as an important thesis thereafter. Indeed, a tension between a historicised sense of nationalism that reflected broadly based support and a more shallowly rooted nationalism that is largely, even essentially, a political programme or governmental project has been crucial to the subject of this book, and remains so. The former can be regarded as organic and in accordance with Burkean principles, even though its manifestations can be malign as well as benign.

Conversely, the idea of nationalism as a governmental project in the sense given above has a more ambivalent relationship with democratic values. Instead, the propagation of a historicised sense of nationalism as a government project can be an aspect of the false consciousness deliberately advanced or encouraged by elites in order to justify their role and power, a process seen, for example, today in the attempt to create a pseudo-nationalism for the EU (see p. 141).

Prior to the nineteenth century, nationalism can be seen as a minority option in societies in which the bulk of the population lacked literacy and had only limited means of political expression.

They were also heavily involved in exhausting menial labour. Yet, this account does not address the extent to which large-scale support for a national community appears to have played a key role in encouraging public action in earlier episodes – for example, ancient Israel, Classical Athens and thirteenth-century Scotland. Religion, moreover, could tap significant currents of support, as in ancient Israel, Protestant England and Orthodox Russia, and could, in turn, be a key source of national loyalty. Thus, in Russia, Orthodoxy helped shape a monarchical, and then national, identity.[3] Nationalism also served as, and was a product of, a rejection of the 'other', as in anti-Catholicism in England, Sweden and the Netherlands. This then developed in terms of ideas of liberty versus enslavement in religion and politics.

In sixteenth-century Europe, it was not so much that Christianity was nationalised (as it was to be in the nineteenth), as that the synergy between church and state that had existed from the conversion of the 'Barbarian' invaders who had overthrown the Western Roman Empire in the fifth century became stronger. Thus, English nationalism was supported by the account of Catholic persecution in John Foxe's *Acts and Monuments* (1563), a much reprinted and referred-to work. Foxe (1516–87) offered a hagiography that contrasted heavily with that which was central to Catholic practice. Ulrich von Hutten, a supporter of Martin Luther, depicted in *Arminius* (1519), its subject, the victor over the legions of Augustus Caesar at the Teutoburger Wald in 9 CE, as a defender of Germany against the tyranny of Rome.[4]

On the Catholic side, there was also printed propaganda that fulfilled a similar role, with pilgrimage books boosting national and local shrines and saints.[5] Such works overlapped with changes in the type of historical work, not least the demise of the chronicle, in favour of more specialist publications, which were aspects of the general expansion of publishing on historical topics.[6]

At the national level, religious accounts, themes and references supposedly demonstrated God's support for individual countries. In England, propaganda and commemorative days, for example of the accession of Elizabeth I in 1558, the defeat of the Spanish Armada in 1588, the Gunpowder Plot in 1605 and the Glorious Revolution in 1688,[7] provided opportunities to stress providential care, as well as the anti-Catholic nature of national identity. Religious assertion and contention also looked back to narratives of church history, particularly accounts of the Apostolic church, which offered arguments for use in doctrinal and organisational controversy.[8]

The same process occurred elsewhere. In Geneva, an independent Calvinist republic from 1536, history provided a way to show the linked history of church and state, as in the commemoration of the failure of the Savoyard attempt to storm the city in 1602. In Venice, events such as the major role of the fleet in the Ottoman (Turkish) defeat by Christian navies at Lepanto in 1571 were presented in an historical account that emphasised the providential role of the city.[9] More generally, religious history and themes strengthened ideas of the nation and, in the era of the French Revolution and Napoleon (1789–1815), provided a model for the mobilisation of popular sentiment.[10] Among France's opponents, these themes also provided a means for mobilisation.

THE NINETEENTH CENTURY

In the nineteenth century, economic change helped transform the parameters of politics at the same time that it created new issues and problems of social organisation and cultural cohesion. Industrial and agricultural change were accompanied by mass migration, between and within countries, by large-scale urbanisation, by the breakdown of earlier patterns of deference and social control, and by a sense of crisis affecting religious belief, although the last was not a serious factor beyond educated elites, and there was a successful, if temporary, co-option of religion to the new nationalism between the 1790s and 1914. In contrast to the eighteenth century, public opinion was now seen as being of key significance.

These changes all helped encourage governments concerned with finding values to fix and affirm public loyalty, not least in the aftermath of the series of popular uprisings seen in Europe from the 1780s. Furthermore, seeking both support and identity, political movements also sought to ground their message in an organic concept of nationhood, one in which past, present and future were linked. Post-Napoleonic *völkisch* nationalism contributed powerfully to this, and literary Romanticism played a significant role in fuelling such ideology. This Romanticism also looked back to eighteenth-century works, such as *Hermannsschlacht* (1769), a glorification of the struggle of the ancient Germans under Arminius (or Hermann) against Roman invasion, written by the poet Friedrich Klopstock. He also sought in *Oden* (1771) and in his patriotic plays to replace Classical myths by Germanic ones.[11]

Governments were somewhat behind the popular culture and popular opinion but responded with legislation and administrative policy. Equality under national law was an important aspect of this process.[12] Civic and ethnic accounts of nation and nationalism were frequently seen as mutually supporting, although not by ethnic minorities.[13]

The presentation of history was not an add-on in this creation and expression of identity or 'nation-talking' but, instead, was integral to it, and crucially so for the integrationist purposes of states. Thus, the teaching of history played a major role in the development of mass schooling that was organised and regulated on a state basis. The state was the prime frame of reference for public history, and a clear teleology – the past leading inevitably towards and therefore sanctioning and legitimating the present – was asserted. In the USA, nineteenth-century educational reformers cited history as indispensable for creating citizenship and not, for example, to critical thinking. Various public-service groups displayed a keen interest in promoting history as a citizen's credential. This was seen with the Daughters of the American Revolution, the Masonic textbook movement and the Progressive educational reformers of the late nineteenth century.

This process was also insistent for would-be states, with the history of nations advanced for those that were not yet independent and that were otherwise expressed in multi-ethnic empires – for example, the Finns, the Irish and the Poles. States have the monopoly of legitimate force, but nations may exist without having this status. However, they faced serious difficulties in political expression,[14] and, in presenting a distinct politics (which was supported by a different history), these nations lacked the legitimacy of sovereignty. Moreover, they could not legally wage war. In modern western Europe, where the function of defence is largely underrated or allocated to international bodies, primarily the North

Atlantic Treaty Organisation (NATO), this functional bar to the assertiveness of nations (real or alleged) no longer pertains.

In nineteenth-century Europe, however, the public understanding and presentation of history tended to focus on wars, and this contributed to a zero-sum gain approach to the past: one nationalism could only do well at the expense of another. There was scant attempt to search for themes of cooperation and mutual benefit, although the fashionable nature of some causes, such as Greek independence (from Ottoman/Turkish rule) in the 1820s, or Italian unification in the 1840s–60s, ensured that specific nationalisms could win international support when rivalry was not an issue.[15] In contrast, historians of France and Germany sought to annex Charlemagne for their national history.

Within countries, the past was shaped to provide a teleological account of a rise to greatness, with setbacks presented as object lessons, not least as opportunities for heroic fortitude that turned the tide – for example, in German accounts, by Frederick II (the Great) of Prussia in the later stages of the Seven Years' War (1756–63).[16] The Nazis were to tap into that tradition in their film treatment of Frederick, especially in *Kolberg* (dir. Veit Harlan and Wolfgang Liebeneiner, 1945).

The use of history, however, was even more important for the attempt to create a new integrationist basis by overthrowing the cohesive practices of imperial states such as Austria, Britain, Russia and Turkey. Thus, German, Italian, Czech, Hungarian, Irish, Polish, Finnish, Greek, Bulgarian and other nationalist movements presented history to emphasise difference with these imperial legacies while, at the same time, asserting the organic and inevitable unity of the hoped-for new, or to be expanded, state.[17] In part, this looked back to the late-eighteenth-century conflation of increased national consciousness with Romantic mythmaking, but the age of democratic politics sharpened demands for a workable past, and the new nationalisms had to be seen as genuine and grounded in experience.[18] It was necessary to compete not only with imperial overlords but also with other national rivals – for example, Lithuanians with Poles within the Russian Empire – and, to both ends, the education, and thus mobilisation, of the masses was seen as crucial. Commemorative celebrations were used to demonstrate an exemplary past. Thus, in Poland, the centenaries of the 1791 constitution, the 1794 Kosciuszko anti-Russian rebellion and, in 1898, the birth of the poet Adam Mickiewicz, as well as the 500th anniversary, in 1910, of the major victory over the Teutonic Knights at Grunwald, all underlined a glorious past.[19]

There was also an assertion of national history at the university level, although this was contested. In the latter case, the suppression by Austrian forces of the 1848 Hungarian Rising led to moves against the teaching of Hungarian history at the University of Pázmány Péter in Budapest, and the Chair of 'Universal and Hungarian History' became that of 'Universal and Austrian History'. Moreover, Polish scholarship was not backed by the Russian government in the large portion of Poland it ruled.

Nevertheless, the general pattern was of greater institutional support for history at the level of nations and would-be states. In Latvia, then part of the Russian Empire, the Commission of Sciences established a history section in 1905, and this focused on the history of Latvia.[20] The need for assertion and the possibility of a political transformation led to pressure for a distinctive and exemplary history, one that built up the coherence of the people in question and also asserted their value and interests. This history was understood in the broadest sense to include ethnography, linguistics and archaeology, and, in turn, these and other fields required an overarching historical account. The process made it possible to fix otherwise assertive but vague concepts, such as *das Deutsches Volk* (German people). Newly independent states, for example Belgium, Greece and Italy, witnessed the same development.[21]

This nationalist project spanned scholarship and public approaches. The degree to which the European university history departments emerged at precisely the same time as the drive for national histories suggests that the divide between academic and public histories may have been less clear-cut than it is now. Academics drew support from state-funded national learned institutes, while, on the German model, many universities were linked to government and saw their function in terms of serving a state-defined and focused concept of the public interest. In part, the development of the research university in the Protestant German lands, from the late eighteenth century, was a top-down process, with education seen by governments as an aspect of a competitive international world. This process was also actively moulded by academics in pursuit of their individual and collective goals, namely a definition of academic merit. In a dynamic, changing world, the public definition of merit helped to provide academics with valuable protection. Seminar directors came to police the system by assessing merit and setting standards accordingly, while the doctorate of philosophy and the new doctoral dissertation expressed the rationale of an increasingly bureaucratic state that helped drive academic structures. An ideology of objective evaluation expressed the dominant bureaucratic mentality.[22] In contrast, the English university system had a different ethos and practice.

The historians who benefited from such state-supported systems made nations the object of philological, ethnographic and historical study and were keen backers of a national approach to history.[23] They focused on the idea of inherent characteristics, and misleadingly so, given the more porous nature of peoples and the more changeable, not to say transient, links with particular territories and cultural features.[24] Textbooks offered an exemplary account and were standardised accordingly, as in the USA in the Progressive era.

It is easy to attribute historians' endorsement of clear-cut national criteria and themes to self-interest, but a cultural affinity with society and an openness to broad-based intellectual trends that favoured this course were more important. The contrast with the present day is readily apparent. Thus, in Britain, leading historians, such as Henry Hallam (1777–1859), author of *The Constitutional History of England, from the Accession of Henry VII to the Death of George II*; Thomas, Lord Macaulay (1800–59), author of *The History of England from the Accession of James II*; and Samuel Gardiner (1829–1902), author of *The History of England from the Accession of James I to the Restoration* and *The Student's History of England*, helped shape the study and presentation of the civil conflicts of the seventeenth century. They did so so that these conflicts could be seen not as a warning of divisive tendencies but, instead, so that they could be incorporated into a national historiographical consensus able to draw on prominent individuals and episodes from a number of backgrounds. For example, Oliver Cromwell could be treated as an exemplary statesman, worthy of memorialisation with prominent statues, and not as a traitor.[25]

A state-defined and focused concept of the public interest was also seen in other institutional aspects of cultural life, not least the foundation of national galleries, museums, theatres and opera houses and the works they staged. In Stockholm, the National Museum, opened to the public in 1866, emphasised the visual arts, with imposing Nordic landscapes and monumental scenes from Swedish history being seen as a way to encourage a sense of national identity. Sometimes, state-sponsored culture proved problematic, however, as in Sofia in 1906, when the opening of the National Theatre witnessed an anti-government demonstration in which pieces of ice were thrown at the ruler, Prince Ferdinand.

Intellectual institutionalisation was also significant. Thus, in Bulgaria, the National Library, opened in 1878, was followed by the Ethnographic Museum (1906) and the Archaeological Museum (1908).

Across the West, within universities, chairs of national history were created, and national history became increasingly important as the Classical-based scholarship presented as 'universal history', receded in relative significance. In France, a chair in the history of France was established at the École Normale Supérieure in 1853. More generally, national history was emphasised in the teaching of and by schoolteachers.

Public spaces contributed to the same goal, especially in town and city centres. There also, the public media are more vulnerable to manipulation, while it is easier to sustain official attention. The national town planning and monuments of the late nineteenth century were frequently as assertive as their inter-war Communist and Fascist counterparts. In 1874, Emmanuel Frémiet's gilded statue of Joan of Arc was installed in Paris. Standing in the Place des Pyramides, close to the Louvre, it powerfully reminded citizens of the Third Republic of the loss of Alsace and Lorraine (in fact, part of Lorraine) to Germany as a result of defeat in the Franco-Prussian War of 1870–1. This was at a time when the symbolic townscape of the capital was being remade after the fall of the Second Empire and the suppression of the Commune.

This statue was also an instance of the powerful role of the arts in creating national iconographies and of the influence of history as providing contents for this iconography. Joan, who was linked to Lorraine, was understood in terms of self-sacrifice for the cause of France.[26]

In contrast, in 1915, Carl Larsson's painting *Midwinter Sacrifice* was rejected for the National Museum in Sweden, in part because of historical inaccuracy and in part because the mythical King Domalde, a figure from the *Edda* (Old Norse texts) who was to be the victim in a pagan sacrifice at Uppsala intended to seek divine support for better weather, was depicted as naked. The painting was not purchased for the museum until 1997.

More generally, statues and buildings normalised and made familiar national and imperial narratives. Thus, at Westminster, Thomas Thornycroft's statue of Boudicca was erected, and in the Grand Place in Brussels, an equestrian statue of Godfrey of Bouillon, a hero of the First Crusade. He had been a Duke of Lower Lorraine and thus provided an appropriate pedigree for the new state. This was an aspect of a more general appropriation of the Crusades.[27] The unveiling of King Alfred's statue in Winchester, the ancient capital of Wessex, in 1901 proved the centrepiece of extensive celebrations.[28]

Paintings also made national and imperial narratives more familiar, not least because they could be readily reproduced. Thus, in Switzerland, Frank-Edouard Lossier (1852–1925) painted scenes from the medieval quest for independence, including episodes from the life of William Tell and from the Reformation. In Sweden, the Age of Greatness provided similar episodes, as in the *Death of Gustavus Adolphus* (1855) by Carl Wahlbom, in which the King appears as both heroic and luminous on the victorious battlefield of Lützen in 1632, and *Bringing Home the Body of King Karl XII* (1884) by Gustaf Cederström, an inspirational depiction of valiant resolution in the face of adversity in 1718. Earlier periods were also depicted as with Carl Gustaf Hellqvist's *Valdemar Atterdag Holding Visby to Ransom 1361* (1882), a clear

contrasting of oppressive foreign rule with virtuous Swedes, and Johan Sandberg's *Gustav Vasa Addressing Men from Dalarna* (1836), a linkage of dynasty with people at a formative period of national independence. The National Museum in Oslo holds Norwegian equivalents, including *Harold the Fairhead in the Battle at Hafrsfjord* (1870) by Ole Peter Hansen Balling; *The Wild Hunt of Odin* (1872) by Peter Nicolai Arbo, a powerful depiction of Norse mythology; *Christian II Signing the Death Warrant of Torben Oxe* (1875–6) by Eilif Petersen; and *Norsemen Landing in Iceland* (1877) by Oscar Wergeland.

Symbolic townscapes served for public celebration, not least triumphal parades. These proved particularly appropriate to the military, which used compulsory military service to affirm the identity of state and society. National standardisation in weights and measures, currencies and postage was a more mundane part of the same process. Newspapers, railways and taxes contributed to the same results.[29] Space was organised and segregated in national terms.

There was also an imperial dimension to the use of history to create and sustain identities. This was the case not only in imperial metropoles, where memorialisation was about empire as well as nation, but also in the colonies. Townships, buildings, institutions and school lessons combined to the same end. Thus, in the Victoria Memorial in Kolkata (Calcutta), built in the early twentieth century, the Viceroy of India, George, Viscount Curzon, sought, as a memorial to the recently dead Empress-Queen, 'a monument and grand building where all classes will learn the lessons of history and see revived before their eyes the marvels of the past'.

In the Russian Empire, grand buildings were part of the policy of Russification. Thus, in Tallinn, the capital of Estonia, a large Orthodox cathedral was built in 1894–1900. Occupying a prominent site, it was a clear display of cultural power, not least with the removal of the statue of the Protestant reformer Martin Luther in order to make way for it. The cathedral was dedicated to Prince Aleksandr Nevsky, who had defeated Swedish and German (Teutonic Knights) forces in 1240 and 1242 respectively and who had been canonised in 1547. He was commemorated with a mosaic on the side of the cathedral (as he was to be in Eisenstein's film in 1938, see p. 53), while the mosaic on the opposite side of the cathedral depicted Count Vsevlod of Pskov, who had campaigned against the Estonians during the thirteenth century.

The British presentation of national-imperial history absorbed Britain's experience as a part of the Roman Empire, presenting that as a key aspect of national development and as an imperial model that Britain subsequently emulated and surpassed. Thus, Edward Elgar's *Caractacus* (1898), an account of heroic (albeit unsuccessful) opposition to the Romans, ended with praise, by H.A. Acworth, to the future British empire:

And where the flag of Britain
Its triple crosses rears,
No slave shall be for subject
No trophy wet with tears.

Britain was apparently better, as it added liberty to empire. In an essay on nationality, in his *Home and Foreign Review* of July 1862, John, later Lord Acton (then a Liberal MP and from 1895 Professor of Modern History in Cambridge), claimed, 'If we take the establishment of liberty for the realisation of moral duties to be the end of civil society, we must conclude that those states are substantially the most perfect which, like the British and Austrian Empires, include various distinct nationalities without oppressing them'.[30] Oppression, however, was a relative concept, not least if historical destiny was at stake, as in an essay on colonies he published in the *Rambler* in 1862:

we may assume (as part of the divine economy which appears in the whole history of religion) that the conquest of the world by the Christian powers is the preliminary step to its conversion. In paganism and in heresy there is a national and political character which identifies the religion with the nation, and requires for it the support of the state [. . .] The conversion of the Germans resembled that of the Romans: their states were broken up, and their local traditions destroyed, and they were converted in the very moment of migration and settlement. In Saxony the absence of migration was made up for by wars of extermination and proselytism [by the Franks under Charlemagne from 772 to 804.] The same means is still requisite to prepare the two extremes of barbarism and cultivation for the reception of Christianity – conquest by European powers. This alone can destroy the tenacity of old institutions, of social division, of moral customs, of political habits. By this alone can the benefit of a higher civilization be conferred on the savage races.

For India, Acton claimed, 'what we must desire, for the sake of religion, is that the oriental career of our country should extend beyond the destruction of Eastern politics, even to the demolition of Eastern society'.[31] Such an approach would no longer be acceptable in Britain nor among prominent Christian clerics, but such a thesis, of clear truth permitting destruction, still seems conducive to radical Islam. It can also be seen in the case of some Western commentators. Thus, the prominent American right-wing commentator Ann Coulter suggested, after 11 September 2001, that the USA should invade Muslim countries, kill their leaders and convert the people to Christianity. This, however, is a very marginal view in the West.

In the nineteenth century, alongside the success of integrative policies and tendencies, some failed; although failure is often in the eyes of the beholder and of later public myth. A focus on twentieth-century Irish nationalism can distract attention from the extent to which Irishness in the nineteenth century was expressed alongside or in support of Britishness. Pressure for Home Rule, rather than independence, was an aspect of this, and large-scale service in the British Army a key instance.[32]

From a Scottish academic perspective that suits the cause of modern Scottish nationalism, it has also been claimed that there was no effective British ideology, a situation that has been attributed to the failure, after the 1707 Union, to fuse English and Scottish Whig historical ideologies in a potent British Whiggism. As a consequence, it has been argued that Britishness was simply Englishness writ large, although there seems little doubt that, whatever the intellectual flaws, British nationalism worked well from the suppression of the Jacobites at the battle of Culloden in 1746.

The Scottish contribution to British imperial expansion and rule was notable, although imperial servants held different views of what they were doing. As a consequence, Britishness was a partnership of pragmatism as much as a union of hearts. At the same time, the decline of Scotland's once potent national historiography has been held responsible for contributing to nationalist failure in Scotland during this period: although aspects of Scottish Whig history continued to exert some hold on the political imagination, they were no longer tied to constitutional principles and lacked the ability to be developed in response to circumstances.[33]

Returning to European history, the forms of power, of course, are not the same as its use. State-building through historicised nationalism in the nineteenth century was not the same as Hitler or Stalin's contrasting uses of history. Nevertheless, there were continuities. Towards the close of the nineteenth century, those who propounded the increasingly common organic notions of the nation became readier to draw on, if not create, an often mystical sense of identity between people and place or, as it generally was, race and country. This was a historicist interpretation because it was usually posed in terms of a long-term identity. Race began to play a greater role in identity from the second half of the nineteenth century.

Organic notions of the nation drew on, and sustained, a range of political and cultural notions and ideas, including the legacies of Romanticism, medievalism[34] (or subsequent periods of greatness),[35] and Social Darwinism, and, in turn, fed into early Fascism. The past was pillaged, as in 1898 when Kaiser Wilhelm II of Germany visited the Middle East and referred to the medieval role of the Teutonic Knights. He also rode into the old city of Jerusalem.

The role of character, both collective and individual, the latter ranging from heroism in battle to leadership in politics, supposedly represented the inherent nature of a people and provided narrative interest to emphasis on the strength and role of nations.[36] These were given a strong racial dimension. The notion of race was an anthropological one and was seen to be objective and ideal and, thus, as possessing distinctive characteristics, including a distinct history. This neglected the socio-psychological character and context of ethnicity, the extent to which it is subjective and, in part, a construction that entails the stereotyping, both of those included and of those excluded. Instead, distinctions between genetics, ethnicity, language and material culture were overridden.[37]

This stereotyping, however, made readily accessible the ideas of nationhood propounded both in existing states and also in challenge to them. Such ideas appeared more necessary because of the volatility and, even more, sense of volatility and uncertainty, arising from the extension of the electorate and, in some cases, such as the North German Confederation in 1867, the introduction of universal adult male suffrage. Democracy created the issue of a tension between politics as consensus problem-management and politics as an affirmation of loyalty to groups and ideas, a tension that challenged national consensus and, thus, underlined the problem of management.

The emphasis on the nation was not only a matter of large states, such as Germany, but also of small ones, for example Montenegro in the Balkans. Its leaders presented themselves as the descendants of a Serb elite that, in response to the Ottoman (Turkish) invasion centuries earlier, had withdrawn to the mountains that were the backbone of their country. On that basis, Montenegro's leaders claimed that they should direct a greater Serbia.

However, as has also been the case more recently, the exposition of historicised nationalism, and of national history, was challenged by variant readings of the national past. This was true even in the aftermath of success, such as in Prussia after the War of Liberation from Napoleon (1813–15). Public recollections then were contested, reflecting the extent to which the war interacted with political division; and this contest was represented in commemoration and depiction.[38]

Disputes over recent history were strongly marked in France where contention over the memory of the French Revolution was bound up in bitter dissension over the legitimacy and purpose of the Third Republic (1871–1940). The positive presentation of a republican tradition in France by the Third Republic is a reminder that a historically grounded nationalism was scarcely a monopoly of the right. This nationalism lacked the socialist internationalism that found favour in some circles on the left but, on the left, there was also a more potent liberal nationalism with a historical consciousness, as well as a socialism and trade unionism with a strong awareness of radical antecedents. Within France, discussion about nationalism was interwoven with competing secular-republican and Catholic narratives of national history and destiny. The Catholic account was at once national and international. The latter simultaneously looked back, with notions of appropriate behaviour and ecclesiology grounded in the Middle Ages,[39] and also forward to the international ideologies of the twentieth century. The Catholic account of the French Revolution was very hostile.

The tension between religious and secular accounts of history were, moreover, seen elsewhere, especially in Italy, Portugal and Spain where there were also clashes between liberal and Catholic perspectives. In all three countries, it was necessary to overcome Catholic, monarchist conservatism in order to propound more secular, liberal nationalism. In Italy, the liberal nationalism was explicitly directed against the Papacy, because of its role, as a temporal power in the Papal States, in opposing Italian unification.[40]

Across the West, alongside state-controlled cultural life, such as the sponsoring of national institutions and monuments, came cultural forms that reflected the artefacts, beliefs and customs of popular society and, thus, the popularisation of culture. These forms themselves were affected by technological developments, as with wax shows, the popular theatre, mass journalism and, eventually, film. Expressions of changes in community practices or 'associational habits', these offered possibilities for nationalist expression (for example, films on Joan of Arc or Henry VIII, such as Carl Theodor Dreyer's *La Passion de Jeanne d'Arc*, 1928) that were probably more influential in encouraging national sentiment than more self-consciously intellectual agendas. These forms were important to the development of cultures of history at the national level.[41] A poster for the British Empire Exhibition of 1924 showed Elizabeth I (r. 1558–1603) being rowed on the Thames towards a Tudor warship, with the caption 'Britain's Past and Present Beckon You to Wembley. British Empire Exhibition'.

REMEMBERING WAR

The past as a reference point was powerfully seen with the First World War (1914–18), not least with German militarism and war-planning. These drew on the legacy of purpose and success in the German Wars of Unification (1864–71) and also looked back to earlier reference points of military achievement, particularly Hannibal's victory over the Romans at Cannae in 216 BCE, which the Germans thought a suitable model. Ethnic resonances of conflict – between Teuton and Slav, and Teuton and Latin – also played a role, and, in turn, looked forwards to Nazi racial imaginings. A sense of historical destiny, as well as institutional complacency,[42] can be linked to the German General Staff's lack of a Plan B in the event of the failure of their plan for victory.

More generally, a disadvantage with 'knowing history', in the form of an apparent understanding of the past and a clear teleological grasp of the future, was that it led to a blinkered and inflexible approach. This assumption was generally optimistic, in the sense that past, present and future appeared readily determined, although teleology (apparently knowing where history was going) could also lead to historical pessimism. The First World War also saw many appeals to historical episodes of valour and success, as with the 1915 British naval poster 'England Expects' with its picture of Horatio Nelson, the victor at Trafalgar (1805).

Historical pessimism subsequently played a role in the recollection of the First World War, and that has been the note most powerfully struck since the 1960s when recalling that war.[43] However, in contrast, the general theme in the inter-war period (1918–39) was the commemoration of the conflict, not least in terms of the sacrifice of those who had died and the impact of the war on societies that experienced a 'lost generation'.[44] This was as one with the long-standing process of memorialisation of war in Europe, which had been accentuated after the Napoleonic Wars and, even more, the mid-nineteenth-century Western wars of 1848–71, which were conflicts in which nationalism had played a major role. The mass politicisation of the mid- and late nineteenth century, with the spread of literacy, inexpensive newspapers and universal education, and the extension of the male franchise, led to a situation in which war was seen to focus the will and energy of committed societies and to require commemoration in terms of both collective and individual endeavour.

Thus, in place of memorialising only prominent individuals and mass graves for the rest, increasingly came monuments to the common soldiers and individual tombstones for them. This was very much the case with the American Civil War (1861–5) and the First World War, with the latter being followed by an unprecedented quest to identify the fallen, especially through photography. Prominent memorials commemorated the fallen, as with the Vimy Memorial inaugurated in 1936 by Edward VIII to honour the Canadians who had died capturing Vimy Ridge on the Western Front in 1917.

Aside from public monuments, letters, memoirs and war poetry were key forms of individual recollection, although sometimes they contested nationalist accounts. Technology also contributed to the same end, with the habitual use of photography to record individuals.[45] Illustrating the variety of forms of recollection, individual messages from the spirit world were also significant, and there was a major vogue in spiritualism after the First World War.

Memorialisation, in turn, led to problems when the results of the conflict cut across existing political lines. That could be seen with the consequences of Irish independence, which not only built on, but also accentuated, existing tensions between competing national identities and the contrasting response to events.[46] A long-term sense of distinctive Irish identity was argued by Eoin MacNeill in his *Phases of Irish History* (1919).

In Ireland, the war led to a large-scale upsurge in demands for independence, to insurrection and finally, under the Anglo-Irish Treaty of 1921, to a partition, with the Irish Free State (now the Republic of Ireland) defining its nationalist origins and its myth of national independence in terms of a rejection of the British Empire. The large numbers who had fought for the latter in the First World War, and the political movement that had hoped to gain Home Rule for Ireland within the Empire through participation in the conflict, were slighted or ignored.[47] Instead, there was an emphasis on the Easter Rising of 1916 against British rule, which, in fact, was very much a minority effort, and on the War of Independence. In practice, the First World War and the struggle for independence were not polar opposites. A number of IRA commanders had served in the First World War, including Commandant Tom Barry, who shot wounded men dead in the road at the Kilmichael Ambush, men he might have been serving with a couple of years earlier. In 1918, there were crowds to welcome the troops home, yet many had voted or were about to vote for the nationalist Sinn Féin party which won seventy-three out of the 105 parliamentary seats in the election of 1918. Moreover, the Treaty of 1921 was ratified by referendum in 1922.

By then, support for the British Empire had fallen greatly, and this led to an underplaying of the commitment in the First World War. This was seen with the National Irish War Memorial to the war dead, which was erected not in the centre of Dublin, as initially suggested, but at the more remote location of Islandbridge. Furthermore, the memorial was not inaugurated for many years.[48] Similarly, after the Second World War, there was hostility to the 80,000 Irish citizens who volunteered to fight for Britain, and their role was ignored by the Irish government.

From a different direction, a tension between individual and collective memories of the First World War, and one that reflected contrasting understandings of nationalism, was seen in the 2000s in the campaign for an official pardon for British soldiers who were executed for cowardice during the First World War. The campaign succeeded in 2006 and was, at once, an acknowledgement of the failure to appreciate the impact of post-traumatic stress disorder (shell shock) and yet also, to a certain extent, the product of an ahistorical unwillingness to understand the practices and values of the period.

In the latter sense, the pardon is part of a wider, but anachronistic, construction of attempts to 'right wrongs' by the use of pardons, appeals against sentences and national apologies. Thus, there is a tension between legitimate attempts to face up to the past and the ahistorical emphasis on apology which is an aspect of a constant indictment of the past based on the ever-changing needs of the present.[49] There is also, frequently, a combination of an understanding that customs were different in the past, with an insistence, on a personal or family basis, that an ancestor should have his name rehabilitated.

It was not only in Ireland that the First World War led to the creation of a new state and to the related establishment of an official narrative of national difference. This was also the case in the newly independent states of eastern Europe: Czechoslovakia, Hungary, Poland, Yugoslavia, Estonia, Latvia, Lithuania and Finland. In these, histories provided an account to support independence. Thus, in Finland, there was a stress on a history of resisting pressures from the east, a stress that appeared appropriate in the face of the Soviet threat.[50] These states were also very different. Whereas Hungary and Poland had strong national histories and identities, Yugoslavia and Czechoslovakia were artificial constructs with little or no national history or culture.

New states meant new institutions, and these included support for the teaching of national history. In constructing these histories, the nation was the key unit and narrative although in Yugoslavia, a federal state, the kingdom's peoples had separate histories presented in textbooks. However, as in already-established historical systems, such as those of Britain and France, the emphasis on the nation did not preclude consideration of other elements, such as social structure. Instead, they could be subsumed into the narrative. There was a potential tension as class, in a Marxist sense, was primarily a narrative about division but, in contrast, a blander social account – of past arrangements, the life-and-times approach – was favoured. It was more compatible with an optimistic portrayal of national history and with one focused on supposedly distinctive national characteristics in, for example, costume or vernacular architecture. Museums catered to this approach.

FASCISM

The common currency in 'knowing history' was a perception of mission, and this was to be abundantly seen with both Fascism and Nazism, although not only with them. Benito Mussolini, the dictator of Italy from 1922 to 1943, saw Fascism both as a modern and relevant ideology and also as a revival of Italian greatness that would lead to national regeneration. Destiny was a theme. In his co-authored *The Doctrine of Fascism* (1932), Fascism was described as 'an historical conception [. . .] Outside history man is nothing', the sort of cliché encountered all too frequently, and still today, not least in works on historiography.

The revived history was particularly that of Classical Rome, which provided the Fascists with a malleable agenda for both domestic and foreign policy, as well as with a tone of power that focused on force. Other periods, however, were also considered. The Middle Ages and Renaissance were shaped as a splendid and exemplary backdrop for Fascist Italy and provided additional instances of how the cultural heritage was used to support the cause of national regeneration and to create a sense of progress and momentum leading to the present. Building, restoration and design schemes and policies sought to provide an appropriate setting, not least to create the sense of an historical Italian symbiosis of beauty and function, past and future.[51] In contrast, the seventeenth and eighteenth centuries were seen as a degenerate period when foreign control of much of Italy (by Habsburgs, Spanish and Austrian, and, later, Bourbons) reflected and ensured national weakness and decline. In part, this was a continuation of the liberal, national account of history held in the late nineteenth century, but it was actively moulded by Mussolini.

Fascism, indeed, was presented as the culmination of the *Risorgimento*, the nineteenth-century movement for national unification, which was central to the national myth. In 1932, the Fascist regime extensively celebrated the fiftieth anniversary of the death of Giuseppe Garibaldi, the military hero of the *Risorgimento* whose social radicalism was neglected in the celebrations. The Exhibition of the Fascist Revolution the same year provided an opportunity to present history as an ongoing process in which Fascism was gloriously situated.[52]

Much emphasis was also placed on the contrast between the national humiliation at the hands of Ethiopian forces at the battle of Adua (Adowa) in 1896 and the success of Mussolini's forces in conquering Ethiopia in 1935–6. This was seen in the film *Scipione l'africano* (dir. Carmine Gallone, 1937), an account of a Roman general in the Second Punic War that counterpointed the Roman defeat by Hannibal at Cannae (216 BCE) with Scipio's victory over him at Zama (202 BCE) which led to the surrender of nearby Carthage. This offered a parallel with the contrast between Adua and Mussolini's victory. The subtext was that Italy was destined to rule in Africa. The cruelties of Italian imperialism were ignored.[53]

The authoritarian conservative Salazar regime, which governed Portugal from 1932 to 1974, focused on the celebration of the foundation of Portugal, as well as on great events in the age of discoveries, such as the life of Henry the Navigator (1394–1460), and on the restoration, in 1640, of Portuguese independence from rule by the King of Spain.

Similar views about mission and regeneration played an important role in other inter-war authoritarian states, such as 1930s Thailand and Japan.

In Japan, triumphs that had paved the path to imperial greatness were widely celebrated in the 1910s–1930s. Admiral Togo, the commander in the total victory over the Russian fleet at Tsushima (1905), which made possible successful Japanese imperialism in East Asia, himself began, in 1925, the subscription fund for the Mikasa Warship Memorial in Yokosuka (the *Mikasa* had been his flagship at Tsushima). Togo died in 1934. Six years later, the Togo Shrine opened in Harajuku, Tokyo. A year later, Japanese imperialism was to be pushed to its utmost as the American, British and Dutch empires were all attacked. Japanese historians who challenged the received view were criticised. Tsuda Sōkichi, a critic of the imperial myth, which he claimed had been invented by eighth-century writers, was sentenced in 1942 to two years' imprisonment for *lèse majesté*.

A historicised confidence in national valour, however, was not to suffice. Having helped bring only fleeting success, it became, instead, a lodestar in a quasi-suicidal effort to hang on and triumph through will. In 1945, that proved an empty policy, and Japanese history as a usable myth of power was discarded as a new system was put in place by the American victors.

THE NAZIS

In Nazi Germany (1933–45), the racial dimension was emphasised, with an understanding of Germany in terms of Aryans and a harshly hostile approach to other Germans. As with Mussolini's Fascism, Nazism was aimed against individualism, which was presented as lacking the characteristics of destiny and, instead, as being destructive of the *Völk*. Thus, instead of history as a progressive account of increasing liberalism, came history as a struggle between racial groups, where a lesson of the past was the sapping characteristics of such liberalism.

Nazism was a movement for Aryan greatness, but, at the same time, the eclectic and frequently incoherent nature of Nazism included other themes and interests, such as that of territorial and military prowess, modelled not so much on the Aryan greatness as on Classical Rome or on Prussia. History was used by the regime and its supporters, notably by Heinrich Himmler who was fascinated with his particular mystical concept of the Germanic past. This use was determined by their agenda, as in the excision of Jews from Germany's history, and the use of film to advance the *Führerprinzip* (the leadership principle), with historical figures encapsulating and advancing Germanness in a prequel to Hitler. This was seen in *Friedrich Schiller* (dir. Herbert Maisch, 1940), with the poet presented as a pan-German able to see beyond the atomistic politics of Germany before unification. Also that year, *Bismarck* (dir. Wolfgang Liebeneiner, 1940) emphasised the importance of firm leadership and its espousal of 'iron and blood' for German unification and strength, rather than the debilitating nature of parliamentary processes, while Bismarck was shown as favouring a Russian alliance to protect Prussia's rear, anticipating Hitler's policy with Stalin from 1939 to 1941. These films were followed by *Der Grosse König* (dir. Veit Harlan, 1942), the most lavish of Nazi films, on Frederick the Great, and an account of the need for fortitude, *Die Entlassung* (dir. Wolfgang Liebeneiner 1942), in which Bismarck's fall is seen as making necessary a new *führer*, and *Kolberg*, with its call for stoical endurance against Russia and its promise of eventual success.[54]

The treatment of film indicated how, under the Nazis, what might have been autonomous centres for memorialisation were sidelined, subjugated or even suppressed. This was particularly seen in the depiction of cultural history, with topics and forms employed to present the past in an admonitory and exemplary fashion. In doing so, the Nazis were copying other revolutions, such as the French and Russian ones. In the former, churches and vaults were desecrated in a violent attack on a now-rejected sense and means of continuity. Moreover, tombs and statues were displayed in the 1790s in the Museum of French Monuments in order to warn of the dangers of wrongly informed and directed art.[55] The Russian Revolution also turned on the Orthodox Church.

RACE AND HISTORY

Alongside Germany, other European states witnessed a similar process of ethnic assertion in the twentieth century as the redrawing of boundaries was sought, in large part on supposed ethnic grounds. This involved the marshalling of history in an ethnic light. Thus, after Germany's ally Hungary gained much of Transylvania from Romania in 1940, the Hungarians stepped up their argument that this reflected historical justice, with the reversal of their earlier loss of this, and other territories, in the Treaty of Trianon of 1920 presented as more than a matter of short-term justice. In 1941, the newly formed Institute of Central and Eastern European History in Budapest University published the *Documenta Historiam Valachorum in Hungaria Illustrantia usque and annum 1400 P. Christum* by Imre Lukinich, a reputable and prominent professor. This gave a history of the Romanians in Transylvania, arguing that, far from being the original population, they had only appeared in the area relatively late and in small numbers, only arriving en masse in the fourteenth century. Therefore, it was truly Hungarian.

Alternative forms of identity were also historicised. Thus, the union of democratic states proposed in 1919–20 by Marshal Józef Pilsudski, first President of newly independent Poland, a federation of nations between Germany and Russia, and designed to limit both, looked back to what was termed the early modern, Jagiellonian[56] concept of Poland as an extensive federal power, rather than to the more limited idea of an ethnic Polish state.

Race-based history confronted a range of issues. In Spain under Francisco Franco, the conservative dictator from 1939 to 1975, the medieval *Reconquista* from the Muslims was presented as recovering what had been lost to the Moors. The Moors were seen as a foreign group that had, in the eighth century, conquered a Christian population that, however, remained. This *Homo Ibericus*, it was argued, had been restored to freedom by the *Reconquista*, and the latter, therefore, did not emerge as another conquest. This presentation had been Spanish practice for centuries. The innovation by the Nationalists under Franco was to equate Communists with Moors, ironically while using Islamic troops from Morocco to help win success in the Spanish Civil War of 1936–9.

The Nationalists' approach underlined the depiction of Spain as a bastion of civilisation and Christendom, a theme that was extendable to the Francoists' presentation of their own regime. The continuation of this theme was seen in the attempts to canonise Queen Isabella of Castile (r. 1474–1504), attempts that continued in the early 2000s despite her involvement in the expulsion of the Jews and Moors from Spain.

More generally, race provided a theme not only for national cohesion but also for external aggrandisement. This was seen with a number of states, notably Germany, which emphasised, in particular, claims in eastern Germany; Italy, which deployed the earlier Roman and Venetian empires to these ends, especially in the Balkans; Hungary, which dwelled on the lands lost after the First World War; and Greece, which stressed both ethnic and historical claims in Anatolia and elsewhere. Unsurprisingly, such agendas led other states that felt threatened to move against their own minorities.

Would-be states also saw an emphasis on the link between people and place. Based on the Hebrew University in Jerusalem, founded in 1925, scholars emphasised the Jewish character of the history of what was then Palestine, particularly the theme of continuity in Jewish settlement. This was an important intellectual support for the Zionist cause.

COMMUNISM

Although race did not play the role seen with Germany, Communist public history was similar to that of Fascism and Nazism in many respects. There was a common emphasis on struggle, an opposition to liberal notions of development and a determination to use the state to propagate the historical ideas of the regime. In each case, history was employed to show the truth of the ideology and also that the seizure of power by the regime was necessary and represented an improvement on a failed, if not degenerate, past. Opposing views of history were seen as falsifications and had to be elided as the past was rewritten to correspond to current ideological needs. These points can also be made about liberalism, although the contexts were very different.

Communists, however, had to incorporate the allegedly universal character of Marxism as analysis and prospectus, for, in their eyes, class struggle was a global force, movement and phenomenon that subverted national borders. This was a challenge to organic theories of the state, but Communist history offered its own malignity. In stressing the continuous nature of class struggle, it was hostile to attempts to construct inclusive notions of nationhood that stopped short of the Marxist mantra, while the Communist view of class consciousness as historically well defined, widely held and international was seriously problematic.

Religion was ignored or condemned, which meant, in the Soviet Union, that the role of the Orthodox Church was denigrated and minimised until the Second World War when it was found expedient to revive aspects of national identity. In the assault on the church, symbols of continuing belief such as church buildings, icons and bells were destroyed. In Russia, as with the French Revolution, radical ideology proposed 'a new man' or revolutionary citizen no longer defined by the communal meaning once promoted by the official church. The destruction of graves, as by the Soviets in Estonia, was also a means to destroy a non-Communist memory. During the Cultural Revolution, temples and cultural relics all over China were smashed and destroyed. In Tibet, this included religious scroll paintings and statues, but the Han Chinese Red Guards also attacked their own cultural heritage.

The extent to which religion offered an alternative history was captured during the pontificate of John Paul II (1979–2005). He canonised more people than any other pope, and the vast majority of them were victims of left-wing anti-Christian agitation. This was a challenge to Communist and allied left-wing narratives, for example in Spain, where John Paul canonised the 'new Spanish martyrs': several dozen victims of left-wing anti-Catholic squads during and before the Spanish Civil War.

This process continued under his successor, leading to controversy in October 2007 with charges from the left that the Papacy was ignoring the partisan role of the church during the Civil War. Four hundred and ninety-eight priests, nuns and monks killed in the 1930s were beatified, a stage toward sainthood. Clergy killed by the Nationalists were not beatified, which was justified on the grounds that they had been fighting for a political cause and were not killed due to their ecclesiastical position.

Although there was little common ground between Communism and international religious movements, it was tempting to seek such ground with secular national histories. Looked at differently, Communist historiography did not free itself from the problem of nationalist mythology. Despite the theoretically global character of Communism and the opposition to 'bourgeois' national identities, seen in particular under Joseph Stalin, the dictator from 1924 to 1953, the history provided in the Soviet Union was largely Russian nationalist, which gave Mao Zedong of China an opportunity to claim to revive a 'real' Communist internationalism that had withered in the hands of the Soviet Union.

Alternative nationalist views were suppressed in the Soviet Union. This was seen in Ukraine in the 1930s, and, indeed, Ukrainian history had been proposed in the latter years of Imperial Russia as a challenge to its historical approach.[57] In 1968, Ibrahim Muminov, President of the Uzbek Academy of Sciences, was dismissed for publishing a book querying the critical orthodoxy about the fourteenth-to-fifteenth-century ruler Temur (Tamerlane) that presented him as a savage barbarian. All copies were removed on the instructions of the Central Communist Committee of Uzbekistan.[58]

The Russification programme of the Stalinist era took forwards the Slavophile themes of the nineteenth century, with their hostility to Western influences, and added particular Communist perspectives.[59] The peasantry was presented in a positive light, but that was because their support for alternative values, especially those of the Orthodox Church, could be ignored. The nineteenth century became an account of the oppression of the masses by the tsarist autocracy and of their growing demand for redress, which culminated in the revolution of 1917. Earlier rebels, such as Stenka Razin, Bulavin and Pugachev, were acclaimed.

A similar approach was taken in other Communist states, with the addition of a positive view of the Soviet Union and, earlier, for Russia. Institutions, such as the Institute for Bulgarian History and the Historical Institute at the Serbian Academy of Sciences and Arts (both founded in 1947), the Montenegrin Historical Institute (1948), the Institute for History in Sarajevo (1959) and the Institute for the History of the Workers' Movement (Zagreb, 1961), provided an opportunity not only to produce an exemplary, approved history but also to police it.

The reporting of foreign news and history by Communist and Nazi reporters, commentators and historians was as one, designed to serve the interests of the dominant ideology. This was also seen as news became history. For example, after Franco's nationalists suggested that the town of Guernica had been dynamited by Basque saboteurs in April 1937, rather than being bombed by the Germans, as was, in fact, the case, the denial of this responsibility became part of Fascist history. The Reichstag fire proved part of the same process.

The past was employed throughout this period in order to strike what were seen as appropriate nationalist resonances. Thus, during the Second World War, the collaborationist Vichy government in France employed Joan of Arc as a symbol of anti-British Catholic nationalism, and, when a house she had occupied in Orléans was destroyed in the wartime bombing, Vichy propaganda referred to British assassins returning to their target. The Third Republic's celebration of 14 July (Bastille Day) as an annual commemoration of the French Revolution and its values was rejected under Vichy which, instead, sought to make it a day for France's war dead. The Resistance in France, in turn, pressed the people to demonstrate in support of the anniversary as a celebration of the Revolution. The Vichy memorialisation put Marshal Pétain, a hero of the First World War as well as Vichy's

Head of State, in a prominent position, but it failed to evoke much domestic support.[60]

Academic history, of course, could not be left alone. Historians who refused to toe the party line were purged in Communist states, as they also were in Nazi Germany; in both, books deemed unacceptable were destroyed. Communist China very much took part in this process. There was also a memorialisation of the Communist past. The full panoply of naming and commemoration seen in other totalitarian societies was repeated in the Communist world. In the Soviet Union, cities were renamed, while the year was organised in terms of Communist celebrations. For example, 7 November became the Revolution Day holiday. In China, 1 October became National Day, celebrating the founding of the People's Republic.

Museums presented national history in the light of Communism – for example, in the Chinese Museum of Revolutionary History (now the Chinese National Museum), built in 1959 to celebrate the tenth anniversary of the foundation of the People's Republic. In 1955, the Museum of the Slovak National Uprising (in 1944) was founded in Banska Bystrica. It played up Communist Slovak participation and the support of the Red Army. More generally, students were made to take courses in the history of the Communist Party. The past became a display of class history and class struggle. This process continued until the last days of Communism. Thus, in 1987, the Museum of Revolution was opened in the Maarjamäe Palace in Tallinn, Estonia. A mural, *Friendship of Nations, Depicting the Achievements of Peoples' Friendship and Socialism*, was painted by Evald Okas.

Memorialisation, however, was not restricted to the Communist years. There was also an attempt to annex nationalist historical themes. For example, faced by the challenge of Nazi Germany, Stalin evoked memories of Russian nationalism, including in film, even though this involved respect for tsars, especially Ivan IV (the Terrible), Peter I (the Great), and Alexander I, the opponent of Napoleon. Ivan's cruelty, not least his use of the *oprichnina*, his private army, for harsh repression, was presented as necessary patriotism in order to protect Russia, a parallel that allegedly justified Stalin's use of the Purges to defend the

Russian Revolution.[61] Sergei Eisenstein's film *Aleksandr Nevsky* (1938) presented a medieval victory over German invaders (on the frozen Lake Peipus in 1242), although, in early 1941, at a time of Soviet alliance with Hitler, the film was banned.

The stress on a Russian national identity became far stronger after Germany attacked the Soviet Union in June 1941. The past was extensively used in a patriotism that therefore did not centre on Communist ideas. The three parts of Eisenstein's *Ivan the Terrible* appeared in 1945–7. At war's end, and also subsequently, Stalin used past Russian positions to support territorial gains and geopolitical dominance, not least in the Far East and eastern Europe. More recently, as another instance of a Communist ruler striking historical nationalist notes, the official biography of the North Korean dictator Kim Jon Il claims that he was born on the slopes of Mount Paektu, a key icon of Korean history, even though he was actually born in Moscow.

The tension between national and class history was replicated and complicated by that between Soviet and non-Russian accounts, and this became more acute as the Soviet Union expanded in the 1940s. In Ukraine, there was a serious tension over nationality from the outset of the Soviet period, and some of this was played out with reference to historical commemoration. Ukrainian memory and accounts clashed with Soviet themes, and the ideology of 'friendship of peoples' could not overcome this tension. This proved a major weakness for the Soviet Union; indeed, a fatal one in its ultimate collapse. A single community with approved common memories could not be created in this fashion.[62] This is a lesson of interest for the EU, although the latter, of course, is not a terror system like the Soviet Union was for much of its history.

Moreover, within the Communist bloc, peoples, unlike Ukrainians, who were not acknowledged as the basis for particular governmental jurisdictions, found their history far more actively downplayed. Thus, the Rusyns (Carpatho-Ukrainians and Carpatho-Rusyns are other names), most of whom lived in Ukraine but with others in Poland and Czechoslovakia, suffered a campaign to deny that they were a distinct people. Their name was banned; they were generally classified as Ukrainians;

and research into their history and culture was discouraged in an attempt to destroy their collective memory.[63]

Similar themes about the tension between national and class narratives,[64] and the failure to acknowledge minorities, can be seen in other Eastern Bloc states. In Bulgaria, religious culture was annexed to state ends, with 24 May being celebrated as Cyril and Methodius Day in honour of the patron saints, or the Day of Culture and Education.

The Communist approach, nevertheless, was different to the state-building nationalist historiography of the nineteenth century. The latter had denied aspects of earlier history as it sought to construct a coherent account from a given perspective as well as to create usable myths, but it had not done so to the extent seen with Communist regimes. Their fusion of Communist ideology with nationalist narratives ensured that, for reasons of policy and ideology, ideas of class had to be nationalised, but, in addition, national myths had to be provided with a class dimension and explication. The regimes were keen not only to dismantle existing socio-economic systems but also to transform the intellectual and cultural ideas of both government and populace.

This was seen in the Soviet Union, eastern Europe and China and also in Communist regimes elsewhere, most brutally in Cambodia. There, the Communist Khmer Rouge declared 1975 Year Zero and swept away the past (and much of the population). In seeking to create a new world that fulfilled their millenarian vision, the Khmer Rouge between then and 1978 both took forward the brutal (and unsuccessful) destruction for the cause seen with China's Great Leap Forward of the 1950s and Cultural Revolution of the 1960s and anticipated the savage methods and abrupt change that Islamic fundamentalists have called for more recently. The Khmer Rouge prospectus was not an affirmation of a history, however partial, comparable to nineteenth-century state-building, but rather a denial of the past in pursuit of a profoundly anti-historical vision. This vision proposed a Manichean contrast between good and evil, with the latter dominating a world that had to be destroyed in order to be renewed.

From Shi-Huangdi's Burning of the Books in 213 BCE, treating history as a blank is one way of negotiating the past in formulating definitions of identity, even if it turns the normal strategy upside down. As First Emperor, Shi-Huangdi (also spelled Qin Shihuangdi, 259–210 BCE) established the Ch'in dynasty and united China, completed the Great Wall and guarded his tomb with 10,000 life-size terracotta warriors. He represented the totalitarian 'legalist' school of thought, which valued society over the individual, stressed the present and rejected the past. Hence, in 213 BCE, he ordered the destruction of all records of pre-unification China in circulation outside the Imperial Library. The decree states that those who had not destroyed them within thirty days were to be branded or condemned to forced labour. The explicit purpose was to erect a barrier between past and present. Unification would thus appear as the norm, the past could not be used to discredit it, and Shi-Huangdi and his successors would be secured in power.[65]

Similarly, the Jacobins of the French Revolution sought to reset the clock to zero in 1793. Under the revolutionary calendar, the new system dated retrospectively from 22 September 1792 when the Convention proclaimed the Republic. The year 1792–3 became 'Year One' of the era of liberty, 1793–4 'Year Two' and so on. The inevitable implication was that the preceding monarchical era was symbolically deleted from human memory as unworthy of chronological commemoration, although no official attempt was made to destroy written records. As the new week consisted of ten days, rather than seven, it was also a rationalising shift to metrication and de-Christianisation.

Although these examples are the opposite of embracing, incorporating and moulding the past, they are alternative ways of dealing with it. The past is being manipulated for present advantage. Whether that requires the presence or absence of historical reference does not affect the principle at stake.

History understood as a sceptical study of the past that is motivated by a quest to understand, a quest that entailed appreciating as different the varied values of past ages, was scarcely acceptable in this perspective. Moreover, such an understanding of history, one that drew on the scepticism of nineteenth-century liberalism and on the appreciation of the past displayed by conservatives, especially in Britain, was of little interest to those who wanted to use the past for present purposes, not least in order to justify sweeping change. This tension remains the case today, and, after a discussion of particular cases in the next chapter, Chapter 4 considers the situation in the Third World as Western and other empires collapsed.

CHAPTER 3

HISTORY WARS AND MULTIPLE PASTS

Sectionalising the topic, as in the following chapters of this book, captures important continuities and questions at the level of major states and of groups of states. In doing so, there is, moreover, a shaping in terms of particular themes, such as the consequences of the demise of colonial empires in the Third World (Chapter 4) and of the Warsaw Pact and of Communist states (Chapter 5). It is also necessary to note the wider prevalence of the 'history wars' that are discussed. For example, they can be seen not only in the ex-Communist states considered in Chapter 5 but also in countries once ruled by authoritarian right-wing regimes, such as Chile, Greece, Portugal, South Africa and Spain, the last of which is considered in this chapter.

Once these regimes had fallen, the new governments and the liberated publics did not have to address the legacy of so insistent and comprehensive an ideology as Communism, in part because, however authoritarian, these right-wing states did not have a regime as powerful and persistent as the Communist ones. Moreover, there was no equivalent to the dominant, or would-be dominant, power of the Soviet Union in the Communist bloc. Nevertheless, the weight of the past is something that still has to be addressed when considering these states and discussing their 'history wars'. In part, this reflects the continuation of a liberal dimension to society in them during the years of authoritarian government and conservative ascendancy, and its ready return to influence once they ended, in part the attempt to exploit the past for political ends, if not revenge, and in part the attempt by conservatives to adapt to newly democratic times. Reference to truth and reconciliation, in short, does not capture the varied cross-currents present in such situations, nor the extent to which only some of them are able to voice themselves in truth and reconciliation commissions.

If history is in fact a civil discourse then it is natural to expect that it atrophied under regimes that starkly policed the public sphere, whatever the politics of the regime. It is also natural to expect that the restoration of an open public sphere would result in renewed historical debate. 'History thinking', from this perspective, emerges as a gauge of the health of civil society. Historical debate does not guarantee a healthy public space, but its absence definitely indicates something amiss. Debate, of course, does not prevent abuse of the processes of historical scholarship, while the propagation of partisan opinions becomes a problem when there is an attempt to close down differing voices.

SPAIN AND THE LEGACY OF CIVIL WAR

The first example comes from Spain where the right-wing dictator Francisco Franco, who seized power as a result of his success in the bitterly fought Spanish Civil War of 1936–9, retained control until he died in 1975. During his Nationalist regime, there was a determined attempt to present the type of history that the Vichy regime of 1940–4 in France would have applauded. There was an emphasis on unity through the victory of the Nationalist cause and on the central role of Catholicism. The Museo del Ejército in Madrid displayed Franco's Civil War car with the description 'The car the General used during the Crusade'. There was also an exclusion of regional perspectives and of the important role of Jews and Muslims in Spanish history.

The harsher aspects of the Francoist approach were, however, moderated from the late 1950s as the divisions of the Civil War, while still stressed, were replaced by a memorialisation linked to an attempted national reconciliation that was designed to secure the stability of the new order. Indeed, there was at times a conscious omission of the Civil War. For example, the university curriculum frequently stopped the teaching of Spanish history in the nineteenth century or quickly moved through the 1930s, presenting them as a lesson about the dangers of liberal rule.

Accounts critical of the Nationalists were not, of course, published in Spain. Thus, a Basque translation of George Steer's *The*

Tree of Gernika: A Field Study of Modern War (1938), a discussion of the brutally destructive bombing of Guernica in 1937, had to be published by exiles in Caracas in 1963.[1] The government also took measures to stop the investigation of the Civil War, including by closing the archives. The situation abroad was not much better, as many relevant archives, not least those of the Soviet Union, were also closed, which made it difficult to follow the politics of international intervention in the Civil War and, indeed, the extent to which each side received foreign assistance.

After Franco's death, although what critics termed *bunkerista* writers, such as Ricardo de la Cierva, continued to offer Nationalist history, there was a widespread determination to move beyond his legacy as an aspect of the creation of a new, democratic Spain. This was termed *El Pacto de Olvido* (the Pact of Forgetfulness), and it was maintained during both the centrist government of 1976–82 and its left-wing and right-wing successors of 1982–97 and 1997–2004 respectively. The last, the Aznar government, in particular, tried to present a consensus view of the past. There was also a failure of novelists and film-makers to discuss the issue, particularly in the 1970s. The anniversaries of key events in the 1930s were left to discussion rather than public memorialisation.

Aside from the removal of the words from the National Anthem – Francoist praise of the Fatherland was now deemed inappropriate – there were, however, cracks in the edifice. An anti-Francoist intellectual consensus developed with, for example, a discreet revolution in the Spanish universities in the 1980s. Moreover, the National Civil War Archive in Salamanca was organised in the 1980s. Ironically, most of the material was originally by Republicans and had been compiled under the Francoists in order to help in the trials of Republican leaders. The opening or, at least partial opening, of foreign archives was also instructive. The fall of the Soviet Union and the end of the Cold War were important, as the Soviet archives clarified much about Stalin's policy. There was also an opening up of non-Soviet material about the Spanish Civil War, including in Italian archives: Italian troops had played a major part in the war on the Nationalist side.

In the 2000s, the uneasy consensus within Spain collapsed. In part, this was a result of political pressure, especially from the regions striving for a proto-nationalism. The assault on the Castilian, centralised account of Spanish history helped lead to the reconsideration of the Civil War, not least because of the prominent role of Catalonia in the resistance to Franco. The Catalans were finally able to get back material Franco had deposited in Salamanca.

There was also an attack on the Pact of Forgetfulness at the popular level. Associations to recuperate the historical memory of the Republicans were founded. Novelistic accounts of the large-scale slaughter of Republicans during and after the Francoist takeover were published in the 2000s in what became a widespread cultural movement. These books became popular, and many were published at the local level. Moreover, the web was extensively used in order to discuss the issue. Much of this focused on the bodies in the large number of mass graves across Spain. The families of Republicans were insistent that their forebears be exhumed, identified and reburied. This pressure coincided with advances in geo-radar equipment, DNA testing and forensic science that made such discovery and identification a stronger prospect. Furthermore, the age of the children of the victims lent a sense of urgency to the situation, with pressure for the identification of their parents before they themselves died. The grandchildren proved the main champions. The first exhumation occurred in 2000, and by 2003 there were exhumations at the sites of Francoist concentration camps. The search for truth was linked to memorialisation, with plaques now explaining how people had died.

As with similar campaigns elsewhere in the world, there was also pressure for restitution of property and for the return of children that had been seized. After the Civil War, such children had been given to the families of Francoist officers, as also happened in Argentina in the 1970s. Confrontations over the confiscation of children encapsulate the passion of history wars.

Politics played a role. The Aznar government opposed what it saw as left-wing pressure for action, not least for a judicial process to investigate the cause of all deaths. After it fell in 2004, its replacement, under the Socialist José Luis Rodríguez Zapatero, whose grandfather was killed by a firing squad during the

Civil War, sought to garner political capital by highly publicised reversals of Aznar policies. On 12 October 2004, an effort was made by the new Socialist government to make more inclusive Spain's National Day, the day on which Christopher Columbus sighted the New World. The annual celebrations include a military parade attended by the King and the Prime Minister, but in 2004 they were accompanied by Angel Salamanca, a veteran of the large Fascist volunteer force sent by Franco to help the Germans on the Eastern Front, as well as by Luis Royo, who had fought for the Republicans in the Civil War. The Defence Minister, José Bono, declared that this was seen as offering 'a symbol of peace and harmony forever'. This was rejected by some of the left, angry at the inclusion of the Fascist veteran; Gaspar Llamazares, the head of the United Left, boycotting the event, which he termed 'an injustice, a historic falsitude by seeking an equivalence between liberty and fascism'. Bono argued, 'Those resentments have to be eradicated [. . .] if you left out all the Spaniards you may not agree with: the *Reconquistas*, the [nineteenth-century] Carlists, the Fascists [. . .] You wouldn't have many people left. It's all Spain'.

In October 2007, legislation by the Socialist government, the Law of Historical Memory, led to a furore. It was designed to permit the overturning of sentences by Franco's courts and to provide state funds for the exhumation of mass graves and for proper burials of the victims. This was criticised from the left as an amnesty and from the right for reopening divisions. The law covers 'all victims of the war killed for religious or political reasons', which includes clerics and others slaughtered by Republicans, but it is directed against the Nationalists.

The new Socialist government also prohibited Francoist memorialisation in the Valley of the Fallen. After the Civil War, Franco spent decades and about £200 million on building the basilica in which he was eventually buried, as well as a monastery and a towering crucifix. The vast edifice, visible 30 miles away, was designed as a monument to the Nationalist dead in the Civil War. Some of the ex-Republicans used as forced labour for the project had died while doing so, and politicians in 2004 focused on this as a way to commemorate the suffering under

Franco. In 2007, rallies at the site in memory of Franco were banned. The general's equestrian statue in Salamanca is due to be removed in May 2008.

Left-wing pressure, in turn, led to a backlash from the right, with writers, such as Pío Moa, who restated the old Nationalist view and attacked the re-evaluation of the history of the 1930s, finding an eager public, in large part because much of the population is deeply polarised. Moa claimed that the Civil War occurred due to the undermining of the political order by the left and, in 2006, 30 per cent of the respondents in a poll in the newspaper *El Mundo*, the paper of the 'populist' moderate right, argued that the Francoist rising of 1936 had been justified. In turn, the revisionists were criticised by establishment historians, most of whom were on the left. The debate was waged vigorously in the press and on the web. Thus, the recall of history reflected and sustained persisting cleavages in Spanish society.[2]

The Civil War, moreover, continued to be part of the vocabulary of Spanish politics. Thus, in 2007, Jesús de Polanco, head of the media empire Grupo Prisa, who had profited greatly from his left-wing connections, accused the conservative opposition People's Party of wanting 'to go back to the Civil War' because of its criticism of left-wing media opinions. This provided an easy way to say that something appeared unacceptable, but, although a powerful charge, the facile comparison was foolish, not least because Spain is in a very different situation to the 1930s, in part because it is a member of international bodies, most obviously the EU.

At the same time, it is important to note the autonomous development of academic ideas that are illuminated by research, although Spanish historiography itself does not put much of a stress on archival work. For example, the emphasis on Republican as well as Nationalist atrocities (there were many of both) is a product of scholarly work as well as partisan controversy.[3] Indeed, it is only thanks to historical research that it is possible to offer any accuracy in a situation satirised by George Orwell when he wrote of the newspaper reporting of the Spanish Civil War (in which he participated on the Republican side): 'I saw great battles reported where there had been no fighting, and complete silence where hundreds of men had been killed. I saw troops who had fought bravely denounced as cowards and traitors, and others who had never seen a shot fired hailed as the heroes of imaginary victories'.[4]

Public controversies in Spain over the past are at once an instance of the truth and reconciliation process and also an example of present politics. The first has become normative as a result of what is held to be the positive instance of such a process in post-apartheid South Africa. Other examples include Chile and Guatemala where there is an Association for the Recuperation of Historical Memory. Yet, there is also both resistance to such a process and attempts to politicise it. This can be seen in Colombia, where the government is only partially responsive to demands that it discuss links with right-wing paramilitaries in the bitter civil war of the 1980s and 1990s. There have been investigations, revelations and arrests, but truth and reconciliation are in short supply in Colombia, in part probably because of the continuing influence of these paramilitaries.

The political dimension operates in part as a cross-current, although it can also be regarded as central to the entire idea of truth and reconciliation. The role of politics could be seen in 1998 when a Spanish judge arranged for the arrest in Britain of the former Chilean dictator General Augusto Pinochet, a move very much opposed by a Spanish government that was keen on reconciliation within Spain. Pinochet was seen on the left as a substitute for the dead Franco. Contradiction in Spain between the impossibility of arresting any member of the Franco government and the possibility of acting against Pinochet was brought into the open in a way intended to embarrass the government.

TURKEY AND THE ARMENIAN MASSACRES

A very different type of divisiveness was exposed by contention over another civil conflict, the murderous treatment of the Armenians by the Ottoman authorities during the First World War. The Christian Armenians were seen as a pro-Russian fifth column (to employ a later term from the Spanish Civil War), and they were brutalised. Aside from large-scale killing and the expropriation of property, many were driven into an arid region where they died.

This became but one episode in the process by which the Ottoman Empire was transformed into Turkey, a state with a clearly proclaimed ethnic identity and one that broke with the multiple ethnicities of the far more cosmopolitan Ottoman system. Thus, the substantial Greek population in Asia Minor was driven into exile after Greece was defeated in 1922–3. Most of the European powers, especially Britain and France, had a major responsibility in egging on or supporting the Greeks. There was, in the end, a formal 'ethnic exchange' of people between Greece and Turkey.

In Turkey, subsequent criticism of the events of the 1910s and 1920s was unacceptable and was seen as a direct challenge to the integrity and cohesion of the state and to the Kemalist tradition of Atatürk, who had established the modern Turkish state, and this view is still taken. Atatürk, President from 1923 to 1938, pressed hard for the assimilation of those living within its boundaries, of whom possibly 15 per cent were of Caucasian origin (which includes Armenians). Distinct cultural traditions received scant support, and education had to be in Turkish. Official Kemalist nationalism denied a separate Kurdish identity and sought to incorporate Kurds into a Turkish national identity by designating them as 'mountain Turks'.

Hitler asked, 'Who now remembers the Armenians?', but the issue came to the fore from the 1960s in part as a result of pressure in the diaspora where it became a key issue in identity. There was strong Armenian lobbying against Turkey in the American Congress, while, as part of the Cold War, the Soviet Union provided backing for the Armenian Secret Army for the Liberation of Armenia: Turkey is a member of NATO. The Turks did not welcome this agitation and, in turn, presented their own view of the relevant history, as in *Armenian Allegations: Myth and Reality*, which was published in Washington in 1986 by the Assembly of American Turkish Organizations. The Armenian cause, moreover, was regarded as a Trojan Horse for that of the Kurds, who also challenged Turkish nationalism. As a result, legal action was taken against those who discussed the Armenian Massacres, while nationalist thugs resorted to force.

A climax of sorts was reached in 2006, with such legal action in Turkey, while, at the same time, in France it was made illegal to deny that the massacres occurred. This legislation did not improve relations between the two states, but it was not motivated simply by a dispute over history. Instead, there was a clear political dimension. Aside from the domestic politics in both France and Turkey, there were international angles. French critics of America found it useful to condemn one of its major allies, Turkey, while those unhappy with the prospect of Turkey in the EU focused on an issue in which the possible member state readily appeared in a poor light. In December 2004, Michel Barnier, the French Foreign Minister, insisted that Turkey take responsibility for the massacres, declaring 'Turkey should face up to the requirement of remembrance. The European project itself is founded on reconciliation', a formulation grounded on Franco-German reconciliation and on German remembrance of Nazi crimes, especially the Holocaust. More generally, the democratisation that is an aspect of convergence with the EU leads to a challenge to the state version of history. Tanef Akçam, a historian who has written of the Armenian genocide, notes that 'the state has a stake in how history is represented, certainly when that history touches on its very legitimacy'.[5]

As a minor aspect of the general tension, there is the question of the care of the part of historic Armenia that is a section of modern Turkey, a sentence the phrasing of which itself reveals the problems of addressing such issues. The area includes key Armenian archaeological sites which are significant to the Armenian collective historical consciousness, for example Ani, which became the capital in 961 CE. Armenians allege that Turks neglect their sites, a charge that can be related to the more general issue of a lack of Turkish interest in the cultural heritage of non-Turks located in Turkey – for example, Greeks (a process that, in fact, is equally mirrored by the Greeks). This treatment by the Turks, however, raises issues about the relationship between Classical and modern Greece. Turkish officials, such as those from the Culture Ministry, in contrast, claim to be mindful of such sites. In the specific case of Ani, they argue that damage to the site is coming from the use of explosives in a quarry across the border in Armenia.

Azerbaijan has definitely been destroying the cross-stones in Armenian cemeteries, most prominently those at Djulfa, where there was large-scale destruction in 1998 and 2002, culminating at the close of 2005 with the total destruction of the cemetery. Such destruction is used by Azeri officials to affirm, inaccurately, that Armenians have never lived in the region of Nakhichevan.

The Armenian issue shows every sign of gathering pace as the anniversary of the mass slaughter in 1915 nears. In part, this reflects the widespread international unpopularity of a Turkish government that is perceived, at least in the West, as harshly intolerant and as overly influenced by the military, although the latter is a powerful agent against Islamisation. By early 2007, eighteen states referred to the massacres as genocide, a description that in part drew on their designation as comparable to the Holocaust. In contrast, the official Turkish version charges that the Armenians killed more Turks than vice versa, a wholly inaccurate account.

More specific political pressures also played a role in the controversy. For example, the rise in Islamic political fortunes within Turkey in the early 2000s increased tension, while, in 2003, the Turkish refusal to allow the USA to use Turkey as a base from which to invade Iraq led to American anger. This was accentuated when Turkey put out feelers to Hamas, Iran and Syria, all, correctly, seen as anti-American. The result was pressure in the USA, leading, in 2007, to a Bill in Congress, declaring the Armenian slaughter a genocide. In response, the Turkish government threatened to limit military cooperation, which led Congress to back down.

Within Turkey, nationalist pressure has increased. The Penal Code, which criminalises insulting 'Turkishness', was used to take action against intellectuals such as, in 2005, the leading writer Orhan Pamuk, who had told a Swiss newspaper '30,000 Kurds and 1 million Armenians died in these lands', a reference to the Armenian Massacres and also the deaths of about 30,000 Kurds at the hands of Turkish security forces from the 1970s. It was similarly employed against Tanef Akçam, author of *A Shameful Act: The Armenian Genocide and the Question of Turkish Responsibility.*[6] In 2006, Elif Shafak was unsuccessfully prosecuted for allegedly insulting Turkishness for using the term 'genocide' in her novel *The Bastard of Istanbul*. In January 2007, Hrant Dink, the (Turkish and ethnically Armenian) editor of the weekly newspaper *Agos*, was murdered by a teenage nationalist for such an 'insult'. The police had failed to protect him. In 2007, there was a surge of support in Turkey for the xenophobic nationalism of the MHP (Milliyetçi Hareket Partisi) party, while hawks pressed for the expulsion of immigrants from Armenia.

The historical issue also affected relations between Turkey and its neighbour Armenia, which gained independence after the fall of the Soviet Union, although Turkish opposition to Armenian control of the region of Nagorno-Karabakh,[7] which it occupied in its war with Azerbaijan, is the key issue in diplomatic relations. Relations at the time of writing are not 'normalised', which means that the border has been closed since 1993, while Turkey also rejects diplomatic relations not only due to Nagorno-Karabakh but also in response to Armenia's campaign for international recognition of what it presents as a genocide. The Turkish government, in effect, is punishing Armenia for making it feel guilty, although the Turks also do not appreciate part of their country being called Western Armenia.

JAPAN AND CHINA

Violence was also seen in some of the demonstrations that recorded tension in East Asia as Japan considered how best to record its military and imperial role in 1931–45. Nationalists both downplayed Japan's responsibility for the warfare of the period and presented a seriously misleading account of its brutality. Anger with and in Japan focused on two issues in particular: the 'Rape of Nanjing' in 1937, in which large numbers of Chinese civilians were cruelly slaughtered,[8] and the enforced prostitution and harsh treatment of large numbers of, mostly Korean, 'comfort women' in order to provide sex for Japanese troops.[9]

The Japanese were apt to downplay both episodes, omitting them from textbooks, which became a prominent international issue in 1982, 2001 and 2005, and denying evidence about the brutality involved. This caused controversy in Japan, with bitter upsurges in the debate over Nanjing in 1972–4 and the mid-1990s, and also angered the Chinese. Within Japan, right-wing nationalists rejected accounts of the Nanjing atrocities. Iris Chang, an American of Chinese descent, who wrote *The Rape of Nanjing: The Forgotten Holocaust of World War II* (1997), was a reviled

The 1963 legislation failed, but political identification with Yasukuni became more prominent from the mid-1980s. The visits, in 2005 and 2006, by Junichiro Koizumi, then the Prime Minister, were regarded as particularly provocative. Although as an MP, Shinzo Abe, the grandson of Nobusuku Kishi, a member of the War Cabinet, also visited Yasukuni, he did not do so when Prime Minister in 2006–7. The museum at the shrine is uncritical about Japan's military past and, instead, depicts it in terms of honour and glory and presents Japanese imperialism favourably.

In June 2007, a visit to the shrine by Lee Teng-hui, President of Taiwan from 1988 to 2000, led to criticism from the Chinese government and from Taiwan's opposition Kuomintang party. As a reminder of the wider ramifications of the issue, Lee went to pay respects to his elder brother who died while serving in the Japanese Navy in 1945 when Taiwan was a Japanese colony. Indeed, due to the colonial link from 1915 to 1945, about 30,000 Taiwanese are commemorated in the shrine. Lee is a supporter of formal Taiwanese independence from China, and, in June 2007, he also claimed that Japanese colonial rule had laid the foundation for Taiwan's modern democratic society. The Japanese legacy is seen by those pressing for independence as supporting the claim that Taiwan is not Chinese.

The mistreatment of the 'comfort women' is also a controversial issue. In 1993, Yohei Kono, the Chief Cabinet Secretary in Japan, a key official, admitted and apologised for the military's role in coercing women into prostitution, while in 1995 the Asian Women's Fund was established to provide financial compensation. In March 2007, however, Abe's attempt to introduce qualifications, by arguing that there was no proof that women were coerced, led to considerable controversy. Although the Chinese government did not react with particular anger, the American House of Representatives pressed for a full apology for the wartime coercion and for adequate compensation. Abe offered a form of apology to President Bush.

There is no sign that American political criticism owes anything to a more critical academic approach in the USA to Japanese history. The key shift in the latter is the displacement of modernisation theory and its view of 1931–45 as an aberration from a more positive record of Japanese development. This theory has been replaced by a more critical analysis of Japan in that period.[10]

Other issues in Japan's treatment of its wartime past include individual attempts to seek compensation for wartime forced labour, which was often murderous. In June 2007, these attempts were rejected by the High Court at Sapporo. The Japanese record in this matter is far worse than that of Germany. Japanese companies, such as Mitsubishi, as well as the Japanese government, have done their best to deny responsibility and, in doing so, have seriously distorted the historical record.

More generally, Japanese attempts to underplay their role and to minimise their brutality in 1931–45 are unacceptable to the Chinese. For the Chinese government, Japanese atrocities provide a useful aspect of nation-building and one that distracts attention from the brutalities of the Communist regime, but they also draw on a deep well of anger in China.

At the same time, it is impossible to debate openly many aspects of the Communist years in China, not only the Tiananmen Square massacre of 1989 but also earlier episodes, particularly the Great Leap Forward. In China, relevant anniversaries of these episodes are ignored, domestic publications banned, foreign works censored, and history is left to personal memories.

Yet, there are also lots of grey zones about what can be discussed, although the boundaries are changing all the time. A simple model of repression therefore does not capture the more messy reality in China. An unsubtle division between 'freedom' and 'totalitarian' is not helpful in this context.

The democratic nature of Japanese public culture is also relevant here. For all the experience of reactionary nationalism in Japan,[11] Japanese students and the public are readily able to explore alternative readings of national history, and the most active critical participants in the debate about Japanese actions during the 1931–45 period are Japanese. In China, by comparison, the government remains actively involved in shaping a historical memory of Japanese aggression against China that shuts out any ambiguities – for example, the many Chinese who cooperated with Japanese rule.

The continuing controversy between China and Japan will be kept alive by anniversaries of the conflict. On one hand, these can be seen as extraneous to 'realist' disputes focused on the issues of the here and now, particularly the political and economic manifestations of regional dominance, such as the fate of Taiwan, which is regarded as crucial to the security of Japanese trade, and also rights of maritime exploitation, especially oil drilling. On the other hand, tensions over the past can be seen as encouraging distrust and rivalry when addressing these issues.

Joining both is an aspiration to assert what are seen as national interests. This means a more robust stance both politically and in terms of identity. In large part, the two cannot be separated. For example, Japanese military deployments and an interest in missile-defence systems are linked to ideological transformation, not least the demand for a revision of Article 9 of the post-war constitution, which commits Japan to peaceful policies. Linked to this is a governmental move, the proposal to transform the Japanese Defence Agency into a full ministry with a seat in the Cabinet.

Yet, assertion is also within a political context, not least that of the responses by others. Thus, Japan's post-war government and political culture were, in part, moulded by the American victors and occupiers. In contrast, post-war relations between Japan and China proved far more difficult. Alongside the Cold War, which divided Japan from China, the earlier experience and nature of Japanese occupation was clearly part of the equation as China was brutally treated, whereas, with the exception of part of the Aleutian chain of islands, the USA avoided occupation. This contrast was also seen in March 2007, when Japan and Australia were able to negotiate a security pact. Chinese opposition to Japanese military transformation draws on a political application of the memorialisation of the Second World War. Furthermore, from the 1980s, this memorialisation within China was extended to encompass the role of the Kuomintang (Nationalists) in the opposition to Japan, as in the museum complex opened near Chengdu in 2005.

Conversely, in Japan, assertiveness resonates with nationalists and others seeking a more positive account of the past. The Second World War thus plays a central role in public discussion, which, in turn, helps encourage demands and remarks by nationalists. The Hall of Shōwa, which opened in 1999, displaying everyday life during the Second World War, was entrusted to the Japan Association of War-Bereaved Families, a conservative body that was far from critical of Japan's wartime policy. Two years later, moreover, a Tokyo banquet attended by prominent figures, including an ex-prime minister, commemorated the death of the progenitor of the kamikaze attacks, Admiral Takijiro Onishi, who killed himself a day after the Japanese surrender in 1945. At the banquet, youths dressed as kamikaze pilots sang war songs from the stage before the general singing of a patriotic song.

In 2007, Yuko Tojo, a granddaughter of General Tojo, ran for election into the Upper House in order to realise his last wish, the establishment of an official memorial day for the country's war dead. She also claimed that 'schoolteachers who refuse to stand for the playing of the national anthem or the raising of the flag are not even fit to be teachers'. Yuko Tojo also regards the post-war constitution as invalid, stating that it 'has forced Japan to lose its spirit as an independent country. We have lost pride and confidence and it must now be revived'. She claimed that prime ministerial visits to Yasukuni were a matter of duty.

Yet, to underline the contentious nature of the past, and the way in which its memorialisation is subject to present politics, the Socialist Party supported an official apology to China and Korea, the Japan–China Friendship Association was highly critical of wartime policy and supported research on it, and the Japan Association for Memorializing Student-Soldiers Fallen in Battle used the Second World War as a basis for advocating pacifism.[12] Contrasting responses to the death of the Emperor Hirohito in 1989, the wartime monarch, made these differences readily apparent.

Memory politics set themes and parameters for competing arguments about present and future. In April 2007, the Prime Minister of China, Wen Jiabao, raised the issue when, on an official visit to Japan, he spoke to the Japanese Diet (Parliament), acknowledging Japan's official regret and apology for its actions in the war but also asking that its government act on those attitudes and promises. This was understood to mean that Japanese prime ministers not visit Yasukuni. Wen noted that the invasion of China in the 1930s was the cause of 'indescribable pain and wounds in the heart of the Chinese people', although he also claimed that the Japanese suffered 'enormous suffering and pain' during the war and were victims of 'a handful of militarists', a conciliatory view designed to lessen tension. Wen continued by meeting Emperor Akihito at the Imperial Palace and drawing to his attention remarks the latter made in 2005 when, in a birthday speech, Akihito emphasised the need for 'history to be handed down in a proper manner'.

The wider background of this has been described in academic-speak in what is a fundamentally important and extremely valuable collection: 'The end of the Cold War also became an important contextual marker in the realm of public memory as Japanese, Koreans, Chinese, Taiwanese, and Vietnamese began to grapple with a new layer of meaning added to the past by the changing present'.[13]

The latter included not only the end of the Cold War but also changing relations between the Asian states. Chinese pressure for Japanese apologies was far from new, but the geopolitical, political and economic contexts in the 2000s were different to earlier periods.

HISTORICAL SITES

Yasukuni is a religious site, and the attitude of Shintoism towards 'historical issues' is different to the position in the secular West. Nevertheless, Yasukuni is also an instance of the more general way in which historical sites play a key role, not only in memorialisation and commemoration but also as the symbolic setting for political action.

Thus, on 14 April 2007, Atatürk's mausoleum in the Turkish capital, Ankara, was the focus of one of the largest public rallies in recent world history. Over 300,000 people, many waving Turkish flags and shouting anti-government remarks, did so in a complaint against the governing AK party (Adalet ve Kalkınma Partisi, Justice and Development Party), whose Islamicist identity is held to be a challenge to the secularist tradition associated with Atatürk. As such, the march was also an affirmation of the prevailing interpretation of Turkish nationalism and was thus used in order to criticise the government's attempt to join the EU. The mausoleum had been the focus for pro-secular marches before, as on 18 May 2006, after the murder of a judge by an Islamic radical. Atatürk's memory and legacy are protected by the Atatürk Thought Association, which, in 2007, claims a million-strong membership. After the Turkish Army, which very much supports this legacy, conquered much of Cyprus in 1974, numerous statues of Atatürk were erected there in order to assert the link with Turkey. Similarly, pictures and photographs of him are much in evidence.

Historical 'sites' of a different type are provided by episodes that are used to support key interpretations of the past which are allegedly of importance for the present. An obvious instance is provided by episodes that contribute to, or are presented as supporting conspiracy theories. Conspiracies rest in large part in the eye of the beholder,[14] but are also key to themes of this book, namely the controversial nature of the presentation and understanding of history, and the close relationship of history with politics.

CHAPTER 4

NEW STATES AND THE
POSSIBILITIES OF LINEAGE

There is no natural and necessary way to organise the rest of
this book. A geographical organisation, indeed, may be queried
in light of the new-found focus, especially, but not only, in the
West, on globalisation and world history. This diminishes the
value of a discussion in terms of geographical blocs. World
history has not only its own academic controversies but also a
more profound public and governmental division focused on the
alleged harms both of globalisation and of Western dominance.
This division might well be the basis of a chapter comparable
to those that follow, but, at present, this debate lacks the historical reference points and national focus of contention that is
so important to history wars. States may appear redundant to
some commentators in an age of large-scale global capital flows,
migration and, more generally, globalisation, but identity politics suggests otherwise.

History wars are differentiated geographically in the remainder of this book, but the shapings of these blocs can be challenged,
while their order is far from inevitable. Indeed, Chapters 5 to 7
originally appeared in a different order. This chapter, however,
was always the first of the geographical ones. That was because
the pressure for a new public history is most acute in states that
are newly independent. Indeed, the failure to put the discussion
of the states covered in this chapter first among the geographical
chapters was a flaw in my *Using History* (2005).

New states face the problem of establishing a workable
past. Such a past is designed to help provide both identity and
legitimacy and is seen as an aspect of the winning of independence. Between 1945 and 1975, much of the world, especially

in Africa and South and South-East Asia, gained independence from imperial rule. This ensured that the states in these regions had to create public histories. The task was made more difficult by the repeated attempt to establish a lineage that spanned the period of Western imperial rule and that linked newly independent states to pre-imperial predecessors. This chapter looks first at Asia and then at Africa, where independence was won later, before offering some general conclusions. The states considered are eclectic, which indicates the variety of the processes considered in this chapter, a variety that can be expanded by discussing other countries.

As in Europe earlier, the creation of public history did not begin with a clean slate. Indeed, there was often a fatal intertwining between the creation of this history and the justification of the position of the governing regime. Such regimes tended to regard their justification and the creation of a new public history as identical, so that the political purpose of the public history did not strike it as illegitimate. Far from it. There was also a clearcut pattern of involvement by public intellectuals who benefited directly from their links to the regime.

A major aspect of commitment was to an exemplary account of the process by which independence had been obtained. This can be seen, for example, in Algeria, India, Indonesia, Israel and Vietnam, as a stress on the independence struggle was used to demand unity, while the role of particular groups in this process was employed to justify their subsequent prominence in national life. Thus, in Algeria, the National Liberation Front (FLN)[1] employed the struggle for independence as a rationale for its power, with the FLN seen as victors over French colonialism, and thus as enabling the Algerians to recover their Arab-Islamic identity and heritage.

In Vietnam, the role of Ho Chi Minh, President of North Vietnam from 1954 to 1969 and the wartime leader of the Communists both against the Americans and South Vietnamese, and earlier against the French, is variously commemorated. This includes his mausoleum and museum in Hanoi, the renaming of Saigon as Ho Chi Minh City, and hats being named after him. Rule by the Communist Party rests on its eventually victorious role in the conflicts of 1945–75 and, in part, is justified by this history of 'national liberation'.[2]

INDIA

In India, the Congress Party could be presented as both cause and end of independence. There was an emphasis in Indian public accounts on the Congress Party's Quit India campaign in 1942 in leading to British withdrawal five years later, and an overlooking of the role of force in ensuring Indian rule of Hyderabad and Goa. Relevant locations, such as Gandhi's cremation place, became national sites of memory. Congress's historical role was subsequently contested by its political rivals.

It was not only recent history that was seen anew in India. There was also a far more critical account of India's history under British rule. This entailed minimising the value of British rule as well as applauding those who opposed it. Thus, empire was presented as a vehicle for British plunder and economic exploitation and, therefore, an economic burden that delayed the development of the country. In place of the British emphasis on progress towards modernity under colonial rule came a public criticism of the latter that frequently drew more on rhetoric than evidence. However, the same point could be made about the British defence of imperialism. Imperial nostalgists, like radical anti-colonials offering polemical anti-British polemic, go for a black-and-white picture of British rule, but, in both cases, this is clearly political posturing rather than historical analysis. Serious mainstream historians of India – Indian, British and others – do not adopt these positions, although, nevertheless, there are important differences and tensions in their treatment which, in part, reflect intellectual suppositions that draw some of their energy from an ideological partisanship.[3]

The Indian public account of history led to a rewriting of episodes in the conflicts of British imperial conquest, in particular, Indian atrocities. These had been discussed by the British in part in justification of their claim to be morally superior and, thus, as legitimating empire. The Black Hole of Calcutta (now Kolkata), in which Siraj-ud-daula, the Nawab of Bengal, imprisoned British captives with fatal results in 1756, played a major role, as did the treatment of British women and children during the 'Indian Mutiny' of 1857–9, especially the massacre at Kanpur, which was commemorated with the Kanpur Memorial Well.

The commemoration of the Mutiny by the British focused on heroism, chivalry and martyrdom in an exemplary Christian and British fashion, the Christianity supporting and defining Britishness and vice versa. Now, instead, with India independent, the emphasis was moved to what were presented as British atrocities, especially the treatment of captured sepoys during the Mutiny, although, in practice, the execution of mutineers was normal across the world in this period. The Mutiny itself was reinterpreted and renamed as a rebellion that was intended to begin a war of independence, indeed as the First War of Independence.[4] In May 2007, the Government Freedom Struggle Museum was officially inaugurated at Meerut, where the rebellion began.

That year, the 150th anniversary of the rebellion provided an opportunity for the government to sound appropriate notes. The Prime Minister, Manmohan Singh, declared 'The fight for freedom united people from different religions and speaking different languages. Hindus and Muslims stood together shoulder to shoulder. We cannot forget the Hindu–Muslim unity that 1857 represented and held out as an example for subsequent generations'. Thus the anniversary was to be used to counter potent religious and caste divisions, and, in particular, Hindu sectarianism.

This led to specific memorialisation, as with a march in May 2007 in which 30,000 people travelled from Meerut to Delhi, to underline how Muslims fought the British alongside Hindus. The link between rebels and the rest of society was also underlined, with Sonia Gandhi, the leader of the Congress Party, declaring 'While the sepoys were in the vanguard, the people of the country were behind them'. The role of Indians in supporting Britain in this crisis of power was ignored, although the suppression of the rebellion depended on this support. In other former colonies, there was also an emphasis on British mistreatment, as in Jamaica, where the brutal suppression of the Morant Bay Rebellion in 1865 was used, as in the 1995 documentary drama *Catch a Fire* (dir. Menelik Shabazz), to define the entire experience of imperial rule to a misleading extent. As far as the Black Hole of Calcutta is concerned, the number of victims has been reduced from 125 to forty-three. At the level of individual rural communities, there was a running-together in local stories of episodes in which the British played a role and a degree of confusion about the resonance of the past. This also indicated its malleability for local purposes.[5]

Contention in India, however, did not solely focus on British rule. There was also the contrast between the dominant Hindu and Muslim accounts of India's past, a contrast that was accentuated by the politics of modern India and by its generally hostile relations with Muslim Pakistan, which had been part of British India. A key aspect of this competing history was the presentation of Muslim rulers, who indeed had controlled much of India, particularly northern India, in the medieval and early modern periods and even subsequently, as with the Nizams of Hyderabad until Indian independence. These rulers were seen by many Indians, especially Hindus, as non-Indian, which led to praise for their opponents, most prominently the Marathas who, in the seventeenth and eighteenth centuries, defied and constrained the Mughal emperors, who were Muslims. As a consequence, there is sensitivity on the part of Hindu nationalists about the treatment of Shivaji, the leading Maratha figure of the late seventeenth century. In 2004, as a result, the Bhandarkar Oriental Research Institute in Pune was attacked, allegedly for contributing to critical work on Shivaji.

The aggressive nationalism and, indeed, fascistic tendencies of Hindu sectarianism was much in display during the years of dominance by the Bharatiya Janata Party (BJP) from 1998 to 2004. This had a major impact in the field of education, with the manipulation of state patronage to advance a BJP agenda in appointments, such as to the University Grants Commission, the Secondary School Board, the Indian Institute of Advanced Study, and the Councils of Social Sciences and Historical Research, and in publications, especially school history textbooks published in 2003.[6] In 1999, the BHP sought, via the Ministry of Information and Broadcasting, to have the role played by Hindu extremists in Gandhi's assassination in 1948 played down in a film, a move that led to a public furore. Much of the Hindutva movement gains energy from expatriate Indians, and, within that community, there is a strong leavening of scientists, engineers and businessmen, rather than scholars, journalists and intellectuals as was often the case with right-wing nationalism in, for example, east-central Europe. Nevertheless, in its debating of history, India is more analogous to (other) democracies than to a country like China where the state controls so much more of how history is presented.

The BJP view of history might have lasting weight in Indian society because the pamphlet history it produces is widely available and popular. This literature is also used in the thousands of privately funded and largely unregulated schools that have sprung up in India. The BJP account of the indigenity (and superiority) of 'Aryans' (rejecting the notion that they were initially outsiders) has an appreciative audience among poorer high caste groups whose status is sliding as society changes. Academics will doubtless continue to rebut this account, and the new Congress government has intervened to re-rewrite the contentious school textbooks. Historical myths, however, are very powerful. In 2007, BJP activists threatened, intimidated and mobbed British tourists whom they accused of commemorating the British role in suppressing the Mutiny, 'the killers of our freedom fighters'.[7]

Hindu sectarianism was not the sole issue. In tension involving the Sikh community, there were attempts to seize the commanding heights of Sikh history. Thus, in 2007, Ram Rahim Singh, the leader of the Dera Sacha Sauda, a Sikh movement aligned with Congress, presented himself in the garb of Gobind Singh, a key seventeenth-century guru. This step was regarded as unacceptable by the Akali Dal Government of Punjab, and they demanded an apology and ordered his arrest on the charge of hurting Sikh sentiments.

The extent to which historical episodes gave rise to different, religiously encoded, social practices was raised in June 2007 when Pratabha Patil, the moderate Hindu Governor of Rajasthan, who was the Congress Party's nominee as President of India, claimed that the purdah system, including wearing the veil, derived from the challenge of medieval Muslim invaders, adding 'times have changed. India is now independent and hence the systems should also change'. This led to criticism from Muslim leaders who saw the remarks as anti-Muslim and accused Patil of rewriting history, while some scholars also suggested that the veil existed in early Indian society.

Twentieth-century Indian history was a matter of contention from the outset, with disagreement over how far and how best to present Indian pressure for autonomy and, subsequently, independence. Udham Singh, a Sikh living in Britain, had been executed for killing Sir Michael O'Dwyer, the harsh former Lieutenant-Governor of the Punjab, in 1940, as a response to the Amritsar Massacre of 1919 in which at least 379 unarmed demonstrators were killed. He was treated as a hero by many Indian contemporaries and has since been seen in the same light. Indeed, an annual conference is held in his memory. Subhas Bose, whose Indian National Army cooperated with the Japanese in the Second World War, is regarded in his home province of Bengal as a great nationalist leader (and Kolkata airport is named after him), but his status elsewhere in India is far more ambivalent.

More significantly, controversy over the partition of India between the new states of India and Pakistan in 1947 and over, in particular, the mass killings, the large-scale refugee movements and the treatment of Kashmir, continues to bedevil Indo-Pakistan relations, not least by feeding into each side's potent sense of grievance.

INDONESIA

Similarly, in Indonesia, a nationalist history has been to the fore. The winning of independence from the Dutch in 1949, after an insurrectionary war, was followed by praise for earlier opposition to the Dutch; and, indeed, Dutch rule was presented as an occupation. As with other states, there was also felt to be the need for a historical backing for unity in what was a new state. Achmail Sukarno, the nationalist, and one-time teacher of history, who became President in 1949 was convinced that the presentation of history had a crucial role to play in the assertion of Indonesian identity. Since the state was the product of a brief period of Dutch imperialism and the word 'Indonesia' was only coined in the nineteenth century, there was a need for a unifying ideology when that imperial control was removed. The longevity of the concept of Indonesia was asserted, with precursors sought, such as the fourteenth-century Javanese empire of Majapahit. As with other newly independent states, there was also a stress on national history rather than on the regional dimension. Nationalism is one of the five guiding principles in *Pancasila*, the new nationalist ideology for Indonesia first articulated by Sukarno. However, in reality, there was no shared past, and this challenges the idea of a common Indonesian identity.

Under Sukarno, the national versus regional dimension was crucial in determining the content of public history, but other disputes also relating to the protean and contested nature of Indonesian nationhood played an important role. In particular, the extent to which the new state should have a Muslim, a Communist or a liberal identity was related to the presentation of its history. Muslims underplayed the Hindu–Buddhist past, while Communists and liberals offered different accounts of the interests and development of the state.

This was resolved in 1965–6 when the Communists were bloodily crushed by the military. General Suharto, who became President in 1968, replacing Sukarno, sought to establish a self-styled 'new order' designed to replace ethnic and religious divisions. Public history matched the content of its nationalism. An authorised national history designed for schools was published in 1977. The key figure in this work, Nugroho Notosusanto, was head of the military history section of the armed forces (and a brigadier general as a result), and became Minister of Education in the 1980s. Museums and monuments were carefully used to this end, and the celebration of Heroes' Day, begun in 1957, carried forward an exemplary view of the past. The heroes were very much drawn from those who had resisted the Dutch, either the conquest or what was presented as the occupation.[8]

KOREA AND TAIWAN

It was not only European imperialism that was at issue in the presentation of the colonial and post-colonial experience. The collapse of the Japanese Empire in 1945 meant the end of control over both Taiwan and Korea, although neither had an uncomplicated passage towards sovereign independence.

Korea, instead, was divided between a Communist dictatorship and what became a conservative democracy, and each struggled to define both an acceptable account for themselves and also one that would work for the whole of Korea, which each claimed to represent. This led to opposition to China over the latter's claim on part of what both North and South Korea saw as their history. They agree that the Koguryŏ kingdom (37 BCE–668 CE) was one of Korea's founding kingdoms and that its territory included part of north-east China. However, in 2002, the Beijing-based Centre for the Study of Borderland History and Geography asserted Chinese academic claims that Koguryŏ was, in essence, a Chinese state. This was unacceptable to both North and South Korea, and the resulting contention saw the customary range of sites of dispute. These included contested monuments as well as natural sites, specifically Mount Paektu, which plays a major role in Korean mythology, as well as textbooks. In the latter, South Korea argues that the Kojoson kingdom started in 2333 BCE, a backward extrapolation of distinct Korean history designed to make the Koguryŏ issue less central. This dispute related not solely to the question of the longevity of Korea as a separate culture and political entity but also to its extent. More generally, the political quest for the reunification of Korea has led to an emphasis on shared history, ancient and recent. The latter includes the theme of victimisation under Japanese rule. Extensive Korean collaboration with Japan has been erased from the record.

Taiwan was returned to China by Japan in 1945, only for the Nationalist Chinese regime of Chiang Kai-Shek to flee there four years later when it was driven from mainland China. In response to (Communist) Chinese claims to Taiwan, its independence is not recognised by many states. Taiwanese independence was thus centrally entwined with Chinese divisions. There was then the problem in Taiwan of presenting a different account of Chinese history, while only controlling a small portion of it, and, eventually, of reaching out towards the establishment of a national historical tradition for Taiwan itself. The latter focused on a constituency that had been marginalised under the Nationalists: ethnically Chinese native Taiwanese (i.e., descendants of immigrants centuries ago), the majority of the island population.

Although contentious, the establishment of a national historical tradition for Taiwan itself has led to a rejection, by the Democratic Progressive Party, not only of rule from Beijing but also of the Nationalist legacy, not least the heroic status of Chiang Kai-Shek, who is seen as a symbol of the goal of reunification. His statues were removed, for example from military bases, and dumped in the Chiang Kai-Shek Culture Park at Tashi, and there was a widespread process of renaming which includes streets as well as the international airport.

As so often, anniversaries proved a central issue. In this case, the 228 Incident is the key: on 28 February 1947, protests against rule by the Nationalists were violently suppressed, leading to the slaughter of possibly 28,000 people. The sixtieth-anniversary commemoration provided an opportunity for the Democratic Progressive Party, the pro-independence government, to criticise Chiang and the Nationalists, whose Kuomintang Party remains powerful. The latter were portrayed as an outside force suppressing a popular movement in 1947, and, indeed, tension between Taiwan and rule from Beijing had been an important feature before the period of Japanese rule, although who the 'real Taiwanese' are is problematic. At the school level, the Chiang regime is now presented as authoritarian.

Marking the anniversary of the 228 Incident, the government, in 2007, announced plans to change a key site of memorialisation, the Chiang Kai-Shek Memorial Hall, the centre of the Chiang Kai-Shek Memorial Park. The hall is to be renamed the National Taiwan Democracy Memorial Hall, and the perimeter wall of the sanctuary is to be removed in order to underline its democratic accessibility. The renamed hall displays evidence of the character of Chiang's regime as a police state guilty of human-rights abuses. Moreover, the changing of the guard there has ceased to be a public ritual. Chiang's portrait may also be dropped from the coinage. These moves symbolised a break with the past that was also a rejection of the link with China. In contrast, although the identity and history of the indigenous aboriginal population (a tiny percentage of the population) have now been noted with the establishment of a Ministry of Aboriginal Affairs, they still only play a minor role in Taiwanese history.

JAPAN

Post-colonial history was also at issue for Japan because, during the American occupation of 1945–52, its political, economic and social structures were transformed. At the same time, as with Germany, West and East, this permitted the presentation of a break in continuity that allowed the post-occupation governments to depict the situation in the 1930s and early 1940s as a disastrous interlude that could be forgotten in favour of a focus on a more exemplary history. Japanese society was not blamed for the war, which poses an acute problem for others in dealing with Japanese accounts of the past. This problem resonates particularly in the USA, given Japanese recriminations about the American use of atomic weapons in 1945. Indeed, there is a Japanese victimhood focused on this issue. This victimhood, however, provided the basis for a refusal to accept other accounts of Japanese policy, especially those from China and South Korea, as well as for a more assertive nationalism. Rejection of Japanese victimhood provides an interesting tie between China and the USA. In June 2007, the victimhood in Japan was challenged when Fumio Kyuma, the Defence Minister, said that the atomic bombings 'couldn't be helped' and 'ended the war', which indeed was the case. In the face of the resulting furore, he resigned within the week. Nagasaki rejected the government in the elections that following month. Kyuma's replacement as Defence Minister, Yuriko Koike, has links with nationalist groups who rewrite school textbooks.

ISRAEL

A distinctive instance of Asian post-colonial history was presented by Israel, not that Israelis, who generally regard themselves as part of the West, would like to accept the geographical constraint of being placed in Asia. Instead, they emphasise culture as more definitive than geography. In Israel, the focus was not on a long period of anti-imperial struggle, because the key opposition to the British in the 1930s had been led by the Arabs. Indeed, the Arab Rising of 1936–9 was in part directed against Jewish immigration. The Holocaust, the wartime slaughter of Jews by the German regime of Adolf Hitler, instead, played a central role in Israeli self-identification, not least with the establishment of Yad Vashem as a Holocaust memorial, museum and archive in 1953, and the seizure, in 1960, and trial and execution, in 1961–2, of Adolf Eichmann, a major Nazi war criminal.[9]

The foundation of Israel was seen as a key episode in escape and recovery from the Holocaust. The Holocaust also provides a frame of reference for considering Israel's predicament in the face of Islamic hostility. It leads to a call for perpetual vigilance but also acts against suggestions of compromise. Thus, calls for action against Iran as it develops its nuclear capacity make reference to Nazi policy, as with the remark by Binyamin Netanyahu, a former Prime Minister, 'It is 1938 [a reference to the Munich crisis], and Iran is Germany'. In the face of the hostility of Arab states, which, at the least, in the War of Independence, 1948–9, intended ethnic cleansing, if not genocide, the Israeli emphasis on the sufferings and endurance of Jews was, and is, not, however, matched by adequate consideration of the plight of the Palestinian refugees. In what the Palestinians called the *Nakba* (disaster), they had been forcibly driven out of, as well as fleeing from, their homes in what is now Israel. Palestinian memory and history is challenged through the destruction of Palestinian villages and landscapes.[10]

Arab writers, in turn, compared the Israelis to the medieval Crusaders. This begs the academic question of the use and abuse of the Crusades, but it is a comparison that provided a resonance that located the Israelis as alien as well as implying that they would be defeated as the Crusaders had been after nearly two centuries.[11] Indeed, Saddam Hussein, who persecuted the Kurds, sought to draw on the prestige of the most famous, Saladin, a victor over the Crusaders who regained Jerusalem for Islam. Saddam named an elite division the 'Saladin'.

Israeli public history invoked a ranking of alleged achievement by ethnic groups, as well as a teleology based on performance. The Israeli position was defended by the association of progress with Zionism, specifically the paternalist argument that Jewish settlers had made fertile land that had earlier been neglected and mishandled by the Palestinians. Conversely, the

Palestinian national myth is heavily focused on the past, not least on a remembrance through grievance as loss. As with other societies suffering loss, family narratives play an important role in sustaining a collective anger.

Another lacuna in Israeli public history was the reluctance to consider the role of political violence, indeed terrorism, in the process by which Zionists challenged the British Mandate – for example, the bombing of the King David Hotel in Jerusalem in 1946. This was more pertinent because the Prime Minister from 1976 to 1983, Menachem Begin, had been the head of the Irgun Zwei Leumi, the military wing of the Revisionist Zionist Movement, while his successor as Prime Minister, in 1983–4 and 1986–92, Yitzhak Shamir, was a member of the Lohamei Herut Yisrael – the Stern Gang to the British.

A far freer polity, society and culture than its Arab neighbours, which, indeed, have shown a reluctance to accept Israel's existence and need for security, Israel also has an independent academic sphere that can encompass revisionist critiques of public myth which are very sharp,[12] especially for a country that is threatened by serious external challenges. The work of Baruch Kimmerling, Simha Flapan, Avi Shalim, Benny Morris and Ilan Pappé, the latter two of whom referred to themselves as post-Zionists, however, was also criticised; Pharon Meggel, for example, termed Kimmerling, the author of *Zionism and Territory* (1983), a 'rewriter' of history. Moreover, veterans' groups have complained about the portrayal of their activities during the 1948–9 war, specifically allegations depicting the treatment of Palestinians as 'ethnic cleansing'. Across the world, such groups are an important constituency in the discussion of recent wars, for example in the USA with the controversy, in 1995, over the Air and Space Museum's presentation of the use of atomic bombs in 1945.[13]

Israeli academic revisionism, and the subsequent controversies, compared far more with the situation in Western countries[14] than with the position across most of Asia. The anti-Semitic nature of some Saudi Arabian textbooks, as revealed in a 2003 survey,[15] are particularly chilling. The same is true of other Arab states, including Palestine.

AFRICA

In Africa, the dissolution of European empires led to the creation of new states that sought to appropriate a pre-colonial past in order to establish an exemplary history. This directed attention to powerful pre-colonial civilisations and states such as Mali and Zimbabwe. Earlier European attempts to explain such African civilisations as the work of Mediterranean peoples moving south were rejected. This rejection was not only in accordance with academic research but also fitted the new political mood with its stress on African achievement and, thus, on the absence of need for European intervention.

Moreover, the historical consciousness of pre-colonial societies was recovered by work on oral history. Research indicated that the earlier notion of tribes was a misleading aspect of Western classification that was designed to aid definition, if not control, and, due to the pejorative connotations of tribalism, to demean African society. A more scholarly and complex account of ethnogenesis could therefore be offered.

However, if the territorial scope and thus ethnic composition of many states was, at least in part, the work of Western conquerors and therefore relatively recent, Western territorialisation and concepts of identity and political authority were (and are) themselves used to particular ends by African nationalists.

This was least an issue in North Africa. Even there, Western imperialism had helped draw boundaries, but it did so as a stage in the shaping by other empires, most recently, prior to Western powers, the Ottoman (Turkish) Empire. The transforming role of such non-Western imperial episodes was more generally the case. This role indicates a flaw not simply with a nationalist public history that blames the West but also with the idea that Western imperial rule can be treated simply as an unwelcome interlude in a benign history of self-rule.

Nevertheless, in opposition to Western imperial rule, a tendency to define and emphasise a contrasting nativist consciousness and continuity was present in much of the literature produced by African commentators, a tendency that was also present elsewhere in the world. Thus, Afaf Lufti Al-Sayyid Marsot, in her *History of Egypt*, claimed that

throughout the eras of alien rule the native Egyptian recognised the existence of a fixed and unchanging territory that
was Egypt, which had fixed natural boundaries, and which
was separate as a territory even when it was the centre of an
empire or amalgamated into an empire as a mere province.
Thus, the native Egyptian, while coping with alien rulers,
also clung to the fixed piece of territory that he identified
and knew as Egypt. [16]

Such claims are not critically scrutinised in much of the literature. Egypt was also an important actual or would-be colonial
power in Sudan, the Horn of Africa, Arabia and the Middle East
in the nineteenth century.

The rethinking of the Western colonial period in Africa led to a
stronger emphasis on resistance to colonial rule. In part, this was a
deliberate 'appropriation' of resistance for the cause of nationalism
and, thus, for the legitimation of the subsequent regime. This process was particularly useful in Guinea in West Africa where Ahmed
Sékou Touré, the long-serving first Prime Minister (1958–72) and
first President (1961–84) of the independent state, was the grandson of Samori Touré, the leader of the Mandinke people who had
fought the French between 1884 and his capture in 1898. As was
generally the case, reference to Samori Touré ignored the extent to
which he had been a tyrant and had oppressed other peoples, who
also provided valuable allies to the French in their conflict with
Touré. In a similar fashion, other imperial powers, Western and
non-Western, had benefited from a considerable degree of local
support, as the Spaniards did when they overthrew the Aztecs of
Mexico in 1519–21, as the British did in India, Malaysia and West
Africa, and the French in Africa and Indo-China, and so on. Such
support was generally ignored in post-colonial public history.

In Namibia (formerly South-West Africa), pressure for action
in response to a historical grievance focused on demands in the
2000s for restitution from Germany for the brutality of the suppression of the Herero rising in 1904 when Germany was the
colonial power. This brutality led to an apology in 2004, although
not the reparations that were demanded. In contrast to the Herero,
the key theme in the public history encouraged by the Namibian

government was the opposition by the South West Africa People's Organisation (SWAPO) to South African rule. This opposition, which began in 1966, eventually led to independence. The monument the government created at Hero's Acre to anti-colonial resistance could incorporate Herero opposition.[17]

More generally, resistance to Western rule was interpreted and reinterpreted in the light of changing social and cultural values. Thus, by the 2000s, there was a greater emphasis on the role of women in resistance. This was seen in Jamaica in the West Indies, with stories about Nanny, a warrior woman, who allegedly led the Maroons – escaped slaves living in the interior – in their resistance to the British.

Consideration of the colonial period in Africa and elsewhere was itself politically problematic, as it posed a question mark against the limited success of post-colonial governments in improving living standards and maintaining stability. Such consideration also directed attention to current relations with the former colonial power.

SOUTH AFRICA

The situation was different in South Africa where imperialism was seen not so much in terms of successive Dutch and British colonial rule, as with regard to the Afrikaners, a white settler society who did not disappear like European imperialism elsewhere in Africa. This ensured complex problems, from the introduction of black majority rule in 1994, over how best to handle not only the presentation of South African history but also the role within it of the Afrikaners. The extent to which they should be able to maintain a different history was also an issue, for their cultural heritage and sense of identity were bound up in such a history.[18] The resulting pressures at the national level were seen in such problems as naming, public celebrations and school curricula. The theme was on reconciliation, as in the designation, as a Day of Reconciliation, of 16 December, when in 1838, during the Afrikaner Great Trek into the interior, there was a key victory over the Africans at Blood River.

At the same time, there is the emphasis on different histories seen, for example, in 2007, with the success among Afrikaners of a song by Bok van Blerk about Koos de la Rey, a Boer general who fought the British. The black response to this, and indeed to the defence of the Afrikaans language, depended in part on whether the black politicians supported distinctive voices of their own, most obviously those Zulu politicians of the Inkatha movement, such as Chief Mangosuthu Buthelezi, who emphasised their particular history including war with the British in 1879. This was a cause at odds with the governing African National Congress's emphasis on South African inclusiveness. In 2004, however, the 125th anniversary of the Zulu victory over the British at the battle of Isandlhwana led to an appropriate memorialisation of the Zulu casualties. This fulfilled a goal long sought by prominent Zulu politicians.

At present, the general context in South Africa is far more positive than in most of Africa, as the Truth and Reconciliation Commission established in 1995 provided a good means for defusing anger, not least by insisting that truth and amnesty were joined in a synergy.[19] Amnesty was offered for outrages by both the government and the liberation movements, but the perpetrators had to admit their crimes and show that they were politically motivated. The process is still incomplete, however, in part because of refusals to appear when the Commission came to an end in 2001. Outstanding cases were transferred to the National Prosecuting Authority, and its activities have been a source of contention, with division over whether political crimes should be prosecuted.

Linked to the Commission, there have been other policies to redress peacefully the impact of apartheid and, before that, colonial rule, through both black economic empowerment and land reform. Each starts from a sense of unfairness that has an historical dimension but that is essentially based on an understanding of the situation today.

Alongside policy issues has come the attempt in South Africa to produce a national history that can serve as the basis for peaceful coexistence rather than what has been termed differentialism. Indeed, the presentation of history has been seen as important to this process.[20] This entailed also the dismantling of the previous historical account, with its emphasis on separate racial historical strands, and its replacement by a multicultural theme: multicultural, but national. There is an emphasis on the same teaching and textbooks in the different provinces of South Africa. Specific points also changed, not least the Afrikaners' presentation of the interior in 1838 as largely empty and of historical white claims to black land. The important role of blacks in the Anglo-Afrikaner Boer War of 1899–1902 was also emphasised in centennial celebrations and publications.[21] Vocabulary has also changed, with 'tribes' rejected as a term that suggests primitive organisation. Forgotten voices have been pushed to the fore. Museums reflect the new trends.[22] The extent to which this history, whether accurate or anachronistic, will bear the expectations placed upon it, however, is unclear. A different world history is also being sought, in South Africa, with interest in the history of non-European peoples elsewhere, including the subject of decolonisation. The stress is on African, not Western, history.[23]

DEMANDS FOR RESTITUTION

Across the Third World, interest in pre-colonial lineage led to demands for restitution, not least the repatriation of material acquired by Western powers. The process of acquisition, whether by research, for example archaeological or anthropological, purchase, or looting, mattered less than the fact that it had been lost. Moreover, the legalistic distinction between antiquities that were robbed and those that were purchased at low prices does not always capture the degree of pressure or deceit involved in the latter. The symbolic value of such loss became a prominent theme and was linked to the expression of grievance and, indeed, at times its manufacture or manipulation.

Thus, Ethiopia has complained about the consequences of two Western invasions. In 1868, a British force, successfully sent to rescue imprisoned hostages, stormed the fortress of Magdala and seized both secular and religious treasures there. The loot included crowns, shields, crosses and manuscripts, as well as tabots, sacred carved blocks of wood or marble. In response to recent Ethiopian complaints, the eleven tabots in the British Museum were moved aside for special treatment and made only accessible to priests, but the museum's position in this and other cases is that, under its charter, it is not permitted to return accessions. This, for example, is the response to the long-standing demand from Greece that the Elgin Marbles acquired by Thomas, 7th Earl of Elgin, be returned to Athens, a demand that reflects the determination of modern Greeks to bask in the reflected glory of Classical Greece. There have also been Ethiopian demands for the return of antiquities seized by Italy during its occupation in 1935–40.

In Italy, however, the attempt to return the 'Venus of Cyrene', a Classical statue, to Libya, from where it was taken by Italian forces in 1912, a year after the Italian invasion, was resisted by Our Italy, a group seeking to retain cultural treasures seen as Italian. In 2007, nevertheless, a court decided that the statue was not part of Italy's cultural heritage and should return. Ironically, the statue has little to do with the culture of Libya, a Muslim state that, however, benefits from tourists visiting Classical sites. The same point can be made about the demand for the return of the treasure from Troy. On the other hand, some non-Arab Muslim states, for example Iran, care a lot about their pre-Islamic culture, and earlier, indeed, the Ottoman Turkish authorities ordered Heinrich Schliemann not to remove the 'Trojan' antiquities he claimed to have discovered in 1873 from Turkish soil.

The demand for returns does not always arise from colonial control. Instead, there is a sense that power was misused at the expense of the complainant, combined with anger about the loss of history, this seen as a fundamental challenge to identity. In part, these disputes also involve an assertion about the latter. Peru's demand for the return of Incan treasures provides an example. The Peruvian government of the 1910s agreed the dispatch to Yale University in the USA of those discovered at Machu Picchu, but its modern descendant claims that they were only loans and should be returned.

This reflects, in part, the strong nativist determination of Peru today to emphasise an Inca heritage that it had earlier cared little about, when, instead, the emphasis has been on the Spanish roots of both country and elite. The same emphasis can be seen in Bolivia, where the President, Evo Morales, seeks to 'refound' the country in order to emphasise its Indian nature.

In 2000, the *Worker's Daily* newspaper of Beijing pressed for the return from the British Museum of hundreds of Chinese pictures which, it claimed, had been smuggled from China between 1911 and 1949. This complaint served to put forward a contrast between Communist care for cultural legacy and the earlier failure to do so. In 2007, China decided to extend the ban on the export of artefacts and antiques from works produced by 1795 to works made before 1911.

Complaints were not always at the national level. For example, in 2007, the Natural History Museum of London handed over to the Tasmanian Aboriginal Centre (TAC) bones and teeth from seventeen Tasmanian Aborigines collected in the early nineteenth century. The Centre had also blocked proposals to carry out scientific tests, such as the extraction of DNA and bone samples, before handing over the remains. Religious traditions (to critics, the fetishisation of the body) clashed with scientific interests. In 2002, France returned the body parts of the 'Hottentot Venus', Saartjie Baartman. Shown in public, she had died in 1816, and some of her body parts were removed and displayed in a museum. She was buried in the Gamtoos Valley in South Africa later in 2002.

Demands for the return of antiquities and remains do not always relate to former colonial powers. There are also disputes between other states. Thus, in 2000, Afghanistan, Iran and Pakistan disagreed over the mummified remnants of a Persian princess discovered in the Pakistani region of Baluchistan and deposited in the National Museum in Karachi. The Taliban destroyed antiquities in Afghanistan, which they saw as idolatry, such as, in 2001, the statue of the Buddha at Bamian. Criticism of their action endorsed a belief that some political movements, and even nations, cannot be trusted to preserve their heritage.

NAMES, DATES AND FILMS

The issue of lineage was also shown in renamings. The patina of Western rule was, it was hoped, removable as the names of countries, towns and landscape features were changed. Thus, Upper Volta became Burkina Faso, Nyasaland became Malawi, East Timor became Timor-Leste, Northern and Southern Rhodesia became Zambia and Zimbabwe, and so on. In Zimbabwe,

Salisbury was renamed Harare, while in 2007 Pretoria, the capital of South Africa, was renamed Tshwane. Each of these changes provided an opportunity to reject the colonial legacy and, instead, to assert a new identity.[24] The assertion of a new identity is generally that of the country in question, although a different and distinctive internationalism may also be sought. Thus, in Kolkata (Calcutta) during the Vietnam War, the Marxist local government renamed Harrington Street, the site of the American consulate, Ho Chi Minh Sarani. In some states, such as Nigeria, new capital cities were established, a process now being followed in Tajikistan and Myanmar, formerly Burma. Similarly, museums were renamed, changed or founded in order to mark the rejection of colonialism. In 1961, a year after independence from Britain, the Museum of the National Struggle was established in Cyprus.

Dates as well as places were at issue. National commemorative days switched abruptly to mark occasions in decolonisation, especially the date of independence, and dates from 'the liberation struggle'. Thus, in Indonesia, 17 August, the date of independence from Dutch rule, is commemorated. Other dates were also significant. In 1967, in Japan, State Foundation Day was created, for each 11 February, which earlier, during the Meiji period, had been the holiday *kigensetsu*, celebrating Japan's imperial line since 660 BCE, and thus national continuity in the shape of an alleged dynastic continuity. Similarly, in 1979, the adoption of Imperial Reign Law ensured that the national calendar would be organised by imperial reigns. Most states did not have such a history to revive but, instead, created a new national calendar, largely focused on the recent past.

Other forms of history were also reconceptualised. King Mohammed VI of Morocco paid 60 per cent of the budget of the film *Indigènes* (dir. Rachid Bouchareb, 2006) which threw positive light on the role of France's North African soldiers in the Second World War, a film released in Britain as *Days of Glory*. Film has also been used to provide a heroic account of other aspects of Islamic history. The life of the Prophet, *The Message* (dir. Moustapha Akkad, 1976), initially disconcerting to Western viewers because, in accordance with Muslim convention (although this is now being challenged), his face is not shown, is one such. I can recall seeing it in Ealing amidst an audience overwhelmingly of British Muslims who applauded very vigorously indeed whenever one of Mohammed's opponents was defeated. On posters, Saddam Hussein allowed himself to be depicted as the heir to Saladin, who created an extensive empire and defeated the Crusaders in the twelfth century, capturing Jerusalem from them in 1187.

In 1981, Mustapha Akkad's film *Lion of the Desert* provided a eulogistic account of the lengthy resistance in Libya to Italian conquest in the 1910s–1930s. The Libyan government contributed substantially to the film, which focused on Omar Mukhtar, a Koran teacher-turned-guerrilla hero. *Lion of the Desert* projected resistance as an honourable cause. Given that Akkad was killed in Amman by Islamic suicide bombers in 2005, it is ironic that his film was used on websites calling for *jihad*, although they have added features that reflected their own presentation of present, and thus past. Scenes depicting women are cut, while the music on the soundtrack has been jettisoned in favour of religious chants.

In turn, Muslims could reject part of the history offered by Hollywood. Aside from the refusal by governments, such as that of Malaysia, to permit the showing of films about the Holocaust, particularly *Schindler's List*, there is also anger about the treatment of Islam and the Islamic world in Hollywood. This extends to the coverage of the latter before it became Muslim. For example, modern Iran claims descent from Ancient Persia, and Iranian commentators were angry at the depiction of the Persian attackers of Greece in Zack Snyder's *300* (2007), an account of the Spartans who resisted at Thermopylae in 480 BCE. President Ahmadinejad claimed 'They are trying to tamper with history [. . .] by making Iran's image look savage'. The film was presented as an insult to Iran's history and civilisation. Whether it was intended by the film-maker, or seen by American audiences, in this light, or as an historical reference to America's involvement in Iraq is unclear.

AFRICA AND THE ROLE OF AGENCY

Africa is still very much in this process of rejecting the colonial legacy, but this also helps ensure a difficulty in addressing problems other than through a frequently misleading and often self-indulgent prism of blaming outsiders. An extreme example is provided by Zimbabwe under Robert Mugabe. This authoritarian and brutal regime tends to see its difficulties as derived from the legacy of British imperial control and the continuing reality of British pressure, rather than addressing very serious issues in its government policies and structures. Aspects of the British legacy that might indeed help greatly in economic regeneration, for example the security of contract that encourages investment, have been neglected. Mugabe's brutality was not only ignored by his supporters in Africa but also by some African-American commentators, including historians. For example, Molefi Kete Asante, a prominent African-American historian and the founding editor of the *Journal of Black Studies*, wrote of Mugabe

> Although he had agitated Britain and the United States by moving against the white settlers who had occupied the land of the Shona people for more than one hundred years, he remained popular among the African people [. . .] By opening the door to more intensive trade with China, Zimbabwe circumvented the stranglehold placed on its economy by the United States and Europe and redistributed the land the whites had occupied illegally since 1898 to the masses of poor Zimbabweans, who had been robbed of their birthright when the whites invaded.[25]

There was no suggestion of complexity in his uncritical treatment of this or indeed most other issues. This is also an aspect of the degree to which the Western post-1945 intellectual agenda that has provided the context for an anti-colonial historiography has not been applied universally. Indeed, this is all-too-reminiscent of the quiescence of so many intellectuals with Soviet policy during the Stalin period.

The historical background of the situation in Zimbabwe requires fuller explanation. Mugabe is a murderous despot, and started early in that role. That is not excused by the brutality of the regime of Ian Smith (Prime Minister from 1964 to 1979) and his predecessors – Southern Rhodesia was a viciously racist place even by comparison with Kenya and Tanganyika – but that is worth noting. Again, the land-reform issue has been used by Mugabe to reward his cronies and has brought Zimbabwe's economy to its knees, and his blaming British agents for everything is wrong. Yet, in 1980, during the Lancaster House talks, it was acknowledged that one of the most pressing issues in what became Zimbabwe was the unjust distribution of land. Mugabe did nothing for many years, but so also did Britain, the former imperial power, which did not finance a smooth transition to a more even land distribution. Mugabe's claim that Britain has a duty to assist land reform as compensation for tolerating Southern Rhodesia is problematic, but it is certainly an issue within living memory and raises the question of whether Britain can cast off its imperial past as having ended in 1947, or, in this case, 1980.

Within Africa, the rejection of colonialism entails a denial of the extent to which, however much cooperation resulted from the pressure from the colonial power, colonialism was influenced, if not made possible and actively shaped, by local cooperation and action. Thus, the colonial era becomes an alien one, a view that is historically inaccurate but politically convenient. This is linked to a sense of history as something that happens to one and for which others can be blamed, an account that leaves no role for one's own agency. Ascribing a historical passivity to Africans is an inaccurate notion that ironically reflects the earlier views of European imperialists. Nevertheless, the tendency to ignore African agency can be seen in modern African accounts of the colonial era, in which, in fact, African cooperation was very important, not least in providing troops.

The slave trade provides a clear instance of this process in the public historical consciousness of Africa: the major role of Africans in the slave trade is ignored, or underplayed and blamed on outside influences. This is not simply an academic omission. In 1961, the National Liberation Front of Angola launched its first guerrilla invasion of Angola, slaughtering Portuguese colonists. Its leader Holden Roberto said, 'This time the slaves did not cower. They massacred everything'. A sense of history as an outside imposition for which others are to blame is also powerfully present in the Arab world, especially when discussing the West.

The documentary trace is also instructive. Although positive efforts were made to preserve and transfer colonial records,[26] the history of colonial policy was largely recorded in archival forms in former imperial metropoles, which is a source of grievance on the part of the former colonies. However, a survey of archives in Africa, carried out by Peter Mazikana in the 1990s for the International Council on Archives, noted not only a shortage of resources on the part of the archives but also problems with a lack of managerial initiative by archivists and of the appropriate attitude on the part of government decision-makers.[27] In short, at least in this case, issues in political culture were at stake, and not the outside oppression that is so readily decried.

In rejecting the West, nationalist state-builders in the Third World have also borrowed heavily from it. The extrapolation of the Western model of the nation-state has indeed been of great value for nationalists elsewhere, although it may well have been a very misleading application. Indeed, it is possible that the states and, especially the political identities, particularly across much of Africa, that were first charted in any detail in the nineteenth century have had their longevity exaggerated by Western assumptions, as well as by the agendas of ethnogenesis that lie at the heart of proximate cultural nationalism. In contrast, some revisionist archaeologists have thrown doubt on the extent and even existence of certain pre-colonial states. Furthermore, modern concepts of nationality have been misleadingly employed to interpret the polities and politics of the past. Moreover, instead of the image of lasting national units, the basis for modern claims for historical lineage, there appears to have been considerable migration for centuries in almost every sphere of human activity across what have since been constructed as national boundaries. Linked to this, there were also multiple civil and sacred identities.

Thus, borrowing Western concepts, and rather recent concepts as well, may be a poor guide to past realities, but this ahistoricism seems necessary to the regimes that run many states. It is scarcely surprising that governments seeking to frame a public history have charted paths that suit their political purpose. In this process, the tension between nationalism and ethnicity has played a major role. Paradoxically, in light of the rejection of the imperial legacy, the major emphasis is on the continuation of colonial boundaries and an opposition to ethnic and regional consciousnesses that challenge the stress on unity, which generally means government control. The decision by the Organization of African Unity to support the maintenance of colonial frontiers is a product of this emphasis. For example, the public history of Nigeria supports federalism and is hostile to separatism, and this provided the context within which the bitter civil war of 1967–70 that stemmed from Biafran separatism is considered. However, in 2000, as a gesture of reconciliation and closure, President Olusegun Obasanjo commuted to retirement the earlier dismissal of the military who had sided with Biafra, a measure that was valuable for pensions as well as recognition.

In Ethiopia, during the left-wing Mengistu government from 1974 to 1991, reference was made to the 'liberation' and reunion of Eritrea with the motherland in 1952, a view that made little sense of the eventually successful separatist movement launched there the following year. The Ethiopian presentation of history also indicated the extent to which an anti-Western, anti-imperial account could be intertwined with the pursuit of regional animosities. Mengistu's government emphasised the historical integrity of Ethiopia and presented it as being under threat from neighbouring and rival Somalia and from Western imperialism. Thus, the threat from Somalia, which attacked in 1977 only to be defeated the following year, was seen as a continuation of earlier Islamic invasions going back to Imam Ahmad Gragn, ruler of Adal, and the Ottoman Turks in the sixteenth century. This threat was also linked to Western pressure. British imperialists were blamed for inventing the notion of a Greater Somalia, which was seen as continued by the contemporary Somalis. Thus, the leading modern rival was allegedly following an agenda laid down by an imperialist manipulator. More accurately, the Italian conquest of Ethiopia in 1935–6 was bitterly criticised. In line with this general approach, past Western links with Ethiopia were minimised or denigrated. The Portuguese, who had provided assistance against Adal, were referred to as pirates.

The rejection of separatism could overlap with the brutal treatment of regions of opposition support. This was the case with Zimbabwe, particularly in the *Gukurahundi* (Early rain that washes away the chaff), the murderous treatment of the region of Matabeleland in 1983. This episode brings up another of the aspects of the weight of history, namely the extent to which atonement and punishment for such misdeeds should be a goal and, indeed, an aspect of politics. Thus, whether Mugabe should be held to account, or even tried, for such action is an item in the broader question of how to ease him from power and to make him history.

There is also the question of remembering victims, as with the Kigali Genocide Memorial in Rwanda that commemorates those slaughtered, maybe 1 million, in 1994. In this case, those who drove out the murderers and ended the genocide now govern the country. In Cambodia, Tuol Sleng, the Khmer Rouge interrogation and torture centre in Phnom Penh, is now presented as a 'genocide museum'.

The ability to manage a peaceful transition of power is an issue in many African states. Linked to this is the problem of offering a critical, indeed objective, account of earlier periods of activity by the regime or its progenitors. In Morocco, a Equity and Reconciliation Commission was established by Mohammed VI after his accession in 1999 to consider human-rights abuses under his predecessor and father, Hassan II (1961–99). Although South Africa was a key trailblazer for such commissions, these processes are unusual in Africa.

Much of this chapter is familiar from the use of public history in the West in the nineteenth and early twentieth centuries, but such a stadial account of history (development through historical stages) is not welcome to most African states. The suggestion that they are passing through stages reached earlier by others is regarded as disparaging and also as failing to appreciate the specific cultural traditions and needs of particular regions. Moreover, the following chapters will indicate that much of the West has not necessarily reached a different stage, at least in terms of the combination of a tolerant and pluralistic public discussion of national history combined with a governmental willingness to forward such a discussion.

IMPERIAL METROPOLES

Alongside the attempt by former colonies to define a new lineage has come that by the imperial powers to come to grips with the legacies of imperialism. For Western imperial powers, the legacies of imperialism now include not only the often critical views of the former colonies but also the ambivalent attitudes of immigrants from them, as well as the debate in former colonial metropoles over imperialism and how it should be presented. This was seen in Britain, for example with the response to the slave trade and also in France with the reaction to the Algerian War. The bicentenary of the abolition of the slave trade in Britain in 1807 led to a commemoration that was very different to that of a century earlier. There was a stress on the Africans rather than on the white abolitionists, and on victimhood and apology rather than solution and salvation through liberal and Christian activism. In 2007, for example, this led to the proposal to erect a national memorial in Hyde Park in order to commemorate the enslaved Africans. Museum exhibitions, such as *London, Sugar and Slavery* in the Museum in Docklands emphasised the slaves' perspective. The foreword to the guide to the London Borough of Camden's 'Struggle, Emancipation and Unity' season noted, 'We remember slavery by reflecting on the resistance of Africans, their celebration in their liberation and their unity in tackling present-day inequalities as a legacy.'

Such issues were not necessarily abstract. For example, in July 2007, elderly Gurkhas who served Britain during the Second World War were denied medical treatment in the National Health Service because they were held to have 'no substantial link with the United Kingdom'. This argument is the product of two strong arguments that have shaped recent decades: that the Empire story is finished and that, anyway, the British record was pretty good. This then fuels a feeling that there is no connection that should allow these Gurkhas to be treated at the expense of British taxpayers and that they should stay in Nepal.

The French reaction to the Algerian War became a more controversial issue during the mid-2000s. On the one hand, in 2006, there was controversy over legislation intended to prescribe the teaching of a positive treatment of French imperialism in the school syllabus. On the other, there was pressure for a more critical account of this imperialism and, conversely, a rehabilitation of the Algerians. In 2005, President Chirac, who, a decade earlier, had apologised for France's role in the deportation of Jews during the Second World War, did so for the 'inexcusable tragedy' of the massacre at Sétif in 1945 that followed an unsuccessful Algerian rebellion against French rule. This was a marked variance with the earlier policy of ignoring the occasion.

CONSPIRACIES AND PARALLELS

Post-colonial history was also interpreted in both former colonies and former metropoles in light of the allegedly continued efforts by former colonial powers to maintain influence. This readily morphed into a presentation of post-colonial history in terms of the Cold War, with an emphasis on the malign role of the superpowers. Thus, for example, the fall, in a 1966 coup, of Ghana's dictatorial and incompetent leader Kwame Nkrumah was blamed on the CIA.

In the Islamic world, there is a widespread tendency to ascribe the failure of the Soviet Union and the fall of the Iron Curtain to the Soviet defeat in Afghanistan at the hands of the Afghan opposition: having invaded in 1979, Soviet forces withdrew a decade later. This defeat then serves as an encouragement to action against the West, which is also seen as secular and, indeed, this interpretation is part of the mantra of Muslim radicals. In practice, this is an instance of the widespread process by which a false perception of the present becomes an instant history, in a mental world in which knowledge is encoded as history, and then this perception serves as a prospectus for the future.

As with much public use of history, this approach tends to be unilinear and, in underwriting the contextualisation and specificity of episodes, tends to exaggerate the transferability of examples and lessons. The frequent Western use of the appeasement of Germany, Italy and Japan in the 1930s is an instructive instance of the same process.[28] This is not the sole flaw in the use of the historical episode of appeasement: as a consequence of the eventual alliance in the Second World War between Britain, the USA and the Soviet Union, appeasement as an historical benchmark is applied to the 'dictators' – Germany, Italy and Japan – but not to the Soviet Union under its own expansionist and brutal dictator, Stalin.

RECOVERING HISTORY

It was not only the imperial experience that was at stake in former colonies. There was also a revival, outside the parameters of imperial control, of other historical themes. These ranged in accordance with the specific nature of societies and cultures. For example, in Lebanon, strong divisions grew anew in intensity after French colonial control ceased at the end of the Second World War. This led to a number of historical narratives, each focused on the claims of particular communities. One that is of contemporary importance is that of the Lebanese Shi'a, which was developed in the 1960s and 1970s by Sayyid Muse al-Sadr, who created the Supreme Islamic Shi'a Council. He focused Shi'a history on the travails of the Lebanese Shi'a, and this was to be important to the evolution of Hezbollah ideas.

While it is understandable that narratives and analyses of history as a movement from imperial control are dominant, it is also the case that there are powerful differences both over this process and also more generally. These differences are generally overshadowed by the episode or trauma of control by imperial powers, frequently deliberately so for political reasons, but it is mistaken to organise history simply in these terms.

This emerges more clearly in the case of 'Third World' countries that were not part of colonial systems even though they were under pressure from imperial powers. This was the case, for example, with Turkey, where there are clashing historical analyses, not least between Muslim and secular approaches.[29] The institutionalisation of history in Turkey was hesitant and certainly far slower than in most of Europe. The Ottoman Historical Society, founded in 1909, was followed in 1933 by the Faculty of Language, History and Geography. The Kemalist orthodoxy, which was the order of the day, left scant room for other interpretations. Turkey, nevertheless, was more liberal, at the university level, than many other authoritarian states, in part possibly because of the very strength of this authoritarianism.

CONCLUSIONS

Looking ahead, it is likely that the role of state-controlled public histories in much of the Third World will be challenged by the spread of access to television and the Internet and by the difficulty of controlling the use of either. Such technology offers the possibility of people 'consuming' a history in which there is a variety of providers, with the state simply as one. Vernacular opinion will not be simply a matter of 'reactionary' memory resisting state propaganda but will be influenced by newly asserted ideas and images. Accepting the point that television and Internet sites often thrive on partiality and conspiracy theories, there will be a greater degree of free expression.

There is a key difference between democracies, which provide lots of opportunity for a variety of opinions to be expressed, and other states. Ill-tempered and often uninformed as discussions on the intersection of history and the present can be in democratic societies, they still take place in a context where much can be said or written. The key element is democracy rather than Western states, not least because of the important difference between China and Japan.

Moreover, where civic society becomes freer, or, at least, less under government direction, then memory activists of different persuasions may well become active in public debate, offering exemplary memories that others internalise. In short, 'history wars' will be waged differently than where the state does not confront such an explicit diversity of views. The situation will vary by country, thus ensuring that the presentation of history becomes an aspect of the very different politics of states. In some cases, the use of history may indeed be a precipitant of these different politics. The extent to which public debate on history requires an end to censorship, an opening to outside media and a wide range for civic activism suggests that authoritarian states, such as Myanmar (Burma) and Syria will offer a very different history to those that have democratic systems, for example the Philippines and Israel.

As interesting may be developments in democracies that have a dominant government party basking in a state-supported national historical myth, such as Singapore. Exposure to the pressure of different foreign-based accounts may become more prominent, not least as the international provision of media services will combine with, or at least operate alongside, the role of transnational activism focused on particular issues. Thus, in public history, as in much else, the role of transnational non-governmental organisations needs to be considered. The same process may affect authoritarian regimes such as China and Vietnam. Nationalism and the state as narratives of public history may thus, at least in some cases, be disconnected, with the former increasingly relying on, but also qualified by, non-governmental accounts.

CHAPTER 5

POST-COMMUNISM
AND THE NEW HISTORY

The fall of the Communist regimes in eastern Europe in 1989 and the collapse of the Soviet Union in 1989–91 brought together a number of post-war trends that provoked new histories, particularly the end of imperial rule, the creation of new, as well as newly independent, states, for example Croatia and Ukraine, and sweeping political changes.

The fall of the Communist regimes had reflected the difficulty of grounding authoritarian regimes in the absence of popular support for their legitimacy and purposes, however much the people were told that there was a dialectical necessity for the success of these regimes and one located in a clear historical continuum. A lack of popularity, indeed consent, particularly in eastern Europe, had made it increasingly difficult for the Communist governments to view change and reform with much confidence. Far from time vindicating the Communist prospectus, with time the sham character of Communist progress became more apparent. Furthermore, instead of being made redundant by the advance of Communism, nationalism re-emerged publicly as a powerful force, both in eastern Europe and in the Soviet Union.

Nationalism, which became a more central political issue from the late 1980s, apparently offered identity, freedom and a route to reform freed from a sclerotic imperial structure. Nationalism also entailed the rejection of Soviet and Communist history and, instead, an emphasis on the histories subordinated, if not denied, by both, as in the Lithuanian law of 1990 for the 'Rehabilitation of Persons Repressed for Resistance to the Occupying Regime'. There was a re-evaluation of recent history and a reconsideration of earlier episodes. For example, in Estonia, Latvia

and Lithuania, there were complaints about the Soviet annexations in 1940, which had been the prelude to brutal and bloody authoritarian rule. These complaints led to a focus on the Nazi–Soviet Pact of 1939 under which the annexations had taken place. This was a pact that the Soviets had done their best to ignore and to sweep from the historical record, because it accorded their regime the same legitimacy and goals as those of Nazi Germany.

The end of Communism also permitted a new history in which past links with non-Communist countries and movements were emphasised. Thus, in Estonia, it proved possible in public to contrast the Swedes, as good imperial rulers from 1581 to 1710, with the Russians who had replaced them and to devote due attention to the British role in 1919 in helping Estonia resist Russian conquest.

The fall of the Iron Curtain also did not mean the end of history, in the sense of ideological division (as Francis Fukuyama unwisely predicted, or at least was held to have predicted), but possibly an end in the sense of the chance of a new beginning, which was Georg Wilhelm Friedrich Hegel's meaning when he referred to Prussia's crushing defeat by Napoleon at Jena in 1806 as 'the end of history'. The end of Communist rule certainly led to a marked revival of history, not least as national history offered a source and cause both for the legitimacy of the new states and for their independence.[1] As such, this provided a powerful new instance of the continuing process by which the contested eastern European past, with its interrelated but adversarial ethnicities, is interpreted in light of the present.[2]

This revival of history was a matter not only of the contents of the presentation of the past but also of its form. Examples were provided by the establishment of new museums and monuments as well as by a transformation of those already there.[3] In Poland, an excellent Museum of the Warsaw Uprising opened in 2004. There remains no national history museum in Warsaw, for, at the time that they were being built in the nineteenth century, Poland was not an independent country. However, funds have now been allocated to build a national historical museum.

Chairs in national history were founded in newly independent states and even in Belarus which remained close to Russia.

Archaeology also served as a way to advance national historical narratives. Moreover, as an aspect of the rejection of Communism, the organisation of archives was transformed. In Hungary, the New Hungarian Central Archives, a depository for post-Second World War documents, was abolished as a rejection of a periodisation based on Communism. The archives of the Communist Party were also placed in the public domain.

The revival of the past entailed the nationalisation of historical figures. In Mongolia, there was a marked emphasis on descent from the great thirteenth-century empire of Genghis Khan. Timur performed a similar role in Uzbekistan with statues of him replacing those of Communist figures, as well as a museum devoted to him which opened in 1996 and the creation of the Order of Amir Timur and the Amir Timur Fund.[4]

In the Caucasus, there was an emphasis on those who had opposed Russian conquest in the nineteenth century. This was also linked to religious assertion. Thus, in 1997, a new mosque was dedicated in Makhach-Kala, the capital of Dagestan, during the celebrations of the 200th anniversary of the birth of Shamil, the most famous resistance leader.[5]

Aside from nationalism, there was also the need on the part of post-Communist states for these states to face the legacy of the recent past and the pressure created by the politicisation of this legacy. The previous century, and, even more, the years from the 1940s were dissected in order to allocate responsibility, and thus blame, and to castigate rivals. The wartime resistance to Germany and its allies was re-examined, and the Communist role in it was downplayed or criticised. Thus, in the castle museum at Bled in Slovenia, the display on Slovene history includes the passage 'The excessive desires for absolute power among members of the Communist Party of Slovenia caused the original, unsullied idea of united resistance to Nazism and Fascism to disintegrate'.

In Slovenia, the collapse of Yugoslavia in 1991 also led to the return of right-wing émigrés, especially from Argentina. They sought to rehabilitate the reputation of the 'Home Guard' which had fought in support of the Germans during the Second World War. This led them to criticise the role of the wartime partisans and also that of Britain which, in 1945, handed over to the partisans those of the 'Home Guard' who had surrendered in German uniforms to British forces in Austria. The partisans killed them. Thus, the legacy of the 1940s affects both domestic politics and attitudes to foreign policy.

More generally, in place of the long-standing Communist focus on eastern European Fascist or authoritarian collaboration with Germany during the Second World War, a focus designed to discredit the right and to highlight resistance by the Communists, came a concentration on the cruelties and iniquities of the post-war Communist era, a theme deliberately struck as a way to condemn the left. For example, the Polish administration of the Kaczynski brothers and their governing Law and Justice Party, in 2007, sought to open the 50 miles of secret-police files from the Communist era. This was also linked to moves against the WSI (Wojskowe Służby Informacyjne, the military intelligence service) and to an attempt to use vetting to remove the alleged secret system of pro-Communist agents of influence in public life, although this attempt was struck down by the Constitutional Court. These initiatives reflected the government's view that such agents had been responsible for a flawed transition to democracy and one that was weakened by the continued power of networks of ex-Communists.

In Romania, the issue of the relationship between the Ceauşescu regime, with its Communist rule in the shape of an authoritarian dictator, and post-Communist governments was a matter of controversy, with claims that there was more continuity than there should be, not least amongst the renamed Communist Party. There was also a determination on the part of the anti Communists to draw attention to the crimes of the brutal Ceauşescu regime. This included the memorial established in 1992 at Sighet, where opponents had been imprisoned. An attempt to discover information about the regime led to a scrutiny of the Securitate (secret police) that was not welcome to its successor, the SRI (Serviciul Român de Informaţii). A national council for the study of the Securitate files was established in 1999, in part with the help of the comparable East German body. The sensitive nature of history was indicated in 1990 when Ioan Petru Culianu, a prominent Romanian historian, was murdered.

In Bulgaria, police files were opened for inspection from 1997, and the Ministry of the Interior released the names of some public figures who had worked for the Communist-era security agencies.[6] In Hungary, the names of those who had collaborated with the domestic and foreign secret police have been occasionally leaked to the press, and several of them later acknowledged their role. Most famous was Péter Medgyessy, Deputy Prime Minister responsible for economic affairs in 1988–9, and Prime Minister in 2002–4. Shortly after he was elected Prime Minister, news regarding his work for the III/II department of the Hungarian Secret Police as an officer under the code name of D-209 was leaked. Medgyessy acknowledged this but claimed that his role was to help Hungary in joining the International Monetary Fund and, in this capacity, that he worked mainly with the KGB.

EAST GERMANY

In some states, the issue of continuing Communist influence played a greater role than elsewhere which, in turn, helped direct attention to the Communist years. In former East Germany, despite concern about its activities and scandals about its informants, the role of the Stasi (secret police) did not become a political issue comparable to that of the secret police in Poland. For example, despite the large-scale oppressiveness of its policies and attitudes, the Stasi was never declared a 'criminal organisation', unlike the Gestapo. Many Stasi members were re-employed in the police, and they benefited from an effective support network. They also disrupt public discussion meetings on East Germany's history by heckling.

Yet, there has been a major attempt to highlight the nature of Stasi activity. The Stasi Records Law was passed by the Bundestag in December 1991, and, from January 1992, citizens could inspect their own personal files. By January 2004, over 5 million applications to do so had been received. The Stasi Records Office also carries out research. In 2007, a written order of 1973 was discovered in Stasi files disproving claims by East German officials that there was no shoot-to-kill policy against those trying to flee. The General Secretary of the Christian Democratic Party, Ronald Pofalla, commented that this provided 'frightening evidence of how inhuman this system was'. Permanent exhibitions on the Stasi system in information and documentation centres are supplemented by a central touring exhibition.

It is also possible to visit Stasi prisons, such as those in Rostock and Berlin-Hohenschönhausen: the latter had earlier been used as a Soviet special camp. In 1992, the prison complex at Berlin-Hohenschönhausen was listed as a historical monument, a measure pressed by former inmates, and the memorial site was established in 1994. In 2000, it became an independent foundation whose purpose is to 'explore the history of the Hohenschönhausen prison between 1945 and 1989, inform about exhibitions, events and publications and prompt visitors to take a critical look at the methods and consequences of political persecution and suppression in the Communist dictatorship'. By the mid-2000s, over 120,000 people, including 35,000 students, visited the site annually, with most of the guided tours conducted by former inmates. The preservation and destruction of the physical remains of oppression were sometimes controversial, as with local opposition in 2000 to the demolition of the last of the watchtowers of the Berlin Wall.

The Association for the Victims of Stalinism sought to direct attention to the plight of those who had been jailed in East Germany, but, against this, left-wing opposition deputies, several former members of the Communist Party, tried to block the provision of government funds to use computers to help fit together the approximately 600 million pieces of Stasi files. These had been shredded in 1989 in order to preserve the secrets of the East German state, not least the extent of informants. The measure, however, was approved in 2007.

On the one hand, the measure can be seen as a necessary closure, that also better enables victims to seek compensation (as well as clarifying issues for historians) and, on the other, as a living in the past that does not reflect, alongside the evidence of brutal oppression, the complexities and compromises of East German society under the Communist oppression. Indeed, interviewed in 2005, Konrad Jarausch, the co-director of the Zentrum für Zeithistorische Forschung (Centre for Contemporary Research) in Potsdam, which seeks to bring together West German and 'positively evaluated' (i.e., not Communist loyalists) East German scholars to work on the history of East Germany, noted the need to take seri-ously its dictatorial character but also 'attempted to address the mixed experiences of the people in their repressive state, because we found out very quickly that for East Germans it was very dif-ficult to dissociate their personal lives from the political system'. Jarausch also pressed the need 'to avoid what had happened in post-1945 West Germany, namely a discrepancy between the dominant critical history and a subterranean apologetic memory [...] handed down as a private narrative of victimhood'.[7]

This is more directly relevant in discussion both of apolo-gies and of 'truth and reconciliation' processes. Part of the con-text, in Germany, was the prior purging of much of East German academe on the grounds that they had supported the intellectual dictatorship of East German communism and the 'colonising' of these posts by West Germans. Museums were also transformed.[8] Rather than seeing this process in critical terms, as is frequently the case, it is worth noting the parallel with West Germany, as it is now widely held that, due both to governmental and popular unwillingness in West Germany and to the exigencies of the Cold War for the occupying powers, Britain, the USA and France, insufficient effort was made to push through de-Nazification after the Second World War.

In Germany, there was also a parliamentary investigative commission established in 1992 by the Bundestag to consider 'the history and consequences' of the East German dictatorship. Property, as both justice and power, moreover, was at issue, both with the resolution of property disputes and with the role of the Treuhandanstalt, the agency with executive competence estab-lished to dispose of state-owned concerns. There were also trials of those involved in what were seen as crimes, both East Ger-man government officials and also border guards. Retrospective justice came understandably in a heavily politicised form, as par-ticular issues were judged in light of current political divisions, as well as of views of German history and historical example.[9]

HUNGARY

In Hungary, the emphasis was on the re-evaluation of the 1956 Hungarian Rising, which had been brutally suppressed by Soviet forces.[10] This re-evaluation was part of the very challenge to and, then, rejection of Communist rule in 1989, as a new public identity was vigorously asserted. Thus, in June 1989, the remains of Imre Nagy, Prime Minister in 1956, who had been executed in 1958 as part of the post-Rising suppression, were dug up and ceremonially reburied. This is a conspicuous and common form of acknowledgement of wrongs, as with the reburials of the Romanovs, the Russian royal family, slaughtered by the Communists. Their tombs can now be seen in the Peter and Paul Cathedral in St Petersburg, where the chapel is a site of reverence.

The eulogies for Nagy in Hungary in 1989 provided an opportunity for a criticism of the suppression of the Rising, and a large crowd of about 100,000 attended. During the speeches, Viktor Orbán, then one of the leaders of the Fidesz Party (Fiatal Demokraták Szövetsége, Alliance of Young Democrats), later Prime Minister (1998–2002), called upon the Soviet Union to withdraw its troops. It was the very first time that a politician in Hungary demanded that, and with this Orbán became, from a little-known member of the opposition, a well-known politician.

Ironically, in an attempt to garner support in the face of popular outrage shortly before the Rising, the hardline Communist regime had, on 6 October 1956, reburied four victims of Stalinist repression including Lázló Rajk, a Communist Interior Minister, in a public funeral, which, itself, became an opportunity to demonstrate widespread pressure for change. The oppression during and after the suppression of the Rising was brutal, but the Soviet Union kept secret the news of the atrocities its forces committed.

Once the Communist regime had gone, and Hungary had become a democracy, then the re-presentation of 1956 and the Communist years gathered pace. Thus, in 1996, a statue of Nagy was unveiled near Parliament, part of a process by which the statuary in Budapest changed guard, with that from the Communist era banished to a museum. Statues and other memorials had also played a role in the events of 1956. Then, demonstrators focused on monuments to nineteenth-century opponents of Habsburg rule, which could be seen as a precursor to the foreignness of Soviet domination. Thus, students marched to Batthyány's Eternal Flame Memorial, while the statues of Sándor Petöfi and Józef

Bem served for displays of opposition: Petöfi was a major nineteenth-century nationalist poet. Also in Budapest, a 1956 Institute was established, and, in 2006, on the fiftieth anniversary of the Rising, a memorial was unveiled where Stalin's statue once stood, and 'cultural' events were organised by the government.

The visit to Hungary, in 2006, by President George W. Bush, underlined the political dimension of the commemoration, as a rejection of Communism. The changing international context had also been shown in 1992 when the post-Communist Russian government of Boris Yeltsin handed over Soviet documents from 1956. The most potent physical legacy of the Rising is the Terror Háza Múzeum (House of Terror) on Andrassy Boulevard in Budapest opened in 2002, in the very building where the secret police once did their worst. This preserves the cells and the torture and execution chambers.

At the same time, the language and labels of the Communist years were discarded in Hungary. Those who were called counter-revolutionaries by the Communists have become heroes. Indeed, in the Terror Háza Múzeum, there is a suggestion that Communism was more harmful than Fascism, not least because more space is devoted to Communist atrocities.[11] Yet, also, as democratic politics has created and revealed fault lines, so the memorialisation of the past has become more complex, not least as there remain unanswered questions about actions and responses in 1956. In comparison, earlier episodes from pre-Communist days are less contentious, not least those focused on the nineteenth-century quest for freedom.[12]

STATUES

Statues were not solely an issue and site of dispute in Hungary, nor only recently. The practice of humiliating or destroying statues, in order to mark and enforce changes, is long-standing and indeed an aspect of the extent to which history is about silencing and silences. Just as documents can be destroyed or ignored, the past being at the disposal of the present, so statues could be destroyed, as that of George III was in New York in 1776, or shunned. The Russian Revolution saw the destruction or removal of statues of the tsars, one of Alexander III, for example, being hidden from view at the Russian Museum. Whereas, in the 1880s, Bohemian Germans erected numerous statues honouring the Habsburg Emperor Joseph II as a past supporter of the German language, after Czech independence in 1918 these were attacked and destroyed by nationalists and, soon, the authorities. The Roman practice of *damnatio memoriae* offered the idea of erasing the name in the inscription on the base of statues, as a clear demonstration of being removed from history.[13] The modern removal of statues to obscure settings, as of British imperial figures in India, offers a parallel. Not to suggest any equivalence, in 2003, statues of Saddam Hussein were toppled in Iraq, as a conspicuous rejection of his authority. The previous year, the life-sized bronze statue of the British explorer David Livingstone overlooking Victoria Falls in Zimbabwe was defaced.

In April 2007, the removal of the Bronze Soldier, a monument to Red Army casualties in 1941–5, and thus to Estonia's liberation from German control in 1944, was denounced by the Russian government as an act of 'neo-fascism' and as 'blasphemous'. To most Estonians, in contrast, the monument, erected in 1947, was a symbol of Soviet occupation in 1940–1 and 1944–91, but ethnic Russians living there, a quarter of the Estonian population, had a very different view and rioted in the capital, Tallinn. This was an aspect of the extent to which the Soviet successor states have inherited its tension between nationalising states and, on the other hand, national minorities with external national homelands.[14]

The townscape of Tallinn is a rejection of Communism. There is a Museum of Occupation, while the former KGB headquarters, now a police building, carries a plaque, 'This building housed the headquarters of the organ of repression of the Soviet occupational power. Here began the road to suffering for thousands of Estonians'. In Freedom Square under tsarist rule, there was a statue of Peter the Great. Under the Soviets, the square was used for military parades. In 2003, however, the Freedom Clock was installed. It shows both the current time and the number of years since Estonia became independent. The Soviets had covered up the consequences of their heavy bombing, in March 1944, of the area round Harju Street, blaming the destruction on the Germans and turfing over the area. It, however, was then excavated and signs were erected to draw attention to the Soviet actions, until in the mid-2000s the area was turned into a park.

In an attempt to assuage tensions over the Bronze Soldier, the Estonian Prime Minister, Andrus Ansip, in May 2007, paid his respects at the monument, which had been moved to a military cemetery, but the Russian Ambassador refused to accept this gesture by attending, while Vladimir Putin, the Russian President, criticised Estonian policy. An attempt at even-handedness was provided when Ansip also attended ceremonies at a Holocaust memorial and at a cemetery commemorating soldiers who had died in Estonia fighting not only for the Soviet Union but also for the Germans. Ansip and President Toomas Hendrik Ilves issued a joint statement calling on Estonians to maintain 'dignity towards oneself and others', adding 'For many, the end of World War II means the victory of freedom over tyranny, and for many it means that one violent regime was replaced by another', an accurate assessment but not one welcome to the Russians.

In turn, on Victory Day (9 May), the annual commemoration of the defeat of Germany in 1945, Vladimir Putin condemned those who 'are desecrating monuments to war heroes, and [. . .] insulting their own people and sowing enmity and a new distrust between nations and people'. Six days later, on 15 May 2007, Vladimir Chizhov, the Russian Ambassador to the EU, criticised what he saw as politics of grievances on the part of ex-Communist states, by which he meant Estonia, Lithuania and Poland: 'It is not a secret that in some of the new member states there are political forces that are still influenced by the phantoms of the past, by historical grievances against the Soviet Union that no longer exists'.

Whether Putin's policies did not in fact suggest that past episodes, even if not those grievances, were, in fact, an appropriate context for viewing Russia, as well as Putin, was not addressed in what was a very aggressive Russian stance. This was taken further in the Kremlin-backed Nashi (Ours) movement founded in 2005 as a youth organisation pledged to restore Russia as a global power. The Nashi Manifesto presents Russia as challenged by foreign attempts to take control. At its summer camp in 2007, posters portrayed Estonia as a fascist state for moving the statue. Urmas Paet, the Estonian Foreign Minister, was depicted in these posters with a Hitler moustache and the slogan 'Who is this if not an enemy?'

In Sofia, the capital of Bulgaria, the prominent mausoleum of Georgi Dimitrov, Secretary-General of the Comintern, the Communist international organisation from 1935 to 1943, and post-war Premier (1946–9), was deliberately destroyed by the government in 1999. Like the monument to the Soviet Army in Sofia, it had been a major site for anti-Communist graffiti. The square next door which, under the Communists was called 'September 9', recording the takeover of the government by the Communists in 1944, has been renamed 'Battenberg Square', in honour of Alexander Battenberg, a German who had become prince in 1879 after Turkish rule ended. In Budějovice in the Czech Republic, the large town square is now named after Otakar II, King of Bohemia from 1253 to 1278. Those it had earlier been named after include the Habsburg Emperor Franz Josef, ruler from 1848 to 1916, the first Czech President Tomáš Masaryk (President 1918–35), and Hitler, whose forces occupied Bohemia in 1939–45.

Renaming is often a dubious process. The monument to victims of Communism erected in the garden of the People's Palace of Culture in Sofia, a replica of the Vietnam War Memorial in Washington, includes names of supporters of the German alliance who had been killed in the 1940s, such as Hristo Lukov, the leader of a pro-Nazi, anti-Semitic movement, assassinated in 1943.[15]

More generally, the issue of actions during the Communist years became an apparently key test of integrity for politicians and others and thus a source of rumour and dissension. This affected the Catholic Church in Poland in 2007, with the resignation of Stanislaw Wielgus, the Archbishop Designate of Warsaw, and was more generally an issue across eastern Europe. The Wielgus resignation also provided an opportunity for the expression of historicised hatreds. To some bigots, the (justified) charges against Wielgus, of active collaboration with the Communist secret police, indicated the work of Jews, foreigners and liberals concerned with disparaging the Church. This was a claim that reflected long-standing prejudices held by some Catholics and that also ignored the ample ability of the Church to damage itself. The issue also brought up questions of contrition and forgiveness that reflect the complex relationship with conduct under a totalitarian past. Pope Benedict XVI, a German (although the relevance of this is unclear) seeking reconciliation within the Catholic world, had declared in Poland in 2006 that nobody should 'sit in judgement on other generations', a call for forgiveness, but that approach can also cover a multitude of sins.

YUGOSLAVIA

Competing views were given a different twist in Yugoslavia as the key issue there became, from 1991, the creation of new states and their attempt to justify their territorial and other pretensions by reference to the past. The assertion of newly independent or autonomous territorial identities overlapped with the feuding characteristics of some ethnic-religious protagonists, to provide a particularly chilling instance of the weight of the past, although, looked at differently, religious nationalism is also very much part of the present and probably of the future.

As under the earlier Communist regime, the relationship with the past in Yugoslavia in the 1990s also included the attempt to disrupt, if not destroy, the historical consciousness of opponents. This led, for example, to the bombardment of monuments that were culturally important. Given the religious divides in former Yugoslavia, it is unsurprising that this destruction extended to churches and mosques, with the Serbs, for example, destroying Catholic churches and the Croats doing the same to Orthodox ones. Indeed, at a far smaller scale, the situation replicated the Nazi assault on Jewish cultural continuity as well as the Jewish role in history that had been such an insidious aspect of the Holocaust.

In Yugoslavia, the fate of baptismal and civil registers was regarded as important as they provided the evidence of who people were and, thus, of the ethnic composition of particular areas. The archives were also damaged, the Oriental Institute building in Sarajevo, with its collection of Muslim manuscripts, being destroyed, having been deliberately targeted, and the contents of the archives in Mostar damaged.

The Yugoslav crisis also saw the looting of history for example and admonition that is such a key feature of its use. Serbian nationalists, who very much employed the past for political ends, looked back to the struggle against the Muslim Ottoman Turks, particularly the heroic, but disastrous, battle of Kosovo of 1389, in order to provide historical reference and resonance for their modern opposition to the Muslims of Bosnia and Kosovo.

The description, in 2006, by Vuk Drašković, the then Serbian Foreign Minister, of Kosovo as 'the Jersualem of Serbia' captured its role in myth as well as history. In 2007, the anniversary of the battle of 1389 proved an opportunity for hardline nationalists in the Guard of Tsar Lazar to demonstrate their rejection of any loss of Kosovo. Lazar I was Prince of Serbia from 1371 to 1389.

Conversely, the modern Turks want a pro-Ottoman account of Balkan history. Croats, Slovenes and others, similarly to the Serbs, also sought heroic resonances from the past and legitimated their new states through history.[16] There are parallels with the way history is drawn upon in 'new' states in the Third World, although the historical context is different.

As far as former Yugoslavia is concerned, there might seem to be a contrast between great powers, which obsess about loss of position, while lesser powers worry more about survival, and the former entertain ideologies of manifest destiny or regional hegemony, while the latter are content to expand a bit here or there. Nevertheless, Serbian nationalists showed in the 1990s that Serbia being a lesser power did not prevent them from having an ideology of manifest destiny and a brutal practice to match. Furthermore, this message had a positive response: the 'emplotters' must have an audience interested in the plot.

The same was true of Croatia. Franjo Tuđman, a former general who had set himself up in the 1960s as a revisionist historian, became President in 1990. He used his history to support his virulent Croat nationalism, in the process attacking the Yugoslav public myth associated with Tito. Instead, Tuđman argued that the Croat role in the resistance to the Germans had been minimised by Tito, and he also played down the iniquities of the Croat Ustaše regime that had collaborated with Hitler. In his book *Bespuća povijesne zbiljnosti* (*The Wastelands of Historic Reality*, 1989),

Tuđman greatly minimised the numbers killed in Jasenovac, the concentration camp in which large numbers of Serbs were slaughtered during the Second World War by the Ustaše regime. As President, Tuđman considered bringing the remains of Ante Pavelić, the head of this regime, back to Croatia for an official state funeral. He was keen to present Croatia as a bulwark of Christian European civilisation and to contrast it with the Balkans that in his view lacked all three characteristics. Tuđman also used historical arguments to justify his ambitions for Bosnia, which he claimed had been part of Croatia, or a Catholic kingdom linked to Croatia, until Muslim settlement after the Ottoman conquest.

History provided opportunities for assertion through symbols, as in 1989 when the remains of Nikola Petrović, King of Montenegro (r. 1860–1918), who had died in exile, were returned to the Montenegrin capital, Cetinje. Aware of the near-universal use across the West of the Munich Agreement of 1938 as a craven and foolish appeasement of Fascism, the spokesmen of Vojislav Koštunica, the Serbian Prime Minister, in February 2007, rejected the proposal by the UN representative for independence for the former Serbian province of Kosovo (which has a majority Albanian population), by arguing that this would be akin to the 1938 loss by Czechoslovakia of the Sudetenland, with its majority German population, which Hitler acquired as a result of the Munich Agreement. The comparison was totally misplaced, not least because the harsh Serb treatment of Kosovo was different to that by the Czechs of the Germans in the pre-war Sudetenland, but that was scarcely going to stop the drawing of such a parallel.

Some of the history thrown forward was far more distant. Thus, in asserting their interests and identity, the Greek Orthodox made reference to medieval rivalry with the papacy; while, in Macedonia, the Greeks backed the Serbs over the position of the metropolitanate of Skopje.

As elsewhere in eastern Europe, the legacy of Communist years was a major issue in Yugoslavia. Tito was disparaged, and there was an attempt to rehabilitate the Chetniks, the largely Serb nationalist royalists who had fought both the German occupiers and the Communists. Their leader, Draža Mihajlović, executed by the post-war Communist government in 1946, was now honoured.

The conflicts of the 1990s, especially the war of 1992–5, which focused on Bosnia, were a more pressing historical issue. With Muslims, Croats and Serbs convinced that, in addition to pre-1990s issues, they were now even more victims, charges of mistreatment served to underline differences and to lessen chances for cooperation. The Bosniaks (Muslims) claim that in 1992–5 there was no civil war in Bosnia and, instead, that they were attacked by the Yugoslav Army, while the Bosnian Serbs claim the opposite. These charges were contested not only within the former Yugoslavia but also more generally, as in the eventually unsuccessful Bosnian case before the International Court of Justice that Serbia was responsible for genocide, although the court did decide in 2007 that Serbia had failed to stop the genocide that did occur. This was presented as a legal decision but can also be seen as a political one. A more recent history was also at issue in Kosovo, with Kosovans claiming retribution for Serbian atrocities in the 1990s including, in 2007, publishing the names of Serbs who had served in the secret police or army.

ANTI-SEMITISM

Anti-Semitism was also an aspect of the post-Communist historical consciousness in eastern Europe. A key aspect of the alleged legitimacy of the Communist regimes had been based upon their role in replacing governments that had been pro-Nazi, and complicity in the Holocaust had been an important aspect of this wartime support for Germany, particularly in Croatia, Romania and Slovakia. In practice, there had been a great deal of anti-Semitism during the Communist years, part of it under the guise of anti-Zionism; but the situation was reconfigured after the fall of the Communist regimes as wartime regimes, such as those of Ion Antonescu in Romania, Ante Pavelić in Croatia, and Jozef Tiso in Slovakia, were rehabilitated. Romanian cities rushed to name cities after Antonescu. Tiso, who had been executed after the war, was publicly proclaimed by those on the far right as a patriot, and in 2000 there was considerable contention over proposals to establish a memorial to him.

In part, this revival of anti-Semitism was a reflection of the ethnically exclusive concept of nationalism, and, in part, a hostility to what were seen as cosmopolitan pressures and, thus, to globalisation. As a result, nationalist opposition politicians in Hungary in 2006–7 actively pushed anti-Semitic themes in an attempt to discredit the government. In 2001, a Holocaust Memorial Day had been instituted by the Fidesz government, but by 2007, now in opposition, Fidesz had links with the far right. The coalition that ran Poland in the mid-2000s included a party with anti-Semitic inclinations. In Russia, the writer Aleksandr Solzhenitsyn, a key figure in the attempt to revive a traditional Russian culture, was critical of Jews, mistakenly blaming them for some of the pogroms they suffered in the 1900s and, more generally, for rejecting his view of assimilation.[17]

All too often, there is an alignment between a xenophobic nationalism and ecclesiastical bigotry or self-interest, as with the close link between the government and the Orthodox Church in Romania, or the government and the Catholic Church in Poland. The rehabilitation of past regimes was also linked to present politics. For example, Franjo Tuđman, the President of Croatia, not only praised Pavelić, but also supported brutal policies of ethnic aggrandisement against Muslims and Serbs. In Romania, the rehabilitation of Antonescu cut across the post-Communist revelation that the Romanians had participated actively in the Holocaust, which, in turn, was a contradiction of the tendency during the Communist years to blame the Germans for the slaughter. An international commission supported by the government that reported in 2004 made the prominent Romanian role in the Holocaust clear.

POLAND

Under the Communists across eastern Europe, history had played a role in justifying the large-scale post-war frontier changes and enforced movement of people that was seen by both Soviets and the new governments as necessary to consolidate the post-war situation. This left a legacy of historical argument and memory, particularly on the part of the numerous deportees, that, in the 1990s, remained as more than a passing echo. An historicist sense of identity and interest was also important, in the 1990s, to relations between the newly independent countries, and also between them and the major states of the region, Germany and Russia.

This was a particular problem for Poland for which historical resonances were pressing in its relationship with each power. This contributed to tension and made cooperation difficult. Thus, the Kaczynskis' government, which was to be voted out in October 2007, regularly opposed and even insulted Germany in the mid-2000s. The father of the Kaczynski brothers fought in the Warsaw uprising of 1944, and, while Mayor of Warsaw, President Lech Kaczynski had demanded reparations from the Germans for the savage wartime destruction of the city. On 14 June 2007, he told *The Times* 'co-operation within Europe should not be dependent on agreement with Germany [. . .] It is Germany that first of all needs to understand Poland'. In contrast, the fact that the Allies (Britain, France and the USA) supported Polish independence in 1918 is deeply engrained in Polish thought. For Poles, cooperation between Vladimir Putin and Gerhard Schröder earlier in the 2000s offered echoes of joint action by Germany and Russia in the partitions of 1772–95 and 1939, while the Germans failed to understand the resonance of this history.

The Kaczynskis offered historical references. The President declared in 2007, 'No, no, I'm not Tadeusz Rejtan. Rejtan failed, you see, whereas we have learnt to be effective in our actions'. Rejtan was an aristocrat who in 1773 failed to prevent parliamentary deputies from supporting the First Partition of Poland by Austria, Prussia and Russia. Also in June 2007, Jarosław Kaczynski, then Prime Minister, argued that the proposed voting formula for the EU based on population was unacceptable because of Poland's heavy losses in the Second World War: about 22 per cent of its population. He told Polish radio, 'It was the Germans who inflicted unimaginable injury, terrible harm on Poland'. Roman Giertych, the Deputy Prime Minister and leader of the League of Polish Families, attacked German Chancellor Angela Merkel's threat to press ahead with the treaty even if Poland would not compromise, claiming that she was forcing the Poles to put their hands up. In contrast, Nicolas Sarkozy in June 2007 appealed to the close historical links between France and Poland.

Equally, the governments of Germany and, even more, Russia found it difficult to abandon a sense that their views ought to prevail in eastern Europe. In large part, this reflected their inherent strength, for example that of Russia in energy supplies, but historical resonances of past concepts of inherent influence also played a role. In Germany, this strength was combined with a sense of victimhood derived in large part from the German refugees driven from eastern Europe after the Second World War.

REVISIONISM

Revisionism remains a powerful element in the political culture of the region, and history simply provides more episodes for revision. As in the nineteenth century, loss of land is a key issue. So also is disruption and loss of possessions resulting from the compulsory movement of people, especially after the Second World War. Thus, in Hungary, the Fidesz party has won support from pressing for what it terms justice for the Hungarians deported from Czechoslovakia, Romania and Yugoslavia from 1945. The equivalent remains a major issue in Germany. In both countries, this issue also represents an echo of inter-war grievances and revisionism. Thus, in Hungary, hostility to the Treaty of Trianon of 1920 and its allocation of Hungarian minorities to Czechoslovakia, Romania and Yugoslavia remains potent. In the 1990s it was possible to buy postcards showing pre-Trianon Hungary at the central train station in Budapest. The inter-war theme of lost Hungary led, in 2004, to the offer of citizenship to those of Hungarian descent living in what had formerly been Hungary. This criticism of Trianon was supported by Fidesz and opposed by the Socialists.

RUSSIA

For Russia, there was also, under Vladimir Putin, President from 2000, an unwillingness to abandon the sense of natural dominance over eastern Europe that had developed during the Cold War. A rethinking of the relationship on the basis of the equality of sovereign states proved unwelcome and is one reason why Russian entry into the EU is not at present credible. Russia's attitude to the Baltic States is very much based on the experience of control by the Soviet Union and, earlier, by Russia.

Indeed, the keenness of the Putin government to reverse Russia's relative decline and to challenge the post-Cold War settlement in Europe, extended to include a rethinking of recent history. Thus, in Munich in February 2007, Putin argued that, far from losing the Cold War and thus being weaker than the USA, the Soviet Union had voluntarily ended it.

There was also a rethinking of public commemoration in Russia. This drew on atavistic impulses that could plunder history for examples at the same time that they called on a sense of historical continuity. For example, to replace 7 November, Revolution Day, the anniversary of the Revolution (which, after the end of Communist rule was renamed the Day of Accord and Reconciliation), 4 November became a new national holiday. It was intended to mark the expulsion of the Polish garrison from the Kremlin in 1612, a key episode in bringing the Russian Time of Troubles to an end, and, thus, a memorialisation of the link between domestic division and foreign exploitation. In turn, pro-Russian elements in republics that had formerly been part of the Soviet Union but were now independent, drew attention to historical episodes that supported their case. In Ukraine, this included the Treaty of Pereyaslav of 1654, under which the Cossacks had turned for Russian protection.

The replacement of 7 November by 4 November in Russia reflected the attempt by the state to keep control of memorialisation by aligning it to the historiography of the new regime. The challenge of local initiatives had been demonstrated in 1991 when the Mayor of St Petersburg decreed that the 7 November holiday become a celebration of the city's new identity. Just as not everyone was happy to see the passing of the name Leningrad, so, on 7 November 1991, a variety of histories was celebrated. Some Communists met at the *Aurora*, the warship that played a key role in the Communist Revolution of 1917; monarchists left flowers at the grave of Peter the Great, the founder of St Petersburg; those marking the victims of totalitarianism organised requiems; and so on.[18] Two years earlier, the Hungarian government had felt obliged by mass protests to recognise 15 March, the date revolution began against Habsburg rule in 1848, as an official national holiday.

Within Russia, alongside the generally private memory of Stalin's brutal mass slaughter, the public search for distant and recent memory, or, rather, the use and misuse of this memory, focused on Russia's international standing. There was far less concern with celebrating aspects of the past domestic situation – and unsurprisingly so, as most of it offered little to a Russia that was experimenting with democracy, or, at the governmental level, with authoritarianism in the guise of democracy. Thus, although the Duma in 2003 agreed to a pension bonus to compensate relatives of victims of Stalin's purges, Putin does not want attention directed to the role of terror in supporting Communism, not least because he had been a KGB officer. Instead, the role of Russia in defeating Nazi Germany was a key theme. This provided a background for demanding influence in eastern Europe and for rallying Russia against the USA. In the same speech on Victory Day (9 May) 2007 in which he criticised Estonia, Putin presented the American challenge as if akin to that from Nazi Germany. The role of Russia in defeating Nazi Germany, however, was differently remembered. Whereas in the 1970s, a statue was erected to commemorate the wartime relief of Leningrad, in the 1990s a monastery was added to the same goal. Putin subsequently compared the tension he claimed was caused by American plans for the location of missile defences in Europe to the Cuban Missile Crisis of 1962.

Under Putin, there was a deliberate and sustained presentation of a nationalist history in order to mobilise support for a more assertive international stand. This was seen, for example, in the Nashi movement (see p. 119) and also in manuals for teachers issued in 2007. The latter support Putin's view that Soviet collapse was a geopolitical catastrophe, defend his policies and provide a troubling historical resonance. Thus, Stalin is presented as 'the most successful Soviet leader ever' and his purges and Gulags seen as essential means to national greatness by helping to mobilise the ruling elite. This is in line with Putin's remarks at a conference for teachers held at his presidential dacha in June 2007. Putin referred to Stalin's purges as terrible but compared them to the American bombing of Hiroshima and added 'in other countries even worse things happened', continuing, 'We had no other black pages, such as Nazism, for instance'.

The attitudes of a Russian protégé, Aleksandr Lukashenko, President of Belarus from 1994 and, in effect, its dictator from 1996, are possibly indicative. He propagated an ideology focused on Communism and his own leadership cult that affected the teaching of recent and earlier history. In 2004, Lukashenko unveiled a statue to one of his heroes, Felix Dzerzhinsky, the founder of the Soviet secret police, at the latter's birthplace. In contrast, his statue in front of the KGB headquarters in Moscow was destroyed in 1991. In Belarus, academic work on historical figures opposed to Russia was judged unacceptable.[19]

THE SOVIET LEGACY

Dealing with the consequences of Soviet power was an issue for other states handling the legacy of the Communist years. These included Soviet atrocities. In 1990, Mikhail Gorbachev admitted the long-denied responsibility for the slaughter of captured Polish officers at Katyn in 1940,[20] and in 2007 Putin spoke at Butovo where thousands of Soviet citizens were shot seventy years earlier during Stalin's Purges, but other episodes remain more obscure, and there is still controversy over the numbers who died as a result of Soviet terror. Nevertheless, the nature and extent of Soviet atrocities were far more discussed in the 1990s and 2000s than during the Cold War when such accounts had, inaccurately, been frequently labelled as propaganda. Bringing this history to light was an important aspect of the post-Communist world,[21] often representing a deliberate attempt to validate the victims and to damn the Communists. In the 2000s, alongside scholars and popular historians, non-academics dwelled on this theme.

This was true for non-Russian as well as Russian writers, for example the novelist Martin Amis in *Koba the Dread: Laughter and the Twenty Million* (2002), which, in part, was an attack on those outside Russia who excused Communism. In keeping with the widespread tendency in modern public culture to give voice to individual experience, there was also an attempt to record those of victims of the Gulags, as in Anne Applebaum's *Gulag: A History of the Soviet Camps* (2003).[22] Frequent reference to the Gulags as concentration camps served to underline criticism of the Soviet system.

It was not only formerly Communist states where the end of the Cold War signalled a change in public history. In Finland, for example, the Lotta Svärd, a women's movement that had pro-vided food and nurses for the army and had taken part in plane-spotting during the wars with the Soviet Union in 1939–44, had been subsequently banned as a result of Soviet pressure. After the Cold War, it was revived, received a medal from the President and was celebrated in a museum. With Finland having to show less concern about its Russian neighbour, it also became more acceptable to mention the close to half a million refugees who had fled Karelia when it was annexed by the Soviet Union in 1940: it is still part of Russia. In Finland in 2007, I was told that this represented losing 'the left arm of Lady Finland'.

More generally, there was also, as a consequence of the end of the Cold War, a return of archival material that had been seized. In 1990, the existence in Moscow of the Special Archive contain-ing materials seized from Germany in 1945 came to light. Some documents had been returned to East Germany in the 1950s, but knowledge of, and access to, the remainder was only provided from 1990.

A common theme in what has been discussed so far is that, far from the end of Communism leading simply to a liberalisa-tion of practices and a depoliticisation of history (and much else), there has, in fact, been a tendency, alongside liberalisation most obviously in discussion, to maintain similar practices of state control, albeit without the directing ideology of Communism. This, instead, has ensured that nationalism has come to play a greater role, with this nationalism having a strong ethnic compo-nent. Yet, the new degree of freedom that was not possible under Communism also needs emphasis. This freedom has included the ability to debate the Communist years and to represent them fic-tionally, as in Florian Henckel von Donnersmarck's critical film *Das Leben der Anderen* (*The Lives of Others*, 2007) about the Stasi. Such debates were challenged by ex-Stasi demonstrators, while there were also attempts to alter critical Wikipedia entries on East Germany, but at least there was debate.

CHINA

Any criticism of the situation in ex-Communist countries simply has to refer to the more dire position in still-Communist states:

the contrast between countries and states is an advisable one in this context as the use of the term 'country' implies consent. If North Korea may be an extreme instance, there is still room to note the degree of manipulation of history in Cuba, China and North Vietnam. In China, the situation is affected by the challenge created by the degree to which the economy has changed and is changing. Partly as a consequence, the Communist Party there does not make it easy to question its orthodoxy. For example, it is difficult for independent commentators to check on the authenticity of the Long March, a key iconic episode in Chinese Communist history and one celebrated in the arts, such as the film of which an English version was broadcast in 2007 under the title *The Great Escape: China's Long March*. In 2006, the Chinese National Museum held an exhibition commemorating the Long March. Yet, the accuracy of the established account is dubious. The passage of the Dadu River in 1935 is a matter of considerable controversy, with the heroic accounts of a crossing of a burning bridge in the face of heavy fire ripe for critical scrutiny.[23]

In 2004, a book on the anti-intellectual, 'anti-rightist' campaign of 1957–8 was banned by the Communist Party's Propaganda Department. Such issues are a reminder of how far, in contrast, the ex-Communist countries have come in their discussion of their past. Tiananmen Square in Beijing retains its monument to revolutionary heroes and the mausoleum of Mao Zedong, while the large portrait of Mao on the Tiananmen Gate is replaced annually.

CUBA

The supposedly heroic past is also on view in Cuba. In 1997, the body of Che Guevara was returned from Bolivia where he had been killed in 1967 while leading a totally unsuccessful attempt to stage a revolution. It was reinterred in the crypt of a mausoleum on the Plaza de la Revolution Ernesto Guevara in Santa Clara. An eternal candle stands sentry within, while the square above is dominated by a bronze statue of the failed leader. The revolution in Cuba that brought Castro to power is also celebrated in the town. As with the bridge across the Dadu River, the focus is on a military occasion, in this case an attack on an armoured train.

The bulldozer used is maintained on a plinth, while four of the restored boxcars from the train are nearby.

In Cuba, the Revolution of 1959 and the subsequent breakdown in relations with the USA were followed by an aggressively anti-American presentation of national and international history. The American intervention in 1898 on behalf of Cuban rebels against Spain was presented as an occupation by imperialists, and the Cuban republic that followed it was seen as neo-colonial. Instead, history began anew in 1959. Thus, traditional Communist themes were combined with nationalist defiance of the USA, the two linked in the portrayal of the USA as an imperial power seeking economic domination. The USA was very useful to Cuban public history, and the government myth it represented, as it linked the notion of a powerful foreign challenge to that of a domestic threat. In North Korea, the emphasis is very much on foreign threats and on the commemoration of the ruling Communist dynasty.[24]

In the non-Communist world, the end of the Cold War, or, rather its weakening, for it is still a residual element in some areas, also led to a rethinking of the anti-Communist character of earlier histories. Thus, in South Korea, there was a downplaying of the earlier emphasis on North Korean atrocities.

RECONCILIATION

Malign as it is (or was), tackling the legacy of Communism is not a separable add-on to otherwise clear national histories. Instead, there is the problem of inherently complex and controversial histories that interact with very different, and clashing, agendas for presenting the past. To cope with these discourses of the strident, it is necessary to produce histories that incorporate the disparate perspectives on offer. Thus, in 1972, under the auspices of UNESCO (United Nations Educational, Scientific and Cultural Organization), a Joint West German–Polish Textbook Commission was established, and, in 1976, following nine conferences, joint recommendations on the presentation of German–Polish relations in history textbooks were issued. The Commission, which was the basis for the Japan–South Korean Joint Study Group on History Textbooks established in 1990, continued issuing material for history teaching, although there were topics that were not tackled publicly.[25] The History Education Committee of the Center for Democracy and Reconciliation in Southeast Europe launched in 1999 a project for 'Teaching Modern Southeast European History' supported by American, British and German government funds. Conferences were followed by the publication of four school workbooks. The goals set out in the 'General Introduction' were clear: 'Through the teaching of history, students must acquire the ability to evaluate human acts and make moral judgements. The development of critical thinking cannot stop merely at raising doubts; it must help to mould responsible citizens with moral values, able to resist any attempt to manipulate them.'

There has also been considerable cooperation between French and German historians. Moreover, the Institute of Civic Space and Public Policy, an international think tank, at the Lazarski School of Commerce and Law in Warsaw brings together authors and publishers from Poland and east-central Europe to correct the many factual errors in textbooks.

These were not the sole initiatives. The Polish city of Wrocław (previously German Breslau) commissioned an account of its history designed to foster reconciliation. Written by Norman Davies and Roger Moorhouse, this was published simultaneously in 2002 in English (*Microcosm: Portrait of a Central European City*), German and Polish.

Unfortunately, there is little similar work on other locations. At the political level, however, there has in some cases been a willingness to downplay the revisionist sentiments of deportees, irridentists and zealous nationalists. This is true, for example, of Polish governmental views on Polish minorities in Belarus, Lithuania and Ukraine,[26] and, in 2003, the presidents of Poland and Ukraine jointly unveiled a monument to the victims of the atrocities of the 1940s. As a parallel, it was not until the late 1950s that a committee of Belgian and German historians agreed that the German destruction of the city of Louvain in the opening campaign of the First World War in 1914 was unjustified, a view the Germans had rejected in 1927.[27]

THE PROBLEM OF NATIONALISM

Across much of eastern Europe, especially in the Balkans, such compromises are often treated as historical betrayals that amount to a deracination that threatens identity. This is not simply due to the Communist interlude. Instead, the legacy of nineteenth-century notions of nationalism remains very powerful, not least in Greece. School textbooks there are compulsory and issued by the government. In 2007, the Greek government was criticised for dropping plans to produce a new edition of a textbook that downplayed accounts in earlier editions of Greek suffering under Ottoman (Turkish) rule and of the 'ethnic cleansing' of Greeks from Smyrna (Izmir) by the Turks in 1922. Right-wing critics had pressed for an abandonment of the plans for this revised edition. Once it was abandoned, other commentators and politicians in turn complained.

The extent to which this legacy of nationalism is to be regarded as a problem is one that readers are invited to consider, for the author cannot offer a pat answer. If, in Chapter 6, the argument, during the discussion of western Europe, is to be critical of the EU and, instead, favourable to national histories, then it is unclear why a different approach should necessarily be taken to eastern Europe.

To argue that nationalism in eastern Europe, at the level of established states, is more malign than in western Europe might not be a view that recommends itself to Catalan, Flemish or Scottish separatists, nor one that makes sense in terms of the strength of Belgian, Italian and other neo-fascists. Moreover, this argument risks continuing an unhelpful and inaccurate tradition of primitivising eastern Europe and using it to project western European anxieties.[28] However, it can also be argued that Western stereotypes about eastern Europe have an important basis in fact,[29] and that the nationalism of some of the latter's states has unpleasant aspects, or that some eastern European nationalisms have only selected features of western European nationalism and, therefore, are not comparable. A long-standing identity and tradition of unity was powerful in Hungary and Poland but not in Czechoslovakia and Yugoslavia, each of which was an invented country. Interference in the Balkans by the Great Powers has helped to create unstable ethno-cultural mixes and deep mutual suspicions. Economic weaknesses can be linked to a political disaffection that provides support for extremists.

The very term 'eastern Europe' is controversial. During the Communist years, the use of the term 'eastern Europe' argued for the unity of the history of the countries of the Soviet Bloc. Critical historians and others in Hungary in the 1970s and 1980s focused on differences and proposed first 'central eastern Europe', then 'central Europe' (which, because of its usage by the Germans in the inter-war period, was very sensitive), and then 'east-central Europe'.[30]

There is also the wider question of the value, indeed legitimacy, of nationalism and, therefore, its associated historical accounts, myths and drives. One approach is to consider nationalism in terms of the supposed challenge presented by a globalism that can be seen as denying individuals much of a sense of value, other than as consumers, or of identity, except through membership in a global community that does not, in practice, fulfil their desire for community. Nationalism, in this light, can be seen indeed in part as a defence mechanism that helps communities and individuals to respond to changes and problems;[31] although the same point can be made about minority consciousness and assertion.[32]

Thus, nationalism can be seen in democratic terms as well as, more negatively, that of ethnocentrism. The two are not necessarily separable as the ethnic dimension, understood in terms of a fixed identity and one linked to ownership of a particular territory, may provide much of the content of the democratic movement. Moreover, flawed, or even false, nationalist history lends itself to organic theories of community that, at least, acknowledge a human diversity. This is lost when ideologies such as Communism propound universal nostrums that challenge cultural specificities. Nevertheless, as eastern Europe shows, an acknowledgement of diversity in the form of cultural identity and historical distinctiveness at the level of the nation-state can be linked to a failure to appreciate or understand diversity within such states, and this failure can be destabilising politically as well as discriminatory.

It is important to probe both the universality of nationalism and its variations. Nationalism is not 'out there' but is part of the universal condition of states, actual or aspirational. For example, it was the Spanish Nationalists during the Civil War who crushed the Catalans and Basques and their aspirations for nationhood. Turning to the variations, there are important differences between 'defensive ethnic' and 'triumphalist ethnic' nationalism, for example between Estonia and Serbia. There are also contrasts over the extent to which nationalism is *völkisch*, in the nineteenth-century sense. In some aspirational nations, such as Catalonia, there have been important moves away from such nationalism, and it was never strong in Scotland. In contrast, in Corsica or Flanders, where there is such *völkisch* nationalism, it is associated, in particular, with hostility to immigrants. This strand was also seen in the Swiss national election in October 2007, with the Swiss People's Party (SVP) taking a stance that was very much focused on opposition to immigration. Critics accused the SVP and its leader of policies and attitudes similar to the Nazis (the practice of family liability for crimes) and the Italian Fascists (adulation of the leader).

Any contrast between ethnic nationalism, seen as historicised, atavistic and bad, and civic nationalism, presented as modern, modernising, benign and good, however, is far too simple, not least as it, misleadingly, proposes a contrast that cannot be readily made.[33] If this distinction is to be made, it is rather the case that there is a continuum, and not a dichotomy, and it is also worth noting that civic nationalism, as well as ethnic nationalism, can be the cause of conflict as the American Civil War demonstrated.

A focus on tendencies, indeed, is helpful, as nationalism (like democracy or religion) can be seen as a category containing contrasting drives. These include both a notion of essentialism (generally racial), with all the negative implications about others and outsiders that that implies, as well as a more liberal, concept of nationalism. As the history of eastern Europe over the past century indicates, this tension does not conform to any simple contrast between left and right.

FORGETTING

From the perspective of historians and others, the reconciliation that addresses the past of conflict and repression can also entail a process of deliberate erasure of contentious episodes. While motivated by a search for good relations, this can create new 'victims', in so far as those whose role is neglected or actively misrepresented can be seen as victims, or at least as having a grievance. An example is the South Korean tendency of late to downplay North Korean responsibility for the Korean War (1950–3) and, instead, to focus on unwelcome actions by their American protectors. Closer to home, there is the extent to which the benefits of the British Empire are downplayed or ignored, while the Germans are presented as the victims of Allied war crimes in the shape of bombing. There is also the downplaying of the evils of paramilitary terrorism as an aspect of the end of the Northern Ireland 'Troubles'. From this perspective, historians emerge as the necessary opponents of false consciousness, with their own obligation to truth in both past, present and, therefore, future, but it is not a role in which they are likely to succeed.

CHAPTER 6

BRITAIN, EUROPE
AND THE FASHIONING OF MYTHS

'History will never forgive him for that'. Clare Short's reference to the 2003 invasion of Iraq when asked, on the radio programme *Any Questions*, on 11 May 2007, to evaluate Tony Blair's 'place in history', was but one instance of the widespread attempt to evaluate Blair in terms of his historical record. For example, *The Economist* of 12 May asked on its cover, 'How Will History Judge Him?', answering, 'For all the disappointments, history will judge Tony Blair more kindly than Britons do today'.

Such remarks are instructive for the confidence they suggest about history operating as a readily understood and coherent force. There is scant sense of the ambiguities of the subject, not least the difficulties of historical research and assessment; and, of course, in a demonstration of their marginality, historians are asked to play little or no role in such public discussion, and also less than their predecessors may have done in the past. In short, glibness is the order of the day, possibly appropriately so in the analysis of Tony Blair.

Looked at differently, history, in the sense of the future assessment of the present, is seen as a key source of validation in present discussion. This was Hitler's conviction,[1] and was also argued, in a very different context, by both Blair and George W. Bush in justifying their Iraq policy. Conversely, visiting London in November 2004, President Chirac of France, their most vocal high-ranking critic, declared 'History will judge whether France was right to oppose the war in Iraq or not'. This conviction of vindication through history contributes to the more general cultural and ideological importance of presenting both the past and also the present in a historicising context.

In contemporary Europe, there is a ready tension between two uses of history. The first is the attempt to fashion new myths intended to serve as the basis for a new prospectus of power at the level of a new political entity, the EU. The second use of history is the advancing of the transformed national accounts discussed in Chapter 5 and the assertion of more long-standing national accounts considered in this. Each acts as a critique of the new European myth. The key new prospectus, nevertheless, is that of Europe, understood as an integrationist project resting on a common culture, although that is not the sole level of such new history. At the national and regional levels, there are also attempts to fashion new myths, but, in many senses, these relate to long-standing tensions and debates at these levels and are not comparable to the European myth.

THE EUROPEAN ACCOUNT

The latter draws heavily on the EU, which is an active and long-standing sponsor of statements and publications claiming that European unification is natural, necessary, inevitable and has already achieved much. Such arguments were advanced from the outset (and were encouraged by the Tindemanns' Report of 1975, with its call for a stress on common cultural traditions) but are increasingly challenged by the expansionism of the Union. The original six members, of what, under the Treaty of Rome of 1957, was initially the European Economic Community, could pretend to a degree of historical cohesion, although, in practice, it was one that was undermined by the religious and political divisions derived from the Protestant Reformation of the sixteenth century, which had shattered the unity first of the Burgundian inheritance in the Low Countries, and then of the German-centred Holy Roman Empire. Despite this, there was a degree to which at least some of the population shared a conception of being European. The Six was seen as an extension or rescue of the national project and not as a rival to it as it has been seen in Britain.

The complexity of the relationship between the EU and individual states can be seen with the comments of those British observers who, at every change of government in France or Germany talked of the 'realities' of national interest being about to resurface, thus 'equalizing' relations amongst France, Germany and Britain. The problem with this approach is that it is seemingly unwilling or unable to recognise that Franco-German (in other words 'European') unity is a French and German national interest and, now, sentiment, such that every pairing of German and French leaders from the 1950s, whatever their political persuasion, have found their way to an understanding that builds on it. New Zealanders and others from the former dominions may grasp the meaning of Europeanism because they lived with imperialism, with being both, say, Canadian and British, and were comfortable with that. In New Zealand, Empire was referred to as 'independence with something else'.

Accessions to what became the EU after the original six members, however, lacked any logic in terms of cohesion. The contrasts in economy and culture between Britain and Greece, or Finland and Portugal, were matched by a lack of a common historical experience. This was disguised by talk of a deep history that looked back to the supposed common characteristics and episodes of European culture, or what Jack Lang, the former French Socialist Minister of Culture, termed Europe's 'soul', such as toleration, the Renaissance and the Enlightenment. The EU's appropriation of Erasmus and Socrates for its higher-education exchange programmes also makes the pretence of an appropriated history.[2] Charlemagne is presented as the 'Father of Europe'. This interpretation in terms of a shared history, however, faces serious drawbacks.

The idea of a common base was flawed as an analysis of the development of European societies, which, in fact, revealed major contrasts and discontinuities. Moreover, if the emphasis was to be on European culture, it was unclear how this was supposed to exclude the European settler cultures, such as those in the Americas and in Australasia, let alone Norway, which voted against membership of the EU in 1972 and 1994, or Switzerland. Lastly, such an interpretation underlined the problem of how best to treat the large and rapidly growing immigrant populations who did not display these supposed cultural attributes and inheritance. Such issues were pushed further to the fore when the EU sought to 'deepen' and extend in new directions from the mid-2000s.

This deepening involved the attempt to draw up a constitution. As with other attempts of the same type, the search for a common purpose in fact encouraged dissension over this purpose. The French and Dutch referenda results in 2005 suggest that the EU has become too pluralist for their vision of it to be secure or activated.

Dissension over a supposed common purpose occurred in particular over the question of whether the EU was to be taken to have a Christian character, a character that was held to be historically rooted in European culture. Ironically, it had required Hitler, or rather the reaction to his policies and short-term success, for the revival of the dream of a Roman-Christian empire to become possible. This might seem an inaccurate rendering of European unification, not least because the EU presented Western civilisation as shaped by the Classical traditions and the Enlightenment. However, alongside the European myth advanced by the EU, which is secular albeit drawing heavily on the ideas of Christian democracy (or, rather, the Christian Democratic parties), came attempts to advance other interpretations of European identity. One of the most potent attempts was that by the Catholic Church to argue not only that Christianity was the crucial cultural dimension of Europe but also that this was truly provided by the Catholic Church. In part, this entailed an attempt to take control of history, for this thesis was directed against other religious and cultural purchases on Europe's past, present and future. As far as Christianity was concerned, there was a marginalisation of both Protestantism and Orthodoxy, and the latter certainly rejected the attempt to see it as peripheral in a Catholic-defined and dominated Europe.[3]

As far as religion itself was at issue, there was an assault on the Enlightenment. This became a bogeyman for many Catholic commentators, serving as a site and cause for secularism. This was a reading that was deeply flawed as far as the eighteenth-century movement itself was concerned, but the Enlightenment served Catholic commentators as a historical occasion to explain where the wrong turn had been taken.

There was also a rivalry with Islam. In September 2006, Pope Benedict XVI, in what, on the whole, was a measured and thoughtful speech, cited, as an illustration, the remarks by a fourteenth-century ruler of Byzantium (the Eastern Roman Empire) to a Persian ruler: 'Show me what Muhammad brought that was new, and there you will find things only evil and inhuman, such as his command to spread by the sword the faith he preached'. Taken out of context, this remark led to widespread agitation in the Muslim world and among Muslims in Europe, agitation that indicated an unwillingness to accept even the possibility of criticism.

The issue was accentuated by the effort to expand the EU to include Turkey, a state which was certainly not Christian and which was scarcely European. This effort encouraged a serious questioning of the extent to which the EU had in fact lost direction. Thus, an argument of identity and difference that owed something to past rivalries, particularly between Christian Greece and Muslim Turkey, fed into a debate over the future of the EU. Pope Benedict referred to Turkey being 'in permanent contrast to Europe', the past thus serving as a reference point for the present and a guide for the future.

Spurious claims about Europe were the case for both near and distant history. For example, it was argued that the EU had kept the peace in western Europe from 1945. This oft-repeated remark was an all-too-typical instance of the preference for assertion over reason that was an aspect of European myth-making. The claim totally underplayed the role of NATO and of American ascendancy in keeping the peace, as well as the (lesser) significance of the British and French nuclear deterrence. In 2007, when Germany held the presidency of the EU, the German Chancellor, Angela Merkel, suggested a standardised history textbook across the EU. To imagine that such a work would be anything other than a combination of the bland and the partisan would be fantastical, but it is in line with the notion that those who, in national referenda, reject European integration should be re-educated, an argument applied to both the Danes and the Irish in the past. In 2007, José Manuel Barossa, the President of the European Commission, employed the argument of historical continuity to argue that the British people should not be allowed a referendum on the new European constitution. He argued that the British had fought hard for parliamentary government in the past and that it would be wrong to abandon it and resort to a referendum.

In part, the EU rests on a false invented history and, in part, on the denial, or at least downplaying, of national history. Centrally, nationalism was seen as a cause of the divisions of 1914–45 and, thus, as a malign force that needed to be transformed with an emphasis on 'transnational' brotherhood in which the history that was recalled was not one of anger and conflict but, instead, of cooperation designed to overcome both. This, however, was always a flawed approach that, in particular, meant less to the French than to their original five fellow members. Britain, with its sense of difference, and its distinctive history, did not readily accommodate to federalist ideology and myths, and the argument that a European identity entails abandoning the memory and grudges of past anger and conflict meant particularly little in eastern Europe. There, history was a vital aspect of not just identity understood in an abstract fashion but rather of the continuity of national groups whose autonomy – indeed, independence – had been challenged, if not denied, for most of the previous half millennium and, in particular, over the past century. This was not a background for forgetting, nor for an emphasis on compromise, dialogue and a downplaying of the past. Rather, however, than treating this as a backward aspect of a Europe moving forward into some form of post-historical identity, it is worth asking not only whether the latter is a mirage, and a dangerous one at that, but also how far it is necessary to understand the role of contested memories and remembered grudges in western Europe as well.

Alongside European myths, indeed, came the contesting of national histories within western Europe. In part, this reflected social and economic changes that led to the weakening or collapse of previously potent social identifiers. This weakening or collapse was linked to a more general lack of confidence in hitherto powerful cultural projects for unity through assertion. There was also a breakdown in many states of the cultural and ideological underpinnings of post-1945 consensus. The challenges were varied, being particularly potent from regional political groupings that embraced autonomy or separatism – for example, Catalan and Scottish nationalists. There was also, from the 1970s, a greater assertiveness on the conservative part of the political spectrum much of which was directed against dominant left-of-centre, or, at least, corporatist accounts.

Thus, in Denmark, the German occupation of 1940–5 has been used to different political purposes, including to strengthen opposition to membership, and the terms of membership, in the EU or to justify Danish participation in the Iraq War of 2003.[4] Notions of Danishness are playing a major role in the Danish immigration debate, while the Cold War is now being discussed from the focus of how politicians, journalists, writers and other leading public figures were allegedly compliant towards Communism, either being unforgivably naive or fellow travellers. These allegations are being used to expose or discredit politicians and other public persons still active and to suggest deceit and treason in left-wing circles today.

Most of the challenge to consensus was not a matter of debate about history. Instead, the end of the long boom in the 1970s followed by the immobility and corrupt elitism of long-standing governments in the 1980s and 1990s helped to lead to anger and to a questioning of conventional nostrums. It was possible to criticise the Kreisky government in Austria, or its Mitterrand (France) or Kohl (Germany) or Christian Democrat (Italy) counterparts, without having any particular views on history. In 1984, however, I had the pleasant experience of being entertained in Vienna by a senior opposition parliamentarian who was convinced that the best way to appreciate the Kreisky system was to understand that of Sir Robert Walpole in Britain in the 1720s and 1730s, another prime minister known for his skill at political manipulation.

At the same time, there were history wars in each country that had political resonances, history wars that looked to the continuation of old rivalries in competing and contested identities. In part, this was a question of names, with the Tories continuing from the late seventeenth century to today in Britain, or the Greens and Whites of Montenegro, the rivals in 1918–19 over unification with Serbia or autonomy, becoming names that continue into its modern politics. Names, indeed, carry historical weight as well as reflecting present consent in particular identities.

FRANCE

In France, the long-standing contest between left- and right-wing views of national past became less prominent from the 1960s as the competing interests became less antagonistic and powerful, not least the Socialist and Communist parties and the Catholic Church, while the institutions of government made a greater effort to insist on a statist and non-partisan approach focused on planning for the future and thus less fixated on the past.[5] In France, there were still long-standing historical controversies, however, although they decreased in significance. From the 1960s, the key issue was the assault on the myth that, during the Second World War, most of the French had supported the Resistance in 1940–4. This was linked to contention over the political complexion of the Resistance. Such contention led to rival – indeed, contested – commemorations of episodes and of heroes such as Jean Moulin, a major Gaullist Resistance figure, responsibility for the capture of whom was bitterly contested.[6] At the same time, scholarship and the publication of memoirs threw additional light on the Resistance.[7]

The sensitivity of the issue was increased by the ambiguous approach to Vichy collaboration with the German occupation taken by François Mitterrand, President from 1981 to 1995, and his failure adequately to condemn the regime, for which he had very good personal reasons. The use of Vichyist themes by Jean-Marie Le Pen's far-right-wing Front National (National Front) movement also underlined the significance of the topic.[8] Tarnishing the Resistance, or questioning its popularity, thus seemed to serve the interests of those who looked back to Vichy, as well as to compromise the nationalist historical account outlined for the Fourth and Fifth Republics. Indeed, the government still memorialises the Resistance with considerable zeal. In May 2007, the new President, Nicolas Sarkozy, instructed schools to read to all classes a farewell letter written in October 1941 by the seventeen-year-old Guy Môquet on the eve of his execution by the Germans as part of a collective reprisal for the killing of a German officer. Sarkozy sees this as an inspiring example of patriotic sacrifice, but opposition politicians and teachers objected to what they saw as the government's appropriating of Môquet, a Communist.

Differing views on Vichy resonate with contrasting accounts of France and French history as a whole, and, in turn, these validate current political preferences. Challenges to an acceptable French historical nationalism came from a variety of directions. Part related to the conduct of France abroad, specifically the character of French imperialism, especially in North Africa. This was politically sensitive because of contention over the consequences of large-scale immigration from the region, not least the extent of disorder in areas dominated by immigrants. Riots in Paris in late 2005 made the issue more acute. The end result was a controversy over the nature of French imperial policy that ended up in legislative debate and public contention. In 2006, there were bitter quarrels about the treatment of Algeria, especially during its eventually successful rebellion against French rule in 1956–62. The response in France had underlined divisions in French society that, earlier, the myth of wartime unity in resistance had sought to conceal. The Algerian War was taught in French schools from 1983, but it was only a small and selective study that was offered and, in general, the war is marginalised, in part to avoid aggravating divisive memories. The controversial nature of the conflict was kept alive by showings of the film *La Battaglia di Algeri* (*The Battle for Algiers*, dir. Gillo Pontecorvo, 1965) and by the expression of the views of participants. In 2000, former generals disputed the employment of torture in Algiers: General Massu admitted and regretted it, while General Aussaresses claimed that it had been necessary. He was subsequently denounced for excusing war crimes in his account of the war.[9]

The legacy of Algeria also had a cultural manifestation with *Indigènes* (*Days of Glory*, dir. Rachid Bouchareb 2006), a major film discussing the role of the Algerian soldiers who fought for France in the two world wars and who were then largely ignored, not least in terms of their war pensions (see p. 97). The entire episode underlined the difficulty of creating an effective historical account in a state with an imperial past where a major legacy of that past is a substantial immigrant population with a sense of grievance. Assimilation was the response in the past but is more difficult now as a policy. Not only is there more individualism, and thus more resistance to incorporating accounts, but, in addition, the expression of difference is both institutionalised and exploited.

In comparison with the Algerian legacy, it proved less contentious, and thus less difficult, to deal with that of France's treatment of its slaves in its Caribbean colonies. In part, this was because slavery, which occurred longer ago, was not seen as an issue to match that of Algeria. In addition, if the legacy of slavery is more divisive in the remaining French colonies, such as Martinique, they are now represented in the French National Assembly and, anyway, are more remote than the *bidonvilles*, in which many Algerians live, surrounding French cities. In 2003, the bicentennial of the death of Toussaint Louverture, the winner of independence for Haiti from France, was commemorated with the Ministry of Culture spending money on the Château de Joux, the prison in which, having been captured by the French, he had died. The château is now presented as a 'site-symbol of the fight for liberty', and he is seen as a precursor of more recent figures including Martin Luther King and Nelson Mandela.

The role of legislative debate over the treatment of French history, specifically Algeria, reflected the extent to which in France memory is seen as an official task in which the state takes the key part. This is more generally the case and contrasts with the position in Britain in which the state does not play as central a directing role or does so in a context of controversy and, indeed, in almost an uncertain, if not an embarrassed, fashion.

The French pattern is far more common across the world than its British counterpart, which helps explain why the British generally underrate the importance of history as a political issue or, at least, central component of the collective memory that helps frame the parameters of public contention. This was accentuated during the long holiday from history from 1991 to 2001 when concern about possible international risks markedly decreased. On the other hand, in Britain, there is great public interest in history, and this is seen in its popularity as a university degree, in the world of books and in the role of references to history in political commentary in the media.

As France indicates, the state's role can itself be a shifting one, with contests not only about the content of governmentally endorsed memory, but also about its form. In France, in the 2000s, there has been a tendency for legislative discussion over historical commemoration, in part reflecting the extent to which the elderly Jacques Chirac no longer seemed able to dominate the public discussion nor to respond to concerns. Similarly, in Spain, regional agencies have been challenging the role of national counterparts.

Public discussion in France was also a response to uncertainty about identity and change. This uncertainty may have owed something to a feeling of decline within a Europe increasingly dominated by Germany, and within a West and a world under the sway of the USA. One manifestation was an interest in the changing nature of French collective memory, and this gave rise to related political anxieties.[10]

Aside from Algeria, another issue from mid-century was the legacy of the student revolt of 1968. Thus, on 29 April 2007, Nicolas Sarkozy, in his successful election campaign for the Presidency, attacked the rival left as the continuation of the spirit of 1968, declaring, 'In this election, it is a question of whether the heritage of May '68 should be perpetuated or if it should be liquidated once and for all'. This was related by him to what he termed a crisis of 'morality, authority, work, and national identity'. Linking the riots of 1968 to those in France in 2005, Sarkozy accused the left of systematically backing troublemakers.

The response to Sarkozy's success was also instructive. Frequent references to Napoleon reflected not only Sarkozy's willingness to strike that echo, in both approach and language, in which he echoed his one-time rival on the right, Dominique de Villepin, but also a general habit of discussing French history in terms of a set cast of individuals and episodes: Joan of Arc and Napoleon, Dreyfus and de Gaulle, the Revolution and Vichy, and so on. Thus, the German weekly *Stern* fronted its issue of 10 May 2007 with a photo of Sarkozy and the title 'The New Napoleon'. The relevant articles did not focus on this theme, but they suggested one way in which he could be presented as Napoleonic when they provided the headline, 'An Egomaniac in the Elysée'.

It is unclear how far such comments matter. For a German weekly to refer to the French President in this fashion does not mean that it is suggesting any comparison with Napoleonic aggression in the early nineteenth century, nor that it is drawing on any deep well of popular anxiety on this head. Indeed, the detaching of historical reference from historical anxiety can be taken as a sign of maturity. Moreover, this can be seen as undercutting the argument in this book that historical references often reflect and sustain identification through grievance and hatred.

Conversely, it can be suggested that this episode simply reflects the conditionality of historical reference. Since the unification of East with West Germany, the country has not had to fear French opposition. If, in contrast, a prominent French weekly had greeted a German electoral result with the cover headline 'The New Hitler', then the situation would have been different. The reference would have been to a more recent episode, but, more crucially, it would have drawn on a stronger anxiety.

It is also worth noting a historical resonance. The term 'Bonapartism' was applied to de Gaulle by his critics, but Napoleon's legacy has become considerably less contentious than it was in the nineteenth century. Then the legacy was strong, thanks, first, to Napoleon III's references to his uncle and then to the Third Republic's self-validation and its concern about the possibility of a military coup, for example in 1888 by Georges Boulanger, a charismatic former general.

The French Revolution remains more controversial. This was made dramatically clear in Paris in 1989 when state-sponsored celebrations of the bicentenary were challenged by posters drawing a parallel between the revolutionaries' brutal suppression of popular opposition in the Vendée in 1793 and genocide, with its obvious echoes in more recent history. Another uprising against the Revolution was the subject of the successful film *Chouans!* (dir. Philippe de Broca, 1988). The extent to which the Revolution led necessarily to tyranny was controversial, not only in academic circles,[11] but also in popular ones no longer willing to accept the doctrine of French statist liberalism. Furthermore, this reinterpretation had an impact on the global understanding of the Revolution as icon and inspiration of modernity.[12]

GERMANY

For Germany, the challenges of recent history were different. As an imperial power, Germany had been more brutal than France or Britain, as the treatment of the Herero of Namibia in 1904–5 indicated (see pp. 91–2), but Germany's colonies had been lost in the First World War before there could be any significant immigration from them, while the scale of the imperial experience was far smaller than for Britain or France. The major immigrant community in modern Germany, that from Turkey, is kept separate by the definition of German nationality and is also in effect in large part segregated into different living arrangements. This community does not play a significant role in the German historical memory, nor in controversy about the past.

Instead, it is a community that has largely disappeared that plays a central role, German Jews, who had played a major part in nineteenth- and early twentieth-century German culture and society. Their role in German historical memory arises from their slaughter by their fellow Germans. The extent to which 'ordinary Germans' were involved in this process has been a matter of contention.[13]

Here it is sufficient to note that the brutal treatment of the Jews was the key aspect of a more generally shameful set of policies and of a totally indefensible wartime conduct, and both have been a subject for controversy. For example, as with the French Resistance, the extent of German resistance to the Nazi regime has been discussed in a fashion that was greatly affected by post-war politics. Seeking, for example, during the Cold War to integrate West Germany into the West as the front line against Communism, there was a tendency to emphasise the role of the resistance (and even to appropriate some Nazis into it) and also to downplay the part of Communists within it.[14] Alongside a positive portrayal of the wartime army, and a differentiation of it from the SS as well as a tendency to present the Nazi years as an aberration, this was an aspect of what has been termed 'the search for a usable past'.[15]

This search was acutely sensitive in a country where a new domestic and international political system interacted with the degree to which most of the population was the same as during the war and, indeed, had views of the recent past that were at variance with what might be judged politically correct.[16] As a consequence, rather than a stress on shame, there was an emphasis on German victimhood, most particularly on the refugees from eastern Europe.

Subsequently, in contrast, there was, from the late 1960s, a growing, but contested, willingness to note the extent of popular complicity in the Nazi regime as well as, from the 1990s, to underline the criminally murderous policy of the Army.[17] This was a matter not simply of historical scholarship and popular impression but also of justice, with cases brought in the 2000s, for example in both Germany and Rome, about wartime German massacres of Italians.

In the 2000s, however, a stress on the Germans as victims re-emerged with an emphasis on suffering at the hands of Anglo-American bombers and advancing Soviet troops. The complete lack of proportionality these comments sometimes reveal is notable, but they also testify to a determination to express and make sense of personal experience.[18] Blame-shifting affected the response to the misleading claim that, in attacking the Soviet Union, Hitler had in fact pre-empted a planned Soviet assault on Germany. Moreover, in response to the stress on the brutal conduct of the German Army came attempts to argue that the Soviet Army was as bad, attempts that ignored the extent to which the Soviet presence in Germany in 1945 was a consequence of the German invasion of the Soviet Union.

The presentation of Allied bombing in terms of mass murder ignored the earlier role of the Germans in bombing, the strategic goals of the Allied Combined Bomber Offensive and its success in hitting German industrial production and destroying the German Air Force. In contrast, Hermann Knell's *To Destroy a City: Strategic Bombing and Its Human Consequences in World War II* (2003), which had a considerable impact in Germany with its account of the British destruction of Würzburg in March 1945, inaccurately presented German policies in the 1930s and the attack on the Soviet Union as defensive and preventive. In October 2004, the issue of whether the British government would apologise for the bombing campaign was stoked up in the mass-circulation German press prior to a visit by the Queen. 'Sagt die Queen jetzt Sorry?' asked *Bild Zeitung*, the leading circulation paper, on 28 October beside a picture of a British bomber and under a reminder of those killed at Dresden. In contrast, recent work by a British author has emphasised the degree to which Dresden was a major centre in the German military-industrial complex,[19] but it also serves for rhetorics of German victimhood just as it was used by the East German government as an issue in anti-Western propaganda. In 1945, Nazi propaganda made use of Dresden, and this theme has been revived by the neo-Nazis of the National Democratic Party (NPD). In 2006, NPD deputies referred to 'a Holocaust of bombs', in response to which a civic declaration outlining a 'framework for commemoration' acknowledges Dresden's role in the Nazi system and its crimes, including against the city's Jews.

Jörg Friedrich's book about the bombing of Germany sold half a million copies in Germany, while, in 2006, the bombing of Dresden was the subject of a major German television programme which included a fictional romance between a German nurse and a British airman. The previous year, the sixtieth anniversary of the bombing saw the re-dedication of the Frauenkirche in Dresden.

Victimhood also saw an overlap between Germany and eastern Europe with a discussion of how best to commemorate those who were driven from their homes in 1945. Such a *Zentrum gegen Vertreibung*, for which Angela Merkel gave the go-ahead in October 2007, entailed controversy both within Germany and also among its neighbours, the Czechs and Poles, who did not regard the Germans they expelled as victims. It is also inaccurately argued by some Germans that 'National Socialism merely provided Poles and Czechs with the incidental opportunity to realise longstanding expansionist plans'.[20]

More generally, whether Germans as a whole should be stigmatised as the perpetrators of Nazism, or whether there is room for a more complex reading and to what effect, is related to the issue of how the Nazi period is used as a touchstone in political debate across the world.[21] Within Germany, the attempt to define an acceptable, coherent and attractive civic nationalism that could present Nazism as an aberration was the core philosophical and historiographical issue around which the *Historikerstreit* (controversy among historians) revolved in the late 1980s.

By the 2000s, the issue of surviving Nazis ebbed as they died out but earlier that had been a key topic. The career of Hans Filbinger (1913–2007) was symptomatic: Minister-President of Baden-Württemberg from 1966, and a critic of the left, Filbinger was correctly named in a newspaper article in 1978 as a wartime military judge who sentenced deserters to death. Filbinger responded by denial, suing for libel, and claimed that 'what was lawful then cannot be unlawful now'. In the face of public criticism, Filbinger, nevertheless, was forced to resign that year, and his rehabilitation in the 2000s was controversial. After his death, controversy continued, with a funeral eulogy by Günther Oettinger, a later Minister-President, that led to an eventually successful pressure for an apology. This was not simply a dispute about the past but also part of the struggle over the future of the Christian Democratic Union (CDU). Angela Merkel, the Federal Chancellor, who demanded an apology, is also a centrist whose views on the CDU are very different to those of Filbinger and Oettinger.

Not only figures on the right were involved. In 1996, Hans Schwerte, a prominent Social Democrat, was disgraced when he was revealed to be a former SS officer. Revelations remained controversial, including, in 2006, in the autobiography of Günther Grass, a major novelist who had made himself the conscience of Germany and who had pressed for an honest appraisal of the German role in the Second World War, that he had spent several months in 1944 in the Waffen-SS.

The Nazi years also shadowed earlier German history, not least with debates over whether they represented the culmination of trends integral to German history or were an uncharacteristic aberration. This involved controversy over Prussia, German nationalism, the impact of Lutheranism and other key aspects of this history and led, for example, in the early 1960s, to a bitter debate about German responsibility for the First World War and about German plans then for territorial expansion.

Post-1945 history was also a matter of contention, not least the degree to which West Germany should be seen as a continuation of earlier periods in German history. In part, contention was a revival of the controversies that had focused on the left-wing activism of 1968. That was more charged than in many European countries because of the legacy in the shape of the violent Red Army Faction (Baader–Meinhof Gang); again, the choice of terms can be significant. Whether its members should be released thus became an aspect of an ongoing engagement with the recent German past, which, in the case of the Red Army Faction, reached its height in 1977. The Italian and British equivalents are discussion about the Red Brigades and the IRA (Irish Republican Army), issues that relate, especially in the case of the latter, to present politics as much as historical discussion.

As elsewhere, the debate in Germany focused also on issues of symbolism. Thus, in 2007 there was a controversy over whether Kochstrasse, the Berlin headquarters of two leading German newspapers, including the right-wing *Bild Zeitung*, should be renamed Rudi Dutschke Strasse after a prominent radical of 1968. The residents voted yes, but the *Bild* went to court to oppose the measure as overly expensive. More generally, the question of what a Europeanised Germany means in historical terms has been so focused on the legacy of the Nazi era that other topics have been pushed to the sidelines. 'Normality' in a German context is an issue, as is the response to the degree to which Germany is becoming multiethnic.[22]

ITALY

Within Italy, the legacy of the Second World War was important to post-war political culture and alignments. The left, in particular, sought a praiseworthy origin in terms of its hostility to Mussolini. The emphasis in Italian public culture was not on cooperation with Germany in 1940–3, but rather on resistance to Hitler in 1943–5. Thus, the focus was on a war of liberation, with the Resistance presented in a heroic light, not least as a redemption from Fascism. This provided an appropriate lineage for post-war democracy which could be located in terms of opposition to Fascism, both during the war and subsequently. This also shifted attention from the Italian imperial role, both pre-war in Libya and Ethiopia, and in Greece and Yugoslavia in 1941–3. In all of these cases, opposition had been harshly treated, not least by brutal and deliberate attacks on civilians held to be supporting opposition. Ignoring this helped the Italians in their self-presentation as victims of the Second World War.

However, there was a competing attempt by the different political parties to annex the positive reputation of the Resistance to their benefit: thus, the Christian Democrats challenged the Communists' effort to present the Resistance as their movement. After the Second World War, moreover, the pressures of Italian politics and the exigencies of the Cold War had helped make it possible to present the *bravi ragazzi di Salò*, those who had supported Mussolini's Salò Republic, the Italian Social Republic, which he headed under German patronage in northern Italy in 1943–5. Its members not only escaped prosecution but also benefited from their emplacement in a patriotic legend, while, conversely, the partisans were often treated critically, especially if they were Communist.

The situation was at once complicated and taken further in the 1990s and 2000s as revisionists sought to contest the post-war orthodoxy. This contesting entailed a more positive approach to Mussolini, both pre-war and during the conflict, as well, in some cases, as a defence of the Salò Republic. Linked to this came a critique of the Resistance. The widespread positive re-evaluation of Mussolini and Italian Fascism, beginning with the work of Renzo De Felice in the 1960s, the differentiation of both from the Nazis and the decline in the reputation of the Communists,[23] were also aspects of the shift that gathered pace following the end of the Cold War, with Italy sharing in the general development of eastern Europe. Alongside politicised rethinking or rather, in many cases, the vocal expression of long-held beliefs, came academic interest in continuities between pre-Fascist and Fascist Italy and the latter and post-1945 Italy.[24]

In the 1990s and 2000s, the far right continued the habit of ignoring Italian atrocities abroad, while also calling for acknowledgement of those that Italians had suffered. In 2005, the government of Silvio Berlusconi responded to the latter by introducing a new national day of remembrance for Italians slaughtered in Istria by Communist Yugoslav forces in the closing stages of the war, as the Yugoslavs sought to secure their interpretation of the much-contested frontier. This slaughter, with many thrown to their death into the *foibe*, limestone chasms, is a key aspect of the memorialisation by Istrian exiles whose view became influential in Italy in this period. As with Germans driven from eastern Europe in 1945, or Palestinian exiles, they find it particularly difficult to express identity other than in terms of a chauvinistic sense of dispossession and victimhood.[25]

At the same time, respectability ensured that, within Italy, the positive re-evaluation of Mussolini and his Fascism can only go so far. Thus, Berlusconi's Foreign Minister, Gianfranco Fini, a former leader of the neo-Fascist MSI-DN (Movimento Sociale Italiano-Destra Nazionale, Italian Social Movement-National Right) party who had proclaimed Mussolini as one of the greatest statesmen of the century, moved politically, merged the MSI-DN with some Christian Democrats, became head of the National Alliance he created and denounced Mussolini.[26]

The legacy of the war was also central to the position of the monarchy. Italy became a republic in 1946 after a referendum that reflected not only left-wing views but also Victor Emmanuel III's failure to oppose Fascism. The referendum itself was highly problematic as it was held before the return of the many prisoners of war, and the Republic won by the tiniest of margins. Yet, the monarchy still plays a role in Italian public history because of its part in the *Risorgimento*. Across the country, streets, squares and buildings are thus named after Victor Emmanuel II, the king who secured unification. In 2007, the former royal family claimed compensation for the property lost in 1946.

SPAIN

Alongside contestation of history at the national level within western Europe came the assault on that level from advocates for regional autonomy, if not a nationalist separatism. This was seen with Scotland and Wales within Britain and also in Spain, particularly with Catalonia and the Basque Country. Under Franco, the emphasis had been on the unity of the country. Because they established unity in the peninsula after the post-Roman divisions, the Visigoths, who ruled most of Iberia from the late fifth century until its conquest by the Moors in the 710s, were much admired by the regime, and Franco praised the Visigoths when founding a museum devoted to them in 1969.

Since Franco's death, however, the Visigoths have fallen decidedly out of fashion.[27] Although Spanish nationalism can be seen, as with the complaints by the government in 2004 over the celebrations for the tercentenary of British rule over Gibraltar, a more regional focus on Spanish history has come to the fore. This is a part of a tension over Spanish identity that can be seen in the lack of words in the Spanish national anthem. The recently opened Museu d'Historia de Catalunya strongly emphasises its subject at the expense of any Spanish perspective. In 2007, a new charter of autonomy for the region of Andalusia declared that it had a 'millennium-long' history and a 'nationality'.

Across Europe, a separatist emphasis could certainly be seen in much of the history produced in such areas and in the public celebration of the past. This is the case, for example, with the cheering Scottish audiences when the English are defeated in the ludicrously inaccurate film *Braveheart* (dir. Mel Gibson, 1995), a film about the Scottish War of Independence in the 1290s and 1300s that has been used by Scottish nationalists. Scotland, of course, is not seen as a region. In Italy, in the 1990s, the separatism of the Northern League led to a distinctive account of regional and national history.

Control over education was important, and changes emerged when it was transferred from the national to the regional level. In Belgium, this occurred from the early 1960s as Flanders and Wallonia became the key governmental areas. This led to a change in the treatment of Belgian history that was made more contentious and problematic by the political context. Flemish nationalists presented Flanders as suffering a millennium of foreign oppression and claimed that, once independent in 1830, Belgium had served as a system to benefit the Walloons. Indeed, in 2007, the new Flemish President, Yves Leterme, declared Belgium 'an accident of history'.

In many respects, the separatist account of history was a traditional one that was rooted in the theories and practices of nineteenth-century nationalism. A more challenging version was mounted in the case of assertiveness by distinctive groups that were religious or ethnic, or both, but lacking any such geographical focus to serve as the basis of separatism. In contemporary Europe, this relates in particular to Islam. In general, this is a product of recent immigration, but in a few states, principally in the Balkans, this separatist attitude had a clear historical dimension.

This was also the case with Spain, where the growing Muslim minority reopened in particular the issue of the *Reconquista*, not least by challenging the Francoist account. Under Franco, heroes included Rodrigo Diaz, *El Cid* (*c.* 1043–99), who was inaccurately presented as a Spanish patriot, when in fact he was a soldier of fortune who fought for Muslim rulers as well as Christians,[28] and also Ferdinand III of Castile (r. 1217–52), under whom much of southern Spain had been conquered from the Moors. Recently, the extent to which the *Reconquista* was in fact a conquest and not the freeing of a subjugated once-Christian population has been debated. Moorish groups have been campaigning to worship in the mosque at Cordoba that was transformed with the *Reconquista* into a cathedral. In contrast, Aznar, the former Prime Minister, has given a speech tracing the challenge from al-Qaeda back to the Moorish conquest of Spain in the eighth century.

While this historical dimension is not present in Germany or Britain, the assertiveness of their Muslim minorities is in part based on a rejection of the current national myths, not least the support for toleration. Repeating again nineteenth-century themes, politicians, in contrast, have argued that national history should be taught in order to integrate the minorities.

IRELAND

The separatist approach to history was taken further in some states that had won independence. Ireland provides a key example in western Europe, and far more so than for Norway, which did not centre its historical account on grievance. Whatever the extent of academic revisionism, the nationalist, anti-British fervour of Irish history is notable, in the public and popular dimension, and this links Ireland to the diaspora. The anniversary of the Great Famine of 1846–8 is the key episode, but the Dublin Rising of 1916 also provides another. The British are presented as the villains, in songs, stories and films, for example, Ken Loach's misleading film *The Wind that Shakes the Barley* (2006), although that is truer of Anglo-American presentations than of Irish ones, which now are more balanced than in the de Valera era.

Museum displays on Irish history concentrate on the glories of Celtic civilisation in the 'Dark Ages', emphasising Ireland's contribution to European culture at a time when Europe was assailed by barbarians. There is then relatively little on the period of English rule, until the story resumes with the struggle for independence and subsequent history. As a consequence, the positive aspects of the centuries of English rule are neglected in favour of an image of lost centuries, their gloom punctuated by cruel episodes, such as the fate of Wexford and Waterford at the hands of Oliver Cromwell and his invading English Protestant troops in 1649 and the Great Famine. This neglects the major role played by the Irish in the development of the British Empire, a situation repeated for Scots in the new Museum of Scottish History in Edinburgh. This approach also ensures that the riches of Anglo-Irish culture, famously represented by the writers Jonathan Swift and Oscar Wilde, are undervalued.

At the same time, among academics and others, controversy over the War of Independence and the subsequent civil war remains potent, not least, for example, the question of whether the IRA was involved in sectarian ethnic cleansing (which they were in Cork) and over the degree to which independence in 1922 was a constitutional or a violent process.[29] Scholarly criticism of the IRA and the eulogisation of armed struggle[30] did not have a comparable impact on the public use of history.[31]

Northern Ireland has both the Republican myth and its Unionist counterpart. They have highly contrasting accounts of the past.[32] For example, Ian Paisley, the most influential Unionist voice, sees the 'Glorious Revolution' of 1688–91 as not simply a key event in Irish history but also as an episode that can be more broadly located in terms of a triumph both for Protestantism over Catholicism and for European religious diversity over Papal attempts at authoritarian uniformity.

BRITAIN

The situation in Britain has varied considerably over the past three decades. Under the Conservative governments of Margaret Thatcher and John Major (1979–97), there were efforts to argue a continuation with the past, not least in terms of a robust patriotism that was particularly asserted by Thatcher. This was linked to her wish to revive appreciation of pre-1945 values and achievements, particularly those of the Victorians whom she saw as responsible for economic transformation. Her appeal to the less recent past owed much to her active rejection of continuity with the recent past of social welfarism, state control of the economy and national decline.

Conservative academics looked further back than the Victorians in their account of national exceptionalism as with Geoffrey Elton's *The English* (1992).

Thatcher's imagining of the Victorian past, however, was a construction that was historically specious. It was not based on any real understanding of the nature of Victorian society which, in very different ways, both Disraeli and Marx understood very well. This did not make her worse than other politicians who also manipulate history, but it does not suggest that she was more historically informed than other recent prime ministers.

The Conservatives were (and are) committed to the role of history in education. In 1988, the subject was included in the National Curriculum, in large part due to the strong advocacy of Kenneth Baker, the Education Secretary, and later an active writer of effective popular history. This inclusion was linked to a commitment to emphasise British political history, and the working group established to advise the minister on the curriculum was instructed accordingly. The group, however, was unhappy with this, and, instead, recommended multiculturalism and a more explicit commitment to the value of presenting contrasting interpretations of history. Thatcher, who was dissatisfied with this, required that the report go out to further consultation, and this led to a stronger focus on British history. Nevertheless, in 1990, it was decided that, at Key Stage 4 (fourteen- to sixteen-year-old pupils), history would be optional, a rejection of Baker's view that history be central, although state schools were still obliged to offer the subject.

In academic circles, the Thatcherite account of national interests and of the past was also related to a positive re-evaluation of
the Conservative leaders who preceded Winston Churchill and
the strand of Conservatism that was displaced by him, with more
favourable treatments of Neville Chamberlain, Lord Halifax and
their allies. This re-evaluation, nevertheless, was certainly not
linked to Thatcherism in foreign policy as her effort to increase
ideological commitments and to push the bounds of possibility
clashed with the pre-1940 policies of appeasement and emphasis
on prudence.

In domestic policy, however, there was a clearer parallel of
academe and politics in terms of a self-conscious rejection of elements of the big government of 1945–79. Thus, Correlli Barnett's
*The Audit of War: The Illusion and Reality of Britain as a Great
Power* (1986) argued that Labour's expenditure on welfarism,
particularly the policies of the Labour governments of 1945–51,
compromised the economic and military future of the country.
This sense of betrayal was one that drew on another historical
work, Martin Wiener's *English Culture and the Decline of the
Industrial Spirit* (1981), which appealed to Thatcherite critics
of Conservative 'Wets' with its argument that the economic past
(and therefore future) had been betrayed by elitist liberal opposition to entrepreneurism. Wiener himself told me that he was
bemused by the politicised reception of his work, although, in
practice it can be said that he had his own politicised view. In
academic terms, his work can be criticised for focusing on failed
management rather than noting the extent of continued economic
growth (in absolute, though not relative terms) and considering
sufficiently the implications of cheap and plentiful labour on production methods.

Under Labour, in power from 1997, there was a transformation in historical consciousness. The espousal of new policies
under the self-conscious New Labour platform was also linked to
a process of asserting a new identity, for Labour and Britain, that
included a different historical consciousness to that which had
hitherto prevailed. Class-based analyses and trade-union sentiment were pushed aside as Tony Blair, leader from 1994 until
2007, made a pitch for the middle ground. In doing so, he delib-

erately broke with the past and embraced the idea of the new, as in 'New Britain'. Indeed, in 1997, Peter Mandelson, Blair's Svengali, declared 'We are defining ourselves by the future'.

This approach had immediate policy implications with the provisions for new government in Scotland and Wales and for changes in the House of Lords. What works was a mantra for New Labour, but within a definite preference for the new. This took both symbolic as well as practical form as in the new Scottish Parliament, which lacks what is seen as the divisive layout of Westminster. Scottish historians responded by emphasising a distinctive national history,[33] although it was also possible to use the Scottish past, for example, the impact of the Union of Crowns (but not Parliaments) between 1603 and 1707, in order to argue that the new devolved governmental system was inherently unstable and that independence was preferable.[34]

The Northern Ireland settlement also led to an avowed break with the past with Blair urging that the legacy of sectarian bitterness be ditched. 'I feel the hand of history upon our shoulder', he declared at the time of the Good Friday Agreement in 1998. In May 2007, in marking the re-establishment of devolved government in Northern Ireland, Blair referred to the need 'to escape the heavy chains of history. To make history anew'. Later that month, on his final tour to Africa as Prime Minister, Blair emphasised the need to look to the future, not the past, declaring, at a press conference in Freetown, Sierra Leone, 'What I have done in the past, what I am doing in the present, I have done for the future. That's the only thing that matters'.

In part, alongside self-assurance that led to a high degree of arrogance, Blair's attitudes reflected a rejection of the past and of national exceptionalism and, less explicitly, of the powerful social and cultural impact of custom, tradition and heritage, an impact sometimes disparaged by being seen in terms of a heritage industry.[35] Blair's attitude can be linked to his Catholic sympathies, which led, in 2007, to his long-considered conversion to Roman Catholicism, because British nationalism was conventionally anti-Catholic as well as xenophobic, the two being closely linked and helping to define Britishness in a process of contrast.[36]

In part, under New Labour, there was also a response to the multiplicity of narratives of the past being offered in an increasingly openly diverse society. These included narratives of ethnic and religious difference and distinction, as well as specifically genderised narratives – for example, 'queer history'.[37] Looked at differently, one of the most impressive things about British culture, which includes both popular and academic history, is that it is relentlessly self-questioning and self-mocking. Indeed, the fractiousness of historical discussion can be seen as a sign of healthy, not troubled, minds. The corollary is that telling people wonderful things about empire and wartime is the type of positive history that will be pursued in totalitarian societies, such as Cuba, that deserve excoriation, rather than in Britain where a more nuanced approach is appropriate.

Under New Labour, institutional 'rebranding' reflected change, with the Department for National Heritage being renamed that for Culture, Media and Sport in 1997. This was linked, that year, to the European pattern by Mark Fisher, the Department's Under-Secretary, who declared: 'we needed to have a Ministry of Culture, which every other European country has'.[38] A lack of interest in history certainly was readily apparent at the time of the Millennium, with the emphasis being very much on present and future rather than on the past, which was deliberately neglected in the contents of the Millennium Dome at Greenwich. Also in 2000, the report on *The Future of Multi-Ethnic Britain* (2000), commissioned by the Runnymede Trust, criticised 'Englishness' as a theme of national identity because of its supposed equation with whiteness.

More consistently, public patronage sought to embrace the new and to downplay the old. This was seen in museums, exhibitions and celebrations. For example, the jingoistic theme of the Last Night of the Proms was deliberately curtailed in the 2000s, a decision that aroused controversy. Indeed, in 2007, Nicholas Kenyon, the Controller of the Proms, remarked that his successor might decide that the Last Night needed to 'move on'. This conformed to a sense not only that the aesthetics of the music and songs, such as 'Rule Britannia', were dated but also the context and reception of the work. To make Edward Elgar acceptable, his imperialism was minimised, a serious misreading of the composer.[39] More generally, empire and war were downplayed as themes in British culture and history, as seen, for example, in the stamps produced to mark the previous millennium of national history, or in clerics banning 'I Vow to Thee My Country'.

Underlying governmental assumptions continued into the 2000s and were publicly advanced. In July 2003, Blair told the American Congress 'a study of history provides so little instruction for our present day'. That November, in an interview published in the *New Statesman*, Jack Straw, the Foreign Secretary, blamed British colonialism for many of the world's international disputes. This was not only a rejection of a positive impression of Britain's past, a rejection supported by only part of the historical literature,[40] but also an irresponsible invitation to grievance on the part of others. Possibly, the nature of English nationalism, specifically what has been seen as the lack of a dominance by the nineteenth-century type of European nationalism,[41] provided opportunities for the Labour government to reject pride in the past and identification through history.

More generally, the process of decolonisation was accompanied by a large-scale jettisoning of the stories, images and myths of empire. Frequently reiterated accounts, such as of the Black Hole of Calcutta in 1765 or of James Wolfe's capture of Québec in 1759 ceased to be recalled, let alone to be iconic. The government proved unwilling to fund the Museum of the British Empire and Commonwealth, while considerable sensitivity surrounded the National Maritime Museum's Trade and Empire Gallery in 1999. Academics, meanwhile, wrestled with the issue of national identity.[42]

Ironically, as Blair came under increased pressure, not least in response to the failure to stabilise Iraq after the invasion in 2003, so he turned to the argument that 'history' would vindicate him. This was a claim shared by a number of statesmen and politicians in the mid-2000s, including George W. Bush and Jacques Chirac. In some respects, it represents a refusal to acknowledge the criticisms, and even constraints, of plebiscitary democracy by public-opinion polls and, eventually, elections. In others, it is linked to an obsessive and self-referencing sense of mission that can be as disturbing or disturbed as the empowerment through grievance already referred to in this book.

The Churchill complex is particularly potent, with Blair and Bush both seeing themselves as latter-day Churchills, a habit earlier satirised on television with Jim Hacker, the fictional minister/prime minister of the satirical *Yes Minister* and *Yes Prime Minister*. Reference to Churchill by, or on behalf of, Blair and Bush is an aspect of an approach that underrates the specificity of particular episodes in an individual career or issue. Such specificity is a key point of academic history, underlining as it does the difficulty of drawing links from one period to another. The Churchill complex was given artistic form when Blair presented Bush with a bust of Churchill in 2001. Bush keeps it in the Oval Office. This approach not only strikes a public resonance but also reflects a lack of knowledge of the complexity of the past: the Churchill they are seeking as a point of reference, for example, is that of 1940 (ennobling defiance of Hitler), not 1915 (Gallipoli) nor 1919 (Russian Civil War).

They were scarcely alone. Thatcher frequently referred to 'Winston' without mentioning that he was a reforming Liberal Home Secretary. Interviewed by *BBC History* in March 2007, John Reid, the (Labour) Home Secretary, chose Churchill as his hero. Not once mentioning that he had been a Liberal cabinet minister and a Conservative Prime Minister, Reid instead sought to annex Churchill, presenting him as 'a bit of a rebel' who became 'a reforming Home Secretary'. That July, Gordon Brown, at his first press conference with Bush, referred to Churchill, 'It's a partnership founded and driven forward by our shared values, what Winston Churchill, who was the first British prime minister to visit Camp David, called the joint inheritance of liberty, a belief in opportunity for all, a belief in the dignity of every human being'. En route from Britain, Brown had quoted Churchill's speech describing the principles of freedom and the rights of man as 'the joint inheritance of the English-speaking world'.

A revised approach to the study of national history was increasingly taken by the mid-2000s, in large part in conscious reaction to what was by then seen as the modishness of New Labour and, in particular, to its negative consequences for a sense of national identity and indeed for popular nationalism. The 2005 London suicide bombings by British-born Muslim citizens contributed to a sense of crisis about the failure of collective consciousness. As a result, Labour politicians, most obviously Gordon Brown in 2006, reached out for an assertion of nationalism that included a positive embrace of the past, with history seen as a way to teach the civic nature and values of Britishness. This reflected civic purpose as well as political calculation, the latter how best to sell a Scottish-dominated Labour Party to an England increasingly concerned about relative neglect and to a Scotland greatly affected by separatism. The rise of English nationalism is indeed a challenge to Labour, which is determined to prevent English parliamentary votes for English laws to match the Scottish position. The St George flags on white vans and scaffolding lorries are an interesting sign of public engagement on this issue.

Brown himself has a history Ph.D. on 'The Labour Party and Political Change in Scotland 1918–29', just as John Reid, the former Home Secretary, has one – on the palm-oil trade from West Africa – and also Blair's one-time adviser, now Brown minister, Andrew Adonis. On the Conservative side, there are also senior politicians with history degrees, including Oliver Letwin, David Lidington and Andrew Mitchell, while William Hague has written two distinguished history books. In 2006, Prince Charles also pressed the case to remember, teach and study British history, as did the 'History Matters' campaign launched by the National Trust, English Heritage and the Heritage Lottery Fund.

Jack Straw, then the Leader of the House of Commons, followed up Brown's lead in *The World Today*, the journal of Chatham House, an article excerpted in much of the press, for example the *Sunday Times* of 29 April 2007 under the headline 'We Need a British Story'. This rested on a sense of exceptionalism designed to focus on Britain, in place of the current emphasis on Scottish, Welsh or English identity. Indeed, Straw claimed that the very problem of British identity derived from national history:

> We are the only European nation – the only one – that has not within memory faced an existential crisis of dictatorship,

occupation, defeat or the moral hazard of neutrality in a just war. A large part of what we describe as Britishness in our story traces back to our own civil war, its resolution in 1688 – and the Treaty of Union in 1707 – but we have not had a crisis of identity like that since, and it shows in the lack of precision of what it means to us to be British.

Straw also argued that an emphasis on history was necessary in order to integrate the multiple identities of Britishness:

A 'British story' must be at the heart of this. It must place stress on the importance of democracy, how it developed here and how it can allow different groups to live together in relative harmony. Above all, British nationality is not about blood and soil, but about common civic values.

To Straw, there was the need to match the historical exceptionalism of other states:

You cannot transmit these ideas without stories. Other countries that do better than ours in defining their sense of citizenship – again, the US is the best example – do so by heroic stories of, for instance, how America came to be America. We must do the same, bringing out the freedom that lies at the heart of the story.

For Straw, the emphasis was primarily domestic, rather than, for example, the wars against Philip II of Spain, Louis XIV of France, the French Revolutionaries and Napoleon which had been so important to earlier exponents of British nationalism alongside, and as part of, a narrative of domestic development:

That means freedom through the narrative of the Magna Carta [1215], the Civil War [1642–6], the Bill of Rights [1689], through Adam Smith and the Scottish Enlightenment, the fight for votes, for the emancipation of Catholics and non-conformists, of women and of the black community, the Second World War, the fight for rights for minority groups, the fight now against unbridled terror.

There is a complicated side to this story – that seeking to secure our freedom through greater prosperity and greater security, we looked like and often were oppressors to the Irish and to many of the peoples of the British Empire. But the very creed of freedom that we preached abroad, if sometimes did not practise, ensured that our colonial episode collapsed under its own very British contradiction, and with less bloodshed than many other decolonisation struggles.

Thus, Straw addressed a reality: that Empire was an exploitative and demeaning experience for many who underwent it. He also found a way to use that positively: rather than coming up with good/bad divisions about Empire, Straw seemed to find a nuanced and overall positive way to talk about the complexities of Britain's recent past and how it has shaped our present.

In turn, Gordon Brown, in 2007, at the outset of his successful candidacy to be Prime Minister, sought not only to affirm his Britishness but also to present a national exceptionalism, telling Radio Four listeners, 'Britain is the country that, I believe, brought liberty to the world'.[43] In his first prime-ministerial statement to Parliament, he declared, 'Britain is rightly proud to be the pioneer of the modern liberties of the individual'. In 2007, there was also talk by Labour ministers, such as Ruth Kelly, about the need for a national day to promote and celebrate the common values of Britishness. This was seen as a way to integrate all ethnic and religious groups.

More than Labour calculations, however, were at stake in the demand for British history. Indeed, the widespread pressure for more public history in large part sprang from a reaction against earlier Labour neglect. This underlay Conservative discussions prior to and after the 2005 election about the need to assert a positive account of national history, in part in response to a sense that national identity was weakening. David Willetts, then Shadow Education Secretary, presented the teaching of history as the way to give the young 'national memory'. In some cases, this reaction was compounded by concern about the direction of Labour's interest when roused. There was, for example, disquiet about the contents of *Life in the United Kingdom: A*

Journey to Citizenship, the Home Office-sanctioned summary of British history, a document that was seen as part of the process of naturalisation.

Other circles and constituencies also called for more national history, not least in response to school curricula dominated by the Third Reich: what Peter Mandler, then Secretary of the Royal Historical Society, termed in 1999 the 'Hitlerisation' of British history.[44] The Qualifications and Curriculum Authority (QCA) came to the same conclusion eight years later. Eighty per cent of A-Level students study the Nazis. More history in schools was also at issue as pupils can drop the subject at fourteen. Indeed, *History in the Balance: History in English Schools 2003–7*, a report by Ofsted (the Office for Standards in Education), noted that only 32 per cent of pupils study history at GCSE (General Certificate of Secondary Education) level (a percentage that is falling), and even fewer after sixteen. Furthermore, although two-thirds achieve A grades at GCSE, a third of A* grades are from pupils educated in the private sector.

The decline in the role of history in the curriculum was possibly linked to the problems created by the multiplicity of narratives about the past (see p. 164), but changes in public policy were more significant. Crucial was the recommendation of the Dearing Committee in 1996 that there should be a greater emphasis on English, Maths and IT (Information Technology) for fourteen-to sixteen-year-old pupils, hitting the idea that history would become compulsory. The Labour government implemented its recommendations. The situation was different across much of the rest of Europe with history being a more important subject there, although Scandinavian historians always complain how little time history gets in the school curriculum there. Furthermore, only in Britain is history a generalist popular degree.

As far as pupils aged five to fourteen are concerned, for whom the subject is compulsory in England, there is an additional threat because the QCA currently proposes allowing schools from 2008 to teach those aged eleven to fourteen themes such as creativity and cultural understanding rather than individual academic subjects. Moreover, as far as history is concerned, the QCA is piloting a GCSE syllabus in which periods of history are replaced by themes such as 'people's diverse ideas' and 'conflict and its lasting impact'.

Currently, in English schools, the National Curriculum requires that pupils develop a 'chronological framework' and make 'connections between events and changes in the different periods'. In Key Stage 1 (ages five to seven), pupils are supposed to learn about people's lives and lifestyles and about significant historical figures in Britain and around the world. They should be taught to place events and objects in chronological order. In Key Stage 2 (ages seven to eleven), pupils are supposed to learn about the Romans, Anglo-Saxons and Vikings; about Britain and the world in Tudor times; and about either the Victorian Age or Britain since 1930. Moreover, pupils are intended to learn European history, for example life in Classical Greece, as well as world history, for example the Aztecs. In Key Stage 3 (ages eleven to fourteen), pupils are required to learn about significant figures and events in British history from the Middle Ages to the twentieth century, including the battle of Hastings, the monarchy from 1500 to 1750, and the Industrial Revolution. They are also supposed to cover the Holocaust.

The Ofsted report, however, observed that pupils had no overview of history, did not cover many major events and lacked a sense of the order in which what they studied occurred. As a result, students lacked both a sense of coherence and an ability to make connections between the periods they studied. Ofsted claimed that students 'often have little sense of chronology and the possibility of establishing an overarching story and addressing broader themes and issues is limited'. Ofsted therefore called for teaching in chronological order within a 'chronological framework' with 'connections between events and changes in the different periods'. The teaching of Key Stage 2 was seen as particularly disappointing. Kate Petty, Principal of Homerton College, Cambridge, claimed, as a result, that Britain was losing a shared identity:

It's the primary view of the great stories in the past, like Alfred burning the cakes, Magna Carta, Columbus sailing the ocean blue – all that sort of stuff. The little tiny stories that make up the common thread which you can pull on, we're expecting students to somehow implicitly know. It's not about A-level knowledge of a particular subject, but a general web of understanding that binds us to a past. That seems to me being lost somewhere in all of this.

Concern was also expressed about the content of the citizenship studies advocated by the government. There is a tension in Britain between positive integrative history and an acceptance of disparate traditions, and, in essence, Labour has switched position. Initially, the New Labour failure to endorse national history to any extent was linked to a greater accessibility to, and for, the disparate views. It was as if there was a vacuum, with history as a national cause being something that was anachronistic and associated with the Conservatives.

More recently, on the part of Labour, has come the approach of history-building by national government. In seeking to establish praiseworthy and integrating values by looking to the past, in short a benign national identity, government, however, in the eyes of critics offers a partial account of national identity. By its nature, the recent governmental approach is one that clashes with the disparate-views one. The latter approach frequently, and often misleadingly or indeed obsessively, presupposes a malign, hostile or, at least, indifferent national culture against which these views are expressed. Thus, in 2004, the Home Secretary David Blunkett, at the first 'citizenship ceremony' for immigrants, provided a positive account when he declared 'Britain has a great tradition as a tolerant and welcoming nation'. While correct in comparative terms (compare Britain with Germany or Japan), this was not a view that found favour with critics advancing the disparate-views approach. For example, the head of the NUT (National Union of Teachers) rejected it at the annual conference held in Belfast in April 2007.

From the perspective of politicians, nevertheless, there is a need to address the issue of nationalism, not only in order to encourage the integration of immigrants but also because of the desire to sustain patriotism and to do so successfully in response to a changing society. Indeed, the issue of patriotism is a key one when considering public history as an approach to an idea of national identity is seen as crucial in eliciting patriotism. It is not true to say 'why else would people fight', as pay, employment and excitement in practice tend to be the key motives in explaining recruitment to the armed forces. Patriotism is possibly more important for the society supporting the military. Given the extent to which terrorism is directed against civil society, this is not an unimportant factor. In June 2007, at a London conference on Islam, David Cameron, the leader of the Conservative Party, argued the case for inspiring a sense of common citizenship in order to overcome increasing Muslim 'cultural separatism' and pressed for history to be taught in a way that celebrated Britain's positive achievements at home and abroad. The tension between a national-identity approach and one focusing on more critical disparate views will continue – whoever is running the government. This underlines the problems of treating history as a national project in a democratised and disparate modern society. Indeed, these problems are a challenge for Conservatives, both because, in response to a situation of cultural flux, they have committed themselves to a historicised concept of national values and because the idea of a trust between the generations is particularly important to British Conservatives at present. It is seen, for example, in the current engagement with environmental issues.

Looked at differently, the concept of the trust between the generations has been altered under Cameron's leadership. Whereas, despite Edmund Burke's remark, in his *Reflections on the Revolution in France* (1790), that 'People will not look forward to posterity, who never look backward to their ancestors', the Burkean strand of the relationship between the generations in practice focuses on that of past and present, the emphasis in the Cameron approach is that of present and future. The same may also be said of the different, and possibly cynical, appropriation by Gordon Brown of ideas of continuity; cynical in part because of his prominent role in the Blair government, the policies of which had scarcely supported continuity.

The contrast between past-present and present-future approaches to the relationship between the generations can be considered in both philosophical and pragmatic lights. As far as the philosophical perspective is concerned, the nature of identity can be seen to rest on aspiration (present-future) rather than legacy, or rather aspiration can be seen to stem from present hopes and not the continuing impact of past (past-present) goals. Such a grounding on aspiration reconceptualises history, in a Blairite fashion, away from constraints and, instead, towards a stage on which hopes are played out. The comparison with Blair would not be welcome to Cameron, but there is a fundamental contrast between the two. Blair put himself at the centre of a historical vision – New Labour, New Britain, etc. – one that rested not only on extraordinary self-will, selfishness and cynicism but also on an ahistorical failure to engage with society and the world as they are. Cameron, in contrast, looks to the future with a more grounded understanding of the present and a perception of the political process in part shaped by a reading of the past. Yet, if Cameron has a better sense of what Britain has become than much of his party, he also faces unreasonable criticism from within the Conservative Party of cynically changing his tune to what the voters want to hear.

Pragmatic issues are also at stake. As Cameron has underlined, British society has changed considerably in recent decades, and this is part of a continuing process. In part, this is due to politics, not least Labour's cynicism and incompetence in addressing the issues of the country's ability to cope with mass immigration, but there are also other reasons for profound change, including economic transformation, environmental challenges, altered relations between the generations, gender questions and demographic shifts. These are not specific to Britain, even if, in detail, the consequences may be distinctive. In attempting to devise policies appropriate for a rapidly changing society and, even more, in establishing a conceptual framework within which such policies can be advanced and discussed, Cameron is arguing that the future must be addressed in terms that do not simply treat it as a continuation of the present. This is an approach that is a challenge to the assumptions of part of the Conservative Party, but there is a need to take Conservative truths of freedom and opportunity, community and independence, and to implement them in a future that will be different.

CHAPTER 7

THE HISTORICAL DIMENSION OF MANIFEST DESTINY

THE USA

Although presenting themselves as breaking free from the trammels of history as they created a new society, in a new country, Americans were, and are, far more affected by the past than they frequently admit. Furthermore, their presentation of their role in the present as historic, a theme exemplified in the title of Hillary Clinton's autobiography *Living History* (2003), underlines a sense of destiny that inevitably also directs attention to the roots and background of this destiny. The presentation of history was also an aspect of American state-building and nation-forming and one that seemed particularly necessary in order to counter separate historical accounts, both by immigrants and within America's distinct regions. More recently, rather than meeting what Jill Lepore has termed, 'our national need for a tidy past',[1] this presentation has played a central role in what the Americans see as culture wars.[2]

From the outset of American independence, the past, in practice, was contested as an aspect of debates and disputes over the nature and role of political authority, with particular controversy focusing on the rights of federal and state authorities. In 1776, America inherited a tension over rights and authority that had been going on, within Britain and the British Empire, from the seventeenth century. Much was involved in the question of how best to interpret the constitution. Indeed, George Washington had offered dire predictions about the durability of the 1787 constitution. When, for example, in the Nullification Crisis of 1832–3, South Carolina claimed that the national tariff was unconstitutional as well as unfair and that individual states could protect themselves from such acts by interposing their authority and thus nullifying the federal law, the terms of the constitution were up for debate.

This was not the sole source of controversy. American events provided a rich crop for further debate, most conspicuously so with the Civil War (1861–5) and its aftermath in terms of Southern reconstruction. This provided at the same time a myth of Southern honour, the 'lost cause', and also the basis for a new attempt at national unification. Concerned to maintain and reinvigorate a failed nationalist myth, Northern politicians and public opinion came to support reconciliation with the South. There were few severe punishments for those involved in the Civil War. Indeed, the senior Confederate commander, Robert E. Lee, received good obituaries in the Northern press after his death in 1870, and in 1898 the surviving Confederate generals were made US generals. In 1913, at the fiftieth anniversary of the battle of Gettysburg, the totemic battle in the Civil War, President Woodrow Wilson declared at the site of the battle, and in the presence of veterans from both sides, that the Union and the Confederacy had 'found one another again as brothers and comrades in arms'.

This reconciliation, however, was at the expense of the African Americans of the South. Their rights were infringed by a resurgent Southern 'Jim Crow' racism that overthrew the reconstruction governments and that had a counterpoint in the white Southern construction of the South's past.[3] Indeed, it was only in 1998 that the 'Spirit of Freedom', the African-American Civil War memorial, was unveiled in Washington. Furthermore, the Southern emphasis on conceptualising, and later memorialising, the Civil War in terms of states' rights, rather than as a defence of slavery, helped ensure that many white Southerners did not confront the issue of Civil Rights in terms of the truth and reconciliation processes encouraged elsewhere in the world. Nor was the role of Christian belief in sustaining both Southern and Northern intransigence adequately addressed. As an instance of the difficulty of choosing the correct term, not least with regard to the current resonance of the words and the need to engage the reader, belief could be replaced by fundamentalism.

Both at the time of the conflict and over the following decades, the Civil War also brought forward the issue of national greatness. While primarily a prospectus for the future designed to cast light on the present, national greatness was also highlighted by the search for an appropriate past. This was seen at the battle site of Gettysburg, when, on the day of Abraham Lincoln's famous speech, 19 November 1863, Edward Everett, Professor of Greek Literature at Harvard, compared the site with that of Marathon. As such, he provided an echo not only of the glorious and successful defence of liberty by the Ancient Greeks against Persian invaders in 490 BCE but also an account that gave Greek civilisation as the progenitor of modern America. This was a comparison that the listeners could be expected to understand, even if they might ignore the role of Classical Greece as a slave-owning society.

Northern opinion, while rejecting the political and economic impact of slavery, did not accept racial egalitarian ideas. American identity and history continued to be focused on whites. A ready sense of identity was challenged, however, by successive waves of immigrants, each of which appeared to offer a different identity. Nineteenth-century concern about the Irish (and about unassimilated Germans in Texas) was followed by anxiety about Poles and Italians, while, on the West Coast, Chinese immigration became a major issue. The response was xenophobia, restrictions on immigration and a conscious fashioning of historical accounts. In the 1910s and 1920s, the challenge to the Roman Empire from barbarian invaders was used as a motif for American developments, although, in fact, there was no comparison between the two.

In the 1920s, aside from a resurgence of the Ku Klux Klan on issues of nativism, there was also a major cultural emphasis on the British basis of American culture. This was, in part, a political project but was also seen in the material culture of the period, not least as celebrated in John D. Rockefeller's sponsorship of Colonial Williamsburg. Aside from offering a reaffirmation of British origins, this emphasis was also designed to teach new immigrant groups the allegedly true nature of America. Thus, history served to provide an incorporating model, although, at the same time, it was one that left the new immigrants second-class and bore no relation to what would subsequently be termed the melting-pot theory of American society.

This presentation of a nation-state in which new whites were accepted provided they conformed to the standards of the old whites was seen as necessary, not only in response to immigration but also as a result of the apparent challenge from far-left politics inspired by the Communist revolution in Russia. By treating left-wing solutions as un-American, however, not only foreign models but also the once powerful American Progressive tradition were marginalised. Although much of early Progressivism had been spawned by nativist, anti-socialist and anti-populist concerns, in the 1920s Republican rhetoric worked successfully to smear Progressives with the taint of 'Socialism', with overtones of immigrant and Communist influences. There was a strong trend to deny class as a force in American history and to explain the opportunity society as somehow nullifying this. There was a counter in the academic specialism of labour history, but it lacked public weight.

This conceptualisation of the USA remained potent until the 1960s when it was challenged both by economic, social, cultural and political pressures and by calls for a more diverse USA. This challenge and the reaction provided the basis for the subsequent 'culture wars' in the USA. Such conflicts concern how memories and events are shaped in terms of long-standing assumptions about identity and value. They are a major theme in the perception and ordering of social developments as well as in the framing of political debates.

In the 1960s, new gender and youth expectations and roles commanded attention across the world, and there was a widespread questioning of authority, fuelled by cultural changes and by medical advances in the shape of birth control and antibiotics (apparently negating a major hygienic argument for sexual continence). The weakness and social conformity of the churches was also significant. Hedonism, focused on free will, self-fulfilment and consumerism, was a powerful element in these new expectations. The net effect was a more multifaceted public construction of individual identities and a more fluid society.

The challenging of earlier norms was, in turn, opposed by a backlash that was characterised by conventional morality and patriotism, for example the reaction against the 'generation of '68' in France. Tension between the radicalism of the counter-culture and the backlash led to the culture wars of the past half-century, both in the USA and more generally. There was an additional historical dimension to this, as such culture wars had occurred before, but this comparative dimension was not probed.

History provided a key theme in these culture wars, although much of the history was not that considered in history courses. Instead, in a pointed reminder of the more widespread role of religion in ordering the past, and linking it to the present, concepts of time and development were central. Fundamental Christians had rejected the theory of evolution from the outset, and this opposition continued to be a potent force. The Scopes trial of 1925 – John Scopes was convicted of teaching evolution in Tennessee where it was forbidden – was kept alive in popular culture. It was the basis of *Inherit the Wind*, a Broadway hit of 1955 that was made into a Hollywood film (dir. Stanley Kramer, 1960), and of *The Great Tennessee Monkey Trial*, a radio play of 1992 that was updated in 2005.

The issue was treated as a litmus test by liberals who, in turn, had their own paranoia, as shown by Edward Kennedy, a member of the Senate Judiciary Committee, when, in 1987, he opposed President Ronald Reagan's nomination of Robert Bork to the Supreme Court. Kennedy offered a nightmare vision that joined past realities to fears for the future, when he anticipated, if the Supreme Court reversed its *Roe* vs. *Wade* judgement, 'a land in which women would be forced into back-alley abortions, blacks would sit at segregated lunch counters, rogue police could break down citizens' doors in midnight raids, children could not be taught about evolution'. This was political rhetoric, not calm analysis, although Bork's book *Slouching towards Gomorrah: Modern Liberalism and American Decline* (1993) was marked both by historical incoherence and by an alarming tendency to cite personal feeling rather than precedent when making judgements.

At the level of school districts, the teaching of creationism (the biblical account) was the issue in dispute. In 1987, the Supreme Court determined, in *Edwards* vs. *Aguilard*, that teaching creationism in the science classes of public schools was an unconstitutional erosion of the boundaries between church and state. This, in turn, encouraged the formulation of what was termed 'intelligent design'. This theory argued that an intelligent being shaped development, or, more subtly, that living things and other elements of nature evinced designs that could not be random, making inference to the Creator a scientific field after all. This was a form of creationism that did not mention God and which was seen as the form most likely to survive legal challenge.

The struggle went back and forth, with public debate and the democratic mandate playing a role alongside judicial decision. In 1999, the Kansas Board of Education decided that creationism should be taught alongside evolution, although the guidelines were repealed in 2001 after considerable public protest had led to changes in the Board's composition in elections in 2000. The topic, nevertheless, remained a live one. A creationist majority was put back in place in Kansas in 2004, and, in November 2005, it voted to introduce criticism of evolution into science lessons. Attention also focused on Dover, Pennsylvania, where the District School Board required that teachers explain intelligent design alongside evolution. This led to a federal court case brought by parents claiming that this decision violated the constitutional separation of church and state. In November 2005, most of the Board was voted out in a local ballot. The following month, the judge rejected the case for intelligent design, arguing that it was a religious theory.

Less distant history was also a source of major controversy, in part as an aspect of a more general debate about the value of multiculturalism in American society, a debate set within and drawing on a fiercely partisan political culture.[4] Thus, in 2007, John McCain issued a campaign advertisement criticising Hillary Clinton's support for the use of tax revenues in order to commemorate the Woodstock music festival of 1969. Multiculturalism became more significant due to a change in the demographic balance. In 1960, whites made up 159 million of the population of 179 million, but by 2000 they were only 211 million of the 281 million, a decline in relative share from 88 per cent to 76 per cent. In the early 2000s, the issue became increasingly prominent. Books such as Victor Hanson's *Mexifornia: A State of Becoming* (2003) and Samuel Huntington's *Who Are We? The Challenges to America's*

National Identity (2004) warned about a change of consciousness and a challenge to Americanness as a consequence of large-scale immigration, although they underplayed the desire of immigrants to become Americans and prosper. Critics of multiculturalism in history lessons referred to a fragmentation that denied any sense of unity, and that made it difficult to produce more than a series of histories of minorities, while supporters focused on recovered voices. This contention was linked to disagreement over the value of bilingual education.[5]

The issue of national identity was scarcely in the background. In May 2007, Barack Obama felt it appropriate, in speeches at fundraisers to support his candidacy for President, to note his visit to Selma for the annual anniversary of the 1965 march and on how, being told on his return, 'That was a great celebration of African-American history', he replied 'No, no, no, no, no. That was not a great celebration of African-American history. That was a celebration of American history'.

The debate over multiculturalism also acted as a background to the controversy over the release, in 1994, of the draft National History Standards, which were intended to act as a voluntary system of guidance to State Boards of Education and other bodies. Instead, however, of providing, as intended, readily accepted outlines and study guides for the teaching of American and world history, the draft standards led to a controversy over alleged political correctness and anti-Americanism. The standards also ignored the established pantheon of heroes, both because the authors contested the interpretations that led to these choices and because they were opposed to the emphasis on great men in history.

The controversy was also politicised, with two Republican senators introducing amendments to ban the employment of federal money for the implementation of these draft standards. They also required that such money should be spent only on those who 'have a decent respect for United States history's roots in Western civilization', which was a critique of the search for other roots, for example African-American ones, and also of cultural relativism. The draft standards were also attacked by the Secretary of Education, by Lynne Cheney, formerly Head of the National Endowment for the Humanities (NEH), and by other conservative commentators. In turn, the draft standards were supported by many liberal commentators. Eventually, after the standards were revised, under the auspices of the Council for Basic Education, not least to provide a different account of the Cold War, and then released in 1996, the controversy became far less heated. Nevertheless, its legacy was divisive, bolstering the convictions of both sets of protagonists.[6] The controversy was also a bitter struggle about federal/state/local power and control, and about teacher qualifications and autonomy. In part, the 'culture war' aspects of this controversy were causative and in part symptomatic.

This controversy was related to wider tensions in the academic world. These included dissension over standards of scholarship, with questionable practices by some historians being used by critics to argue (generally in a very sloppy fashion) that the profession as a whole was unscholarly. This was a crucial issue in the public realm, with an anti-professionalism and a populism becoming increasingly assertive. The influential gun lobby took grave exception to Michael Bellesiles's book *Arming America: The Origins of a National Gun Culture* (2000), which challenged the association of American identity with personal ownership of guns by arguing that in the colonial and early national period many Americans did not own guns, while those who did did not make much use of them. The archival research on which the thesis was based, and Bellesiles's interpretation, were both subject to considerable and powerful scholarly criticism that also served as an opportunity for more political attacks.[7] In 2002, the NEH withdrew its name from an NEH-funded fellowship at the Newberry Library that had been awarded to Bellesiles. Lynne Munson, the NEH Deputy Chair, referred to the need for 'high scholarly and ethical standards', while Bellesiles claimed that the NEH's measure 'should send chills through academics everywhere. The spirit of Joe McCarthy stalks the halls of the NEH [. . .] I regret that my name has been associated with an agency that values so little the principles of the First Amendment, due process, and academic freedom'.[8]

More generally, the charge on the American right was that the academic profession was overly liberal and that this liberalism led to a bias in teaching, marking and appointments and was an aspect of the misleading of the young and the corruption of an intellectual tradition. Conservative commentators such as David Horowitz listed cases of alleged bias. There was, indeed, a failure on the part of much of the profession to confront particular issues, such as the degree of support for Communism or Communist powers among officials in the mid-twentieth century.[9]

Recent history was a matter not only of educational policy but also of political contention and legal action. The last ensured that the bitter Civil Rights conflict of the 1950s–1960s continued to echo. In May 2007, James Fowler, a former state trooper, was indicted for shooting Jimmie Lee Jackson in Marion, Alabama, a shooting that was a key episode in encouraging pressure for civil rights. Fowler's lawyer George Beck complained, 'I think some-body is trying to rewrite history', a reference to the policies of the District Attorney, the first African American to hold the position. This was one of a number of prosecutions that sought to tackle white racist crimes from the period of demands for Civil Rights.

More distant issues are also contentious, not least the Civil War. In 2000, in response to discussion of the Interior Appropriations Bill, the National Park Service submitted to Congress a report assessing the educational information at Civil War sites and recommending that much be updated, not least to illustrate the 'breadth of human experience during the period, and establish the relevance of the war to people today'. Representative Jesse Jackson Jnr. and other members of Congress had complained that many sites lacked appropriate contextualisation and, specifically, that there was often 'missing vital information about the role that the institution of slavery played in causing the American Civil War'. Emphasising slavery, rather than states' rights, as a cause of Southern secessionism in 1861 is a way to criticise ante-bellum Southern culture and thus to present the South as 'un-American' or 'anti-American'. This underlines the extent to which controlling and defining the past became an aspect of current politics. These criticisms are contested from the 'white South' with its aggressive and self-righteous sense of historical grievance.

The long-standing resonance of issues of race not only sustained contention about slavery but also led to continued demands for contrition and apology. Jimmy Carter closed *The Hornet's Nest: A Novel of Revolutionary War* (2003), the first novel by an American president, with a factual epilogue in which he noted the unfair treatment of the Native Americans and ended, not with a triumphant affirmation of liberty but with the remark 'the ravages of slavery and its aftermath would affect the nation for another 150 years'.[10] The emancipation of the slaves also became a matter of organised memorialisation by African Americans, not least with 'Juneteenth', a holiday marking the day in 1865 when General Gordon Granger arrived in Galveston to deliver the news of the Emancipation Proclamation, which thus made Texas slaves free.

In Virginia in January 2007, the proposal for an expression of state contrition for slavery was sponsored by African-American members of the House of Delegates, at least two of whom were descended from slaves. One, A. Donald McEachin, presented this as

> part of a healing process, a process that still needs to take place even today in 2007 [. . .] No one is asking any individual to apologise, because certainly there are no slave holders alive today and there are no slaves alive today [. . .] But Virginia is alive and well, and Virginia was built on the backs of slaves, and Virginia's economy boomed because of slavery, and it is Virginia that ought to apologize.

Other delegates held different views. In January 2007, Frank Hargrove, a Republican, argued that his ancestors were French Huguenots who came to the USA in search of religious freedom. He remarked,

> The present Commonwealth [Virginia] has nothing to do with slavery [. . .] Are we going to force the Jews to apologize for killing Christ? Nobody living today had anything to do with it. It would be far more appropriate in my view to apologize to the Upper Mattaponi and the Pamunkey [Native Americans who lost their lands]. I personally think that our black citizens should get over it. By golly, we're living in 2007. Nobody can justify slavery today, but it is counter

productive to dwell on that. Political correctness has kind of gotten us into this area.

This was very much a minority view and one for which Hargrove was greatly criticised. The following month, the Virginia General Assembly voted unanimously to express 'profound regret' for the state's role in slavery – in other words, remorse but not apology. The resolution passed the House by ninety-six to zero votes and cleared the forty-member Senate on an unanimous-voice vote. The resolution claimed that government-sanctioned slavery

> ranks as the most horrendous of all depredations of human rights and violations of our founding ideals in our nation's history, and the abolition of slavery was followed by systematic discrimination, enforced segregation, and other insidious institutions and practices toward Americans of African descent that were rooted in racism, racial bias, and racial misunderstanding.

The measure also expressed regret for 'the exploitation of Native Americans'. Hargrove, who had received much criticism for his remarks in January, voted for the measure and successfully co-sponsored a resolution calling on Virginia to celebrate 'Juneteenth'.

The issue of slavery also led to a contesting of attempts to provide positive impressions from Virginia's pre-1865 history. These attempts were central to American public history as Virginia shares with Massachusetts the position as key progenitor of narratives of nationhood. This continues to be the case today. The 2007 literature for the 'Monticello Fund' refers to 'The Gift of History' and claims that donors 'help us to share Thomas Jefferson's ideas and ideals with people around the world'. Of recent years, such claims have had to address the role as slaveholders of Jefferson and other 'founding fathers'. This is a different context from the more celebratory atmosphere that surrounded the launching, with the first volume published in 1950, of the project to publish all of Jefferson's papers.

The Virginian expression of 'profound regret' for slavery, which was followed by Maryland, was the first by a state but part of a pattern of action designed to break with the segregationist past. In 1989, Virginia became the first state to elect a black governor, while in 2004 the Legislature atoned for the 'Massive Resistance' movement against desegregation by creating a scholarship fund for African Americans whose schools were shut down between 1954 and 1964.

The controversy over regret for slavery overlapped with the celebrations in 2007 of the 400th anniversary of the first permanent English settlement in the future USA, Jamestown, celebrations that were deliberately termed a commemoration. Aside from massive corporate sponsorship, Virginia spent $100 million of taxes on the commemoration, partly in the hope that it would revive tourism in the area. The establishment of Jamestown is now presented in part as leading to a despoliation of the Native Americans and also to the spread of slavery: the first slaves arrived in 1619. Thus, A. Donald McEachin, a sponsor of the Virginia motion for profound regret, declared of the visit of Queen Elizabeth II of Britain, 'Leaders and heads of state have a responsibility to set the tone and it would be a welcome move for the Queen to express regret'.

Native American representatives, who, in 2006, had sent a delegation to Britain, underlining their separate history, also demanded an apology, while the Jamestown exhibition presented the Native Americans as 'in harmony with the life that surrounds them', in contrast to a divided and elite-run Britain. Members of local tribes had served on planning committees to help shape the way their history is shared with the public. Steve Adkins, the Chief of the Chickohominy tribe, who serves on the official Jamestown commission, told the *Washington Post*, 'We want to be the ones to tell it'. He and his colleagues were keen to present the Powhatan as part of a complex civilisation with agriculture, trade and political systems long before the English arrived.

There was, however, no apology, although the Queen matched the organisers' concept of Jamestown as a 'symbol of convergence of civilisations'. The Queen met representatives of both the African American and Native American communities to recognise, as her spokesman put it, 'that they formed part of the early history of America'; while, at the lunch in her honour, she referred to Jamestown in terms that matched the theme of the anniversary. On the Queen's previous visit, for the 350th anniversary in 1957, there had been no such pressure, but, as Sandra Day O'Connor, a former Justice of the Supreme Court, who was prominent among the greeters, noted in 2007, the USA had only just then begun its 'long struggle for racial equality'. Indeed, having claimed that 'the establishment of the rule of law derived from Great Britain is the great and lasting achievement we celebrate today', she pointed out that in 1957 'the Governor of Arkansas attempted to prevent African-American students from attending Little Rock Central High School'. O'Connor argued that the stain of slavery received its start in America in Jamestown, an instance of the extent to which the values and issues of the Civil Rights era serve to make it difficult to praise pre-1960s American society.

The contrast between 1957 or 1907 and the 2007 commemoration can be compared with that between the 1892 celebrations of the 400th anniversary of Christopher Columbus in the New World with the controversy surrounding the 500th anniversary in 1992: there was savage criticism of the consequences for Native Americans of his voyages.[11] A visit to Jamestown in 2007 also allowed President George W. Bush to present his views on national history in a public forum. Declaring that Jamestown's legacies included representative government, private property rights, free enterprise and the rule of law, he added 'These values took root at Jamestown four centuries ago. They have flourished across our land, and one day they will flourish in every land'. As it was Mother's Day, Bush reminded his audience to call their mothers if they had not already done so.

Bush adapted his theme for the wider world when, on 17 October 2007, he made a speech at a ceremony in which the Dalai Lama was awarded the Congressional Gold Medal, declaring, 'Through our history we have stood proudly by those who offer a message of hope and freedom to the downtrodden and repressed.'

At Jamestown, the Queen was given a ceramic disc made by a Yorktown artist, Michelle Erickson, featuring the images of a Native American man and woman and an intertwined thistle and rose, representing Britain. The Queen's speech to a Special Joint Session of the General Assembly at Richmond on 4 May is of particular relevance for this book, not least the following:

> While it remains difficult to say what it was about those early years which caught that vital moment in the evolution of this great country, it must surely have had something to do with the ingenuity, the drive and the idealism of that group of adventurers who first set foot on this fertile Virginia soil, and the will of the Powhatan people to find ways to coexist.
>
> When I visited fifty years ago, we celebrated the 350th anniversary largely from the perspective of those settlers, in terms of the exploration of new worlds, the spread of values and of the English language, and the sacrifice of those early pioneers.
>
> These remain great attributes, and we still appreciate their impact today. But fifty years on, we are now in a position to reflect more candidly on the Jamestown legacy.
>
> Human progress rarely comes without cost. And those early years in Jamestown, when three great civilisations came together for the first time, Western European, Native American and African, released a train of events which continues to have a profound social impact, not only in the United States, but also in the United Kingdom and Europe [. . .] It is right that we continue to reassess the meaning of historical events in the changing context of the present, not least in this, the 200th anniversary, in the United Kingdom, of the Act of Parliament to abolish the transatlantic slave trade.

In Richmond, the Queen also met Oliver Hill, a centenarian Civil Rights leader, who had been active in school integration in the 1950s. As a sign of what can be seen as the move beyond past practice, as equality, or as political correctness, one of the two footmen in colonial dress on the open-topped carriage in which the Queen and Prince Philip rode through Williamsburg in 2007 was a woman.

Some of the television history programmes produced for the anniversary presented a benign account of Jamestown, not least as the origin of representative government, and neglected the role of slavery. On the other hand, arguments that whites engaged in genocide at the expense of Native Americans and in a cultural genocide of African Americans risk being ahistorical. Thus, in her polemical *George Washington's War on Native America* (2005), Barbara Alice Mann calls for an indictment of the first president for genocide.[12] This misunderstands his position, policies and actions, and the nature of genocide.

Such controversies were played out in terms of existing cultural and political tensions, with a downplaying of the autonomy of disciplinary issues and the past. This was part of a more general process in which both liberalism and conservatism are in part shaped as monoliths by outsiders who offer a false coherence (matching that of polemicists within each tendency), which fails to address the gradations and divisions of these tendencies. In other words, there is a more general false consciousness of agglomeration, seen, for example, in the treatment of the 1960s, both by those who see it as inspiration and by those who are appalled by it. The same is also true of other periods of time and of individual presidencies, for example 'the Reagan years'.

'Hollywood' was another instance of agglomeration, as critics implied that its presentation of past and future was mired in politically correct, left-wing and anti-American prejudices. This general charge sometimes freed those making it from the problem of having to substantiate their claims in a systematic fashion. Some major films, such as the sympathetic account of Lee and Jackson, the key Confederate military heroes, in *Gods and Generals* (dir. Ronald F. Maxwell, 2003), were far from left-wing in tone or content.

It was certainly the case that filmic accounts of the past were frequently wrong, not only in particulars but also with reference to the more general slant of the work. Thus, *The Patriot* (dir. Roland Emmerich, 2000) presented British imperial control of the future USA as inherently vicious, while *Munich* (dir. Steven Spielberg, 2005) failed to underline the terrorist nature of the Palestinian targets of Israeli retaliation for Palestinian terrorism at the Munich

Olympics. The film also provided an opportunity for presenting the Palestinian cause and implied, with 'There is no peace at the end of this' against the backdrop of the World Trade Center, that the terrorist attacks on New York in 2001 were the latest stage in a war of reprisal in which Israel was partly culpable, which is a highly problematic account and one that ignores the contrasts between al-Qaeda and Palestinian terrorism.

The self-conscious presentation of American history came to play a greater role as a political issue from the 1990s. For example, the meeting, on 30 June 2005, of the Subcommittee on Education and Early Childhood Development of the Senate Committee on Health, Education, Labor and Pensions heard an undertaking that when the 'No Child Left Behind' legislation came up for reauthorisation, history would be added as a core element in the initiative's teaching programme, while the Executive Director of the National Assessment Governing Board announced that, from 2006, the Board would ensure that its US history test would be conducted every four years. This would be the basis for intended legislation to authorise a pilot study that would provide state-by-state comparison of US history and civics' test data, the approach taken in the proposed American History Achievement Act.

This emphasis on the need for history can detract attention from the problems posed by the subject itself, not least the extent to which history involves questions as well as answers. An understanding of the process of history indeed is only offered by narratives that are alive to contrasting interpretations and to the problems of using evidence. This, however, is of scant interest to those who seek to use history to support the manifest destiny of their particular political interpretations.

An interesting vignette on the extent to which history played a role in discussion of policy at the very top of American politics came from an article in the *Sunday Times* of 4 March 2007 by Irwin Stelzer. This described a lunch held at the White House to discuss Andrew Roberts' *A History of the English-Speaking People since 1900* (2006) because, according to President George W. Bush, 'history informs the present' and his goal was to see what history could teach him. Those present included Roberts and the historian Gertrude Himmelfarb. Stelzer reported that

Roberts offered a number of lessons of history. First: do not set a deadline for withdrawal from Iraq. That led to the slaughter of 700,000 people in India [in 1947], with the killing beginning one minute after the midnight deadline. Bush wondered if there were examples of occupying forces remaining for long periods other than in Korea. Roberts suggested Malaysia where it took nine years [for the British] to defeat the Communists after which the occupying troops remained for several years. And Algeria, added Bush, citing Alistair Horne's *A Savage War of Peace: Algeria 1954–1962*, for the proposition that more Algerians were killed after the French withdrawal than during the French occupation. Second lesson: will trumps wealth. The Romans, the tsars and other rich world powers fell to poorer ones because they lacked the will to fight and survive. Whereas the Second World War was almost over before Americans saw the first picture of a dead soldier, today the steady drumbeat of media pessimism and television coverage are sapping the West's will. Third lesson: don't hesitate to intern your enemies for long periods. That policy worked in Ireland and during the Second World War. Release should only follow victory. Lesson four: cling to the alliance of the English-speaking peoples. Although many nations are engaged in the coalition in Iraq and Afghanistan, troops from Britain, Canada, Australia and New Zealand are doing the heavy lifting. The closing note was more sombre. Roberts told Bush that history would judge him on whether he had prevented the nuclearisation of the Middle East. If Iran gets the bomb, Saudi Arabia, Egypt and other countries would follow. The only response was a serious frown and a nod.

The Vice-President, Dick Cheney, who was also at the lunch, was observed carrying Roberts' book when he visited Kabul in early 2007. Bush's concern with history and legacy was also shown by his plans for his presidential library which outline the establishment of an institute that will present his views.

The habit of reference to the past is at once encouraging and discouraging, encouraging as it indicates the extent to which the present is understood as part of a continuum, and discouraging as all too often history is treated in a unlinear fashion: lessons are drawn without sufficient care to consider alternative expositions and, also, indeed the very unpredictability and specificity of context that ensures multiple discontinuities in the past and between past and present. Thus, in seeing Iraq as a latter-day Nazi Germany, Bush employed the term 'Axis of Evil' in his State of the Union speech in 2002. Saddam was presented as a latter-day Hitler, and, in 2003, misleading comparisons were drawn over Iraq with the Marshall Plan, the Werewolves (the Nazi resistance), and the Nuremberg trial of Nazi leaders. This was an aspect of a more widespread process of reading between past and present to suit the needs and emotions of the latter, needs and emotions that in part had been shaped by an understanding of the past. Thus, for example, when human rights became a concrete issue they were shaped in parts of different 'narratives [. . .] As Americans saw during the Balkan wars of the 1990s, for some of us the Bosnians were "Czechs" (1938); for others, "Jews" (1941); for still others, "Nazi collaborators" (1941–45)'.[13]

An important frame of historical reference in the USA arose from the argument that the USA was an empire and that therefore it was pertinent to look at past empires for historical comparisons, most frequently Classical Athens and Rome,[14] and Britain over the past quarter-millennium. In part, this was a critical reaction against the optimistic account of American power that had followed the end of the Cold War and a criticism that implied that America had abandoned its historical identity and role; but there was also, in the use of imperial references, a search for a more laudatory discussion of America's role in the world. Whereas anti-imperialism was a strong element in American attitudes to Britain at least to the 1950s, it became customary to refer to the USA as an empire[15] and to imply or argue explicitly that this imperial power was positive, and had a distinguished and encouraging pedigree in terms of former benign empires. This very pedigree also served to present the USA in a teleological light, as the progression, if not culmination, of an historical process, indeed of history itself. This was the stuff of periodical articles, speeches at conferences (including a very pleasant one I attended at Chicago in 2005, the dinners were superb), and a few books. For some, this provided the psychological fulfilment of appearing to be men of the moment.

Most prominent were two books by Niall Ferguson, *Empire* (2003) and *Colossus: The Rise and Fall of the American Empire* (2004), which, aside from providing a positive account of the British Empire (the subject of *Empire*), pressed for the USA to recognise its imperial position and responsibility. Very much an outsider's book, *Colossus* was written by a British historian who had little grasp of the exigencies and complexities of American domestic politics nor of the difficulties of the global intervention-ism it pressed for, a point that could more generally be made of the entire 'neo-con' impulse. Ferguson's theme played well in the USA among those pressing for such intervention and appeared to provide scholarly support for their assumptions and, indeed, prej-udices. A somewhat different British account of the two empires was provided by Rowan Williams, Archbishop of Canterbury.

> It is one thing to take over a territory and then pour en-ergy and resources into administering it and normalising it. Rightly or wrongly, that's what the British Empire did – in India, for example. It is rather another thing to go in on the assumption that a quick burst of violent action will some-how clear the decks and that you can move on and other people will put it back together – Iraq, for example.[16]

Ferguson's arguments did not command much academic support during the build-up to war with Iraq in 2003 nor in the immediate aftermath, and, as both that commitment and the international situation subsequently deteriorated, there were a series of studies that sought to offer a more sceptical account of what empire could achieve and, indeed, of the role and value of empires. In part, this was political and politicised. Critics on the left restated long-expressed attacks on the use, indeed fact, of American power. These attacks went back to disquiet about 1890s expansionism and its aftermath, not least the counter-insurgency conflict in the Philippines, although, for many critics, the point of reference was 1968 and opposition to the Vietnam War.

Such a political locating of the debate is easy and convenient, not least for pro-interventionists who wished to damn their critics as left-wing and anti-American, the two misleadingly presented as synonymous. It was, of course, the case that some, possibly much, of the criticism was indeed partisan. Nevertheless, this was a misleading simplification, not least because it neglected both criticisms of American policy from the right, an aspect of the neo-conservative misuse of conservatism and mistreatment of (other) conservatives, and also downplayed the extent to which there was a degree of professional autonomy in much academic writing.

Judging from many books produced in the aftermath of the Iraq War, such autonomy, however, was certainly under pressure, not least from the determination of many historians to show that they were engaged, or that their work was relevant because of its reference to current issues, or that these issues provided a resonance that also offered insights on the past. Thus, the Abu Ghraib prison-abuse scandal, an episode that, at least in part, indicated that misconduct would be exposed and punished, was interpreted somewhat differently by the scholar Ann Stoler. In her introduction to *Haunted by Empire: Geographies of Intimacy in North American History* (2006), a work that considers personal relations under imperialism as an extension of the public aspects of power, she wrote, 'The violence of colonial intimacies marks these contributions giving deep historic resonance to the Abu Ghraib prison-abuse scandals'. This led to the argument that 'the power to manipulate social classifications, and the often violent and abusive regulation of intimate realms, emerge as a defining, not an errant, component of imperial power'.[17]

The evidence for such a proposition is limited, but that did not stop it being made as it appeared germane to the moment. Now that imperialism has been allocated and annexed to the American experience, so discussions of it will in part be seen as explicitly political whatever their intention. This is a key instance of the present apparently illuminating the past. The debate about American imperialism failed to give due weight to the scholarly insight that empires in practice operate not simply through coercion but also through eliciting cooperation. A failure to appreciate that ensured that the use of empire, a comparative term, to describe the USA was not as helpful as it could have been.

This was also a problem with the definition of modern history in terms of civilisations, most famously in *The Clash of Civilizations and the Remaking of World Order* (1996) by the American political scientist Samuel Huntington. As a defining organisational principle, such claims of cultural clashes, while readily grasped, rest on a structuralist perspective, and present identity and power in terms of clear-cut blocks. This is a dated view that corresponds to the classic age of geopolitics and, by emphasising structural conditions and inherent drives, crucially underplays the role of agency. Furthermore, there is the danger of confusing the rhetoric of obvious rivalry for the complexities of overlapping cooperation and confrontation. Huntington, however, met the popular need to address current concerns, offer a relatively clear panorama and apparently anticipate future trends.

More specifically, the nature of America's past provides plenty by way of emotive issues and, therefore, references. Race is a key issue because it is one that can be extrapolated to encompass many other disputes across the world, irrespective of the appropriateness of such extrapolation. Thus, when the position of Arabs in Palestine in the mid-2000s is compared to the earlier segregation of African Americans by Condoleezza Rice, this is powerful in American terms but lacks credibility as an academic point. So also indeed did the practice in the 1960s of drawing parallels between African Americans and the Jews oppressed by the Nazis, not least through the use of the term 'ghetto'.

Another key issue and discourse is the resonance of past conflicts. Supposed lessons from the Vietnam War were used from 2003 by supporters of maintaining a large American military presence in Iraq. In August 2007, President George W. Bush told the national conference of the Veterans of Foreign Wars that a failure of will in Iraq would have disastrous consequences comparable to those of failure in Vietnam.

Then, as now, people argued that the real problem was America's presence and that if we would just withdraw, the killing would end.

The world would learn just how costly these misimpressions would be. In Cambodia the Khmer Rouge began a murderous rule in which hundreds of thousands of Cambodians died of starvation, torture or execution. In Vietnam, former American allies, government workers, intellectuals and businessmen were sent off to prison camps, where tens of thousands perished.

One unmistakable legacy of Vietnam is that the price of America's withdrawal was paid by millions of innocent citizens whose agonies would add to our vocabulary new terms like 'boat people', 're-education camps', and 'killing fields'.

Bush also claimed that the Vietnam withdrawal had emboldened al-Qaeda to believe that the USA would not persist in the war against terrorism, while he presented the 'advance in freedom' in post-war Japan and Korea as evidence that American commitment could succeed: 'The ideals and interests that led America to help the Japanese turn defeat into democracy are the same that lead us to remain engaged in Afghanistan and Iraq.'

Critics of the Iraq commitment made more frequent references to the Vietnam War. Thus, in campaign speeches, John Kerry, the unsuccessful Democratic presidential challenger in 2004, compared the occupation of Iraq to Vietnam. For the British, the equivalent was the Suez Crisis of 1956. In each case, the historical failure, however, undermined the argument for making a greater effort in order to prevent failure, because it ensured that the public resonance was a negative one. Conversely, the theme of persisting in Iraq drew on the memorialisation of the Second World War, with the sixtieth anniversary of D-Day and the inauguration of the memorial for that war on the National Mall serving in 2004 to affirm the value of struggle. Earlier, President George H.W. Bush had referred to the 1991 Gulf War as one to 'put Vietnam behind us', by which he meant that, in the American public response, there was no repetition of incapacitating division.

AUSTRALIA

Australia provides a parallel instance of manifest destiny, although there are contrasts, not least in the far lesser role of religion in

Australian public discussion compared to the USA. Furthermore, in Australia, there is no equivalent to the African Americans, that is, involuntary immigrants who became a disadvantaged group suffering discrimination. The very different relationship of the two states to Britain is also important. Ironically, this has not had the consequences that might have been expected. Instead, because the USA attained independence in 1783 and did not fight Britain after 1815, the role of the rejection of imperial control in the American historical account is relatively modest and has been overshadowed by many later issues.

In contrast, the slackening of imperial links has played a much greater role in Australian public history, in part because this occurred over the past century, while the public history is less focused on domestic issues than in the American case. Both world wars play a major role in Australia, especially the unsuccessful and traumatically costly Gallipoli expedition of 1915, the subject of Peter Weir's iconic film *Gallipoli* (1981), and the 'Great Betrayal' of the Second World War, when British priorities for imperial defence clashed with Australian interests. This alleged failure to provide sufficient support for resisting Japan then encouraged a further emphasis on Gallipoli as an example of British perfidy in an earlier generation.

Race plays a more prominent role in current contention over Australian history. A conservative position was strongly advanced by John Howard, the Prime Minister until November 2007, who was concerned that a positive interpretation should be advanced. He argued that this should replace what he presented as a liberal multiculturalism that, under the goal of offering an account that accepted Aboriginal perspectives, was negative about Australian achievements. In contrast to what he presented as the 'Black Armband view' of the liberals, Geoffrey Blainey, a prominent iconoclastic and conservative historian, who is favoured by Howard, discerned, in 1993, what he termed the 'Three Cheers view of history'. Blainey had been criticised for suggesting in 1984 that the rate of Asian immigration was threatening assimilation and, in face of the resulting furore, resigned from his post at the University of Melbourne.

In his Australia Day Speech in 2006, Howard called for a 'root and branch renewal' in the teaching of Australian history at school level, claimed that it was in danger of being 'a fragmented stew of themes and issues' and pressed for the return of a narrative structure. This was followed by the federal government pressing for a compulsory three-year coverage of national history for pupils aged from fourteen to sixteen. Julie Bishop, the Education Minister, was in no doubt about the message, that Australia has a distinctive recent history that is 'overwhelmingly positive [. . .] a beacon of hope that has integrated people from all corners of the world'. In this debate, academic, political and public cross-currents play a major role. However, Howard's attempt to establish a new curriculum that would offer history as a narrative-structured subject, separate to social studies, failed.

On a separate theme, the Howard government spent much money in the early 2000s on redeveloping the Australian War Memorial. To critics, however, this was of a piece with the commitment of that government to a military posture, including the contentious dispatch of forces to Iraq in 2003.

Land rights are a particularly charged issue in Australia, not least as they bring into contention Aboriginal and non-Aboriginal views as well as questions about past meanings, specifically in the case of the interpretation of legal judgements. Thus, there have been arguments that Aboriginal myths should be accepted as historical truth on the argument that they are 'true histories' in the sense of 'the authoritative bearers of the truth about history'.[18] The government wishes to integrate Aboriginal history into the national account, but it is hard to do so without raising difficult questions. Pressure from Aborigines for their voice to be heard is readily apparent. In 2004, I noted the juxtaposition, on King George Terrace in front of Old Parliament House in Canberra, between official remembrance, such as the statue of King George V, and the Aborigine 'Embassy', a prominent show of Aborigine anger and rejection of the Australian state. On 11 October 2007, Howard sought to offer a solution. In a speech to the Sydney Institute, he declared his opposition to making a national apology on the ground that it would 'only reinforce a culture of victimhood and take us backwards', but also suggested a referen-

dum to change the constitution to include 'a statement of reconciliation', acknowledging prior Aboriginal settlement.

The impact of changing views can be seen by comparing
the centenary of the beginning of British settlement in Tasmania
with the bicentenary. On 22 February 1904, in front of several
thousand spectators, the Governor unveiled a monument to the
founder of the colony and praised the settlers. No Aboriginal people are known to have been present, and no mention was made of
the subsequent massacre of Aborigines on 3 May 1804.

In 2004, in contrast, no formal ceremony was held to mark
the landing at Risdon Cove, the site of both the landing and the
massacre. Indeed, on 3 May, the massacre was commemorated
from the Aboriginal perspective. The monument erected in 1904
was covered with a white sheet splattered with blood, as a mark
of respect to the victims of the massacre, and the Secretary of the
Tasmanian Aboriginal Centre declared, 'They killed us off in this
place 200 years ago, stole our land, took away our people and
imposed their religion on us. But our presence here today shows
they have not destroyed us'. Moreover, from the academic perspective, settler narratives no longer dominate the account.

After Aboriginal pressure, including the disruption of a re-
enactment of the 1804 landing held in 1988 to celebrate the bicentenary of the establishment of the first British colony in Australia
(in New South Wales), Risdon Cove was declared an Aboriginal
Historic Site and transferred to the Tasmanian Aboriginal Land
Council. This, however, was challenged in the early 2000s by
Reg Watson, a leading member of the Anglo-Keltic Society, who
claimed that the government was bowing unnecessarily to Aboriginal pressure. Similar charges were made by Pauline Hanson,
the leading right-wing populist Australian politician.[19]

Public policy played a major role in the controversy over the
National Museum of Australia, which opened in 2001, the centenary of federation. The Howard government, which had commissioned the museum, regarded its contents as overly devoted
to the Aborigines, not least in the First Australians Gallery, the
largest of the museum's permanent exhibitions. There was also
criticism from journalists and from the former academic Keith
Windschuttle, mostly on the grounds of inaccuracy and political

bias, for instance for giving Labor's Gough Whitlam credit for the 1967 referendum that changed the constitutional position of Aborigines, when he was only Opposition Leader at the time and the referendum was actually an initiative of the Liberal Party government. Windschuttle also castigated the museum for making the centrepiece of its exhibit on Frontier Conflict the so-called 'Bells Falls Gorge massacre', which years before was revealed by an academic historian to have been a legendary event for which there was no contemporary evidence of any kind. Windschuttle also criticised the museum for its attempt to present national history solely through a politically correct version of social history and for omitting political and economic history.[20]

In 2004, the Director, Dawn Casey, an Aborigine, was replaced. She had been undermined by Howard allies appointed to the museum's council. That the museum incorporated the zig-zag employed in Daniel Libeskind's Jewish Museum in Berlin, providing a possible parallel between the fate of the Jews and that of the Aborigines, led eventually to additional controversy.[21]

There was also a related controversy over the treatment of the Aborigines by historians. Windschuttle, the most prominent critic of the standard treatment, was vigorous in his assault on the profession and their writings. He followed his *The Killing of History: How Literary Critics and Social Theorists Are Murdering Our Past* (1996) with *The Fabrication of Aboriginal History. Volume I: Van Diemen's Land, 1803–1847* (2002), a lengthy work, in which he claimed that Henry Reynolds, Lyndall Ryan[22] and other prominent scholars had exaggerated the number killed by the early colonists. Windschuttle argues that the charge of genocide cannot be sustained against Australian colonists, that the Aborigines did not resist the colonists with guerrilla warfare and that historians have invented incidents that never occurred and have given bogus footnotes to cover what they have done. In short, he decries academic misconduct and historical inaccuracy. Windschuttle regards the decline of the indigenous Tasmanian population as due to the impact of venereal and other diseases as well as the sale of women to Europeans. The government is presented as attempting to defend the natives, and their violent response to European settlement is seen as irrational violence. Although

Windschuttle's own political views in some ways shape what he writes, he argued strongly in *The Killing of History*, in a positivist fashion, for the importance of the empirical foundation of historical writing, while his work on the frontier includes a great deal of primary research, especially in the Tasmanian archives.

Aside from attacks by Aborigine commentators, Australian academics, in turn, were very critical and keen to argue that Windschuttle was part of a wider assault on academe and liberal values. *Whitewash: On Keith Windschuttle's Fabrication of Aboriginal History* (2003), edited by Robert Manne, argued that Windschuttle's account did not stand up to scholarly discussion. There were also claims that Windschuttle had been taken up by influential circles in the media, especially the *Australian* newspaper, as part of an assault on the academic profession, and, indeed the debate was extensively covered in the press. At the July 2004 meeting of the Australian Historical Association, Stuart Macintyre, a prominent left-wing scholar who had published *The History Wars* the previous year, claimed that the history wars in Australia were in accord with 'the political dimensions' of the Howard government's 'abandonment of reconciliation, denial of the stolen generations [of Aboriginal children], its retreat from multiculturalism and creation of a refugee crisis'.[23] The battle has been extended to the perceived bias of the Australian Broadcasting Corporation, the national broadcaster, and Windschuttle's appointment to the Board has been controversial. Meeting Windschuttle in September 2006, I was struck by his view that Australian academic historians were overly driven by their political views.

NEW ZEALAND

As far as New Zealand was concerned, the Ministry of Culture and Heritage deployed its historians to help make *Frontier of Dreams* (2005), an optimistic, teleological and celebratory television series on national history. It obviously helped in the funding that the relevant minister, Helen Clark, was also Prime Minister. The costs were high, as the production for each of the thirteen-part hour-long episodes was lavish. This was public history, and, although relatively even-handed, as well as competently presented, it was somewhat simplistic. Nevertheless, public criticism of *Frontier of Dreams* was limited, because the role of the series in nation-building was accepted. Indeed, this nation-building was regarded as a necessary stage by which New Zealand moved away from its British heritage.

Earlier, the state-supported *New Zealand Historical Atlas* (1997) was produced with the support of the New Zealand Lottery Grant Board and the Department of Internal Affairs, which administered the project through its Historical Branch and collaborated with the Department of Survey and Land Information. The emphasis in the atlas's coverage is instructive, with more of a stress on pre-contact (with Europeans) history and of an understanding of the Māori perspective in the colonial period than is usual in general histories. As the introduction, by Malcolm McKinnon, noted,

> Māori history not only asks different questions, it looks at quite different kinds of information, events, recollections. [. . .] the two plates that present a Māori explanation of origins and the five plates presenting geological and natural history. The *Atlas* is primarily a product of the contemporary culture of empirical scientific enquiry, and it is that approach which is the foundation of the geological plates. But a large part of the *Atlas* is concerned with the Māori experience of New Zealand, and it is not possible to comprehend that experience unless we gain some understanding of how Māori themselves interpreted the world around them.[24]

New Zealand governments led by Helen Clark have been in office since the end of 1999 and have been preoccupied with fostering national identity. Much effort has been put into commemorating New Zealand's war record, with a series of publications, centred around interviews with veterans, playing a central role. Moreover, the government has been represented annually at Gallipoli on Anzac Day, 25 April, the anniversary of the Allied landings on that peninsula in 1915, when large numbers of Australian and New Zealand soldiers lost their lives.

In New Zealand, the government's policy is a response to, and part of, 'history wars'. It is a way of blunting the sometimes contentious atmosphere surrounding different Māori and Pākehā (New Zealand European) perceptions of the country's past. Although these differences are less angry than the comparable ones in Australia and the USA, they regularly flare up on Waitangi Day, 6 February, the commemoration of the signing of the Treaty of Waitangi between the British Crown and a large number of Māori chiefs. Anzac Day is a much less contentious commemoration than Waitangi Day and also draws in Māori. There is a case for saying that Anzac Day has become New Zealand's National Day more than Waitangi Day. Much effort has also gone into commemorating the history of the 28th (Māori) Battalion in the Second World War. Government policy was also designed as a way of bridging the gap between the anti-war and anti-nuclear left and more conservative sentiment in the community. Clark has a genuine interest in New Zealand's role in the world wars and has changed a lot since being a 1970s peacenik.

'History wars' or 'culture wars' are less salient in New Zealand now than they were in the 1980s and 1990s. In part, this may be because the New Zealand government has avoided as vigorous, partisan and divisive a stance as the riposte against 'politically correct' history seen with the Howard government in Australia. The more measured initiatives of the New Zealand government may have contributed to the situation there, although the tone of discussion reflects a constituency that is wider than that of the government. *Frontier of Dreams* had a teleological element, but neither it nor other present-day projects, such as the government-funded online encyclopedia of New Zealand,[25] are simplistically progressive.

The *Dictionary of New Zealand Biography*, which had support from the New Zealand Lotteries Board and the Historical Branch of the Department of Internal Affairs, was a successful attempt to offer an intelligently inclusive account. The five volumes which appeared between 1990 and 2000 were very different from either the Australian, British (the *Dictionary of National Biography*, old and new) or Canadian biographical dictionaries, as each volume attempted to capture a cross-section of society across roughly twenty- or thirty-year periods, with gold miners, bushrangers, trade unionists, publicans and women rubbing shoulders with the usual crop of worthies.[26]

Nor are recent general histories of New Zealand simplistically progressive. Among them, Philippa Smith's *A Concise History of New Zealand* (2005); Michael King's *A History of New Zealand* (2004), which got deservedly good reviews from the liberal left to the centre-right; and James Belich's two-volume study *Making Peoples: A History of the New Zealanders, from Polynesian Settlement to the End of the Nineteenth Century* (1996–2001), stand pre-eminent. Of course, by taking New Zealand as the point of reference, King and Belich suggest to the reader the continued validity of framing history in terms of New Zealand, but that is an accurate response to the experience of its people. Smith, in contrast, broke away from the tradition of New Zealand exceptionalism and placed New Zealand history in its regional and global contexts, being particularly sensitive to New Zealand's close historical relationship with Australia.

The situation in New Zealand may also reflect a working-through of two big issues that seized the country in the 1980s: the anti-nuclear issue and the Māori-rights issue. Anti-nuclearism is now the political orthodoxy. There has been a definite drop in Waitingi flarings-up in recent years and in rhetoric about 'biculturalism'. Although the divisions over Māori rights resurfaced in full force during debate in 2004–5 on a Bill regulating ownership of the foreshore and seabed, there is acceptance, rough and ready, but more marked than in the past, that Māori have a distinctive place in both society and in the state. Economic good times, which have seen Māori unemployment fall to historically low levels, have contributed to an easing of tensions in Māori–Pākehā relations: there is not a direct link between Māori preoccupations with matters of mana – standing, influence, ownership and respect on the one hand, and questions of socio-economic disparity on the other – but there are indirect ones.

Debate amongst New Zealand historians has continued to be vigorous on race relations. The 'Treaty Industry' as it is sometimes negatively termed, with reference to the Treaty of Waitangi, has produced both a huge corpus of research and, more recently, a body of fine works reflecting on this research, with some of the contributions critical of what they see as a 'presentism' which brings with it an overly simplistic view of the colonial past in terms of Māori as victims.[27] This, however, is a debate conducted more soberly than the popular one and has few intersections with the latter. King focused heavily on Māori issues and sometimes appeared to forget New Zealand's majority population and dominant Pākehā culture. Smith is more balanced in this sphere.

Writing about New Zealand, McKinnon also offered a stadial (stages) account of national history that is of more general application:

> Does a New Zealand historical atlas imply a single 'New Zealand' history? At any time over the period from c. 1860 to c. 1960, almost certainly. The idea of a nation as a central reality around which historical explanation should revolve was very powerful. This outlook was originally a positive one, linked to the excitement of political change, of people becoming citizens rather than subjects, of a wish to emancipate the past from the dominance of the Crown and the church. But later on it lost vitality being as often used to shore up rulers as to emancipate people. Further, while each nation proclaimed its distinctiveness, the special quality of its history and its people, it did so in forms which were indistinguishable from those used by any other nation. There was a sameness in the difference. Nationalism made assumptions about geography as well as history.[28]

CANADA

The situation in Canada is more complex. Although the Native/ First Peoples dimension is less prominent[29] and problematic than in New Zealand, there is the major issue of French Canada. Québécois nationalists, who became more prominent from the 1960s, stressed their French roots and identity in order to make a separatist cause. Memories and histories of French Canada, however, have only limited popular and intellectual interaction with those of anglophone Canada. This both reflects and sustains tensions in Canadian national consciousness.[30] In the 1980s–1990s, a Native history or history of the First Peoples, was established that recognized the legitimacy and autonomy of the aboriginal culture and its development alongside European traders and settlers. Moreover, the role of the Natives/First Peoples became more prominent in general histories, and these histories no longer saw past and progress solely in terms of European settlement.[31]

CONCLUSIONS

A stadial account of the presentation of progress in and through national history can be found across the world. This invites the question as to whether 'history wars', in which such accounts are contested, are in part to be located in the more general 'culture wars' that have been, and are, fought out over whether the situation described in such stadial accounts should be seen as valid or must be reversed. Separate to this is the issue of whether such a stadial account is teleological and also whether it implies that some societies are advanced and thus others, at least relatively, backward. In short, on a transnational scale, does a comparison of national histories reveal some countries to be limited by and in the nature of their public history, offering as many do a xenophobic anti-modernism? Moreover, is transnational progressivism (left-wing, post-national internationalism) to be seen as a non-democratic, indeed post-Western, challenge to liberal democracy?[32] Readers are invited to consider these points. There is no point foreclosing debate by suggesting clear answers where none exist.

CHAPTER 8

CONCLUSION
THE WEIGHT OF HISTORY

Necessary or a burden; good, bad or indifferent: the weight of history can be seen very differently, and it is, of course, in part each and every one of these descriptions. Running together history and memory, Friedrich Nietzsche argued in 1874 that history was a burden that enslaved the spirit by leading to a fixation on the past that weakened resolve and induced mental paralysis.[1] At the psychological level, he argued for the value of forgetting as a positive force.[2] A century later, Hayden White took up the argument.[3]

More prosaically, the extent of historically grounded wrongs, of empowerment through grievance, of atavistic hatreds and of identities through opposition, which are all mentioned in this book, and which could be extended, encourages a feeling that history is a curse. For many years, this, indeed, was a response that the British readily voiced in reaction to the sectarian divides of Northern Ireland. The 'Could they not get over this?' view was a powerful sentiment and one that was far from new. During the crises of the Napoleonic War, for example, British commentators had expressed the same view about Protestant–Catholic divides in Ireland, although, in part, this reflected a failure to understand Ireland's issues. In 1807, Colonel Hawthorne wrote from Dublin:

> a divided or distracted people like us are not calculated to meet such an invader as [Napoleon] Bonaparte [. . .] the 12th of this month instead of lamenting over the fatal consequences of the battle of Friedland [a Napoleonic victory over Britain's ally Russia], the Orange Yeomanry of the kingdom were celebrating a battle [of the Boyne, 1690]

fought upwards of a hundred years ago, with every mark of triumph and exultation as if Ireland had no other enemy than its Catholic inhabitants.[4]

A similar response about the dangerous failure to overcome past issues has been seen in reaction to the existential challenge posed by the demands of al-Qaeda for the withdrawal of non-Muslims from formerly Muslim lands, especially al-Andalus, southern Spain. That these lands had only ever been Muslim as a result of conquest in the eighth century was ignored by al-Qaeda, which, of course, deplores the fact that Spaniards are now free to choose their religion. There is, indeed, a direct and total antagonism between the high value placed on freedom in the West and theocrats who oppose toleration. In 1998, the World Islamic Front had called for a *jihad* 'against the Jews and the Crusaders',[5] which is an aspect of the extent to which notions of a clash of civilisations are only made understandable in and by history.

In al-Qaeda demands, there is also no sense that distant time was anything other than an immediate issue. Whereas episodes such as the Palestinian movement (forced and voluntary) from Israel were within living memory, this was certainly not true of the final extinction of al-Andalus in the fifteenth century, nor of holy warriors held up for emulation such as the medieval Mamluks of Egypt or Muhammad Ahmad, Mahdi of Sudan in 1881–5. Today, the Shias anticipate the return of the Mahdi to establish a just Muslim government at the end of the world, this Mahdi being Muhammad bin Hassan, their twelfth Imam, who was born in 868 and who has rested hidden for over a millennium.

In contrast, whereas the French conquering Algeria, from 1830, in part saw themselves as latter-day Crusaders, not least in creating a Christian settler society, this was not true of the Americans or British in Iraq from 2003. There is also the question of the relevance, let alone applicability, of past episodes. If, in the face of the Arab Rising in Palestine, the British authorities blew up a section of Jenin in 1938, it is unclear that that justifies similar Israeli methods today, or whether any comparison is ahistorical or helpful, either for propaganda or for instructive reasons.

Conversely, drawing a distinction between the fifteenth century and the period covered by the memory of those still alive can be regarded as presentism and as a breach not only of the injunction 'never forget' but also of the role of an understanding of 'deep time' in inculcating group identity. This is true of religions as well as nations. If movements such as Islam, or, for that matter, Christianity and Judaism, are to be seen as long-term entities, historically grounded through revelation and theology, then it is easy to understand how an organic appreciation ensures that past events become present grievances and, thus, wrongs to be righted in the future.

This was seen in Britain in 2006–7 with the leaders of the Church of England treating that body's attitude to the slave trade prior to 1807 as a matter for present contrition. In 2006, the church agreed to apologise to the descendants of slaves for the church's involvement in the slave trade. The idea that nobody alive was responsible, and, indeed, that another age had a very different set of values, were of nought in the face of this ahistorical assertion of corporate responsibility which represented an ostentatious attempt to identify with victims rather than perpetrators.[6] Moreover, the importance of the slave trade in the creation of the modern world was emphasised, and overly so, as in the International Slavery Museum opened in Liverpool in August 2007. Slavery and the slave trade thus became a means by which to criticise globalisation and modernisation.

At a personal level, I encountered this issue in what was clearly a mismatch of perceptions when interviewed by the London radio station Radio Colour in early 2007. I was asked, in the sense of told, whether, in recompense for the slave trade, the British government should not support the learning of African languages in Britain and was informed that black men had a strong sense of grievance as a result of the slave trade. My response that it had been made illegal 200 years ago, that it was time to get over the grievance, and that the comparison with the Holocaust was a false one as the intention of the Holocaust was genocide, was not warmly applauded. This is understandable given the role of this episode in a particular rhetoric of difference, grievance and victimhood, and a rhetoric that serves to contribute to a sense of identity today.

In contrast, for example, the chronologically far more distant conquest of Britain by the Romans from 43 CE and the subsequent treatment of the population is not a theme in British discussion, although in academic circles there has recently been a discussion of it in terms of an exploitation and foreign domination that was not, as it was subsequently to be presented, an anticipation of Britain's later imperial success.[7]

Should collective grief become public policy, and, if so, whose grief? These questions need rigorous examination. There is a necessary presentism: past 'wrongs' cannot be righted by generations not responsible for them. In practice, and here especially in the context of victimhood and grievances, the search for tailor-made versions of the past that suit present preferences, and maybe needs, is also an attempt to free the past from the shackles of facts. As such, it entails freeing both past, and present, from the stranglehold of intellectual discipline, as facts of course do not speak for themselves (in any case, which facts?) but have to be analysed. Rejecting the complexities and fact-based nature of historical analysis serves political ends. Moreover, as another instance of self-indulgence, this rejection is also part of the pernicious (and really anti-rational) legacy of postmodernity. The popularity of counterfactual ('What if?') history, moreover, takes a part as it can represent 'the seduction of being able to manipulate the past'.[8]

Technology also plays a potent role. The role of the Internet in facilitating the circulation of contending and usually presentist versions of the past is considerable. Through ostensibly democratising the presentation of history, it actually undermines our understanding of the complexities of the past.

The bicentenary of the abolition of the slave trade brought up also the contrast between a historicised sense of grievance, which it was easy to express, or, in critical eyes, indulge, and the more complex reality of problems in the modern world. At the same time as Britain was being denounced for the trade, there was scant reference to the key role of African cooperation in it, and there is little research on it, which is interesting in itself. In Britain, the outlawing in Ghana in 2001 of the practice by which women, known as *trokosi*, were enslaved to traditional priests attracted scant attention. This practice also exists in several other West African countries. A lack of strong interest in the role of slavery in Africa is also true of the presentation of other aspects of the slave trade such as the museum on the island of Gorée in Senegal that tells the history of a branch of the trade dominated by France, or, indeed, commemorative events on 23 August, which has been designated UNESCO Slavery Remembrance Day.

Conversely, it could be argued that a determination to pin more blame on African involvement is also a form of grievance politics of the form 'Don't blame us, the natives were doing it too'. This raises the question of whether some or many of the cases presented as counter-arguments to the grievance lobby are actually also grievances, just of another sort. The lack of 'positive' assessments of Empire and its record can be seen in this light. Possibly, 'positive' and 'negative' are not the terms in which we can most usefully assess historical phenomena. Putting that aside, it is clearly problematic to argue that the demand for apologies for the slave trade is political, and not historical, without noting that so also is the demand that Empire should be celebrated as bringing positive benefits overall to its subject people.

This is linked to the 'grievance' that an ungrateful world/ethnic-minority peoples in Britain/independent post-colonial nations are not giving the British credit for all the wonderful things they did for their colonised peoples. Sometimes, this approach is related to the argument that the British 'stood alone' against Germany in 1940–1, which ignores the fundamental contribution of the Empire and serves also as a way to come to terms with the 'loss' (i.e., dismantling) of Empire after 1945. More generally, it is almost humorous to see how the 'British' Army, even depicted in India, has, in most war dramas, scant 'imperial' component. Underrating the problematic nature of the imperial past also underplays the extent to which it is important in understanding how Britain's majority (as well as minority) communities have come to where they are today.

Alongside modern discussion of the slave trade, African regimes are doing little to criticise the dictatorial and destructive regime of Robert Mugabe in Zimbabwe. That he is also deliberately propagating what will be a false history made this contrast doubly ironic. Mugabe's claim that the economic travails of Zimbabwe were due to British pressure was a nonsense and one that gave no weight to the mistakes of his own government's policy, but it was a claim that was apparently accepted by many other African states. The contrasts between the extensive memorialisation of the iniquities of the slave trade in Britain and the far more hesitant engagement with the devastation wrought by Mugabe were instructive. The needs in public history for a clear good and bad played a role in the preference for criticising the slave trade. Furthermore, the idea of devoting time to the complexities of issues such as the destructive impact today of First World tariffs on African producers, for example cotton farmers in Burkina Faso and Mali, was clearly not an attractive one.

A very different example of ecclesiastical memory is provided by the case of Galileo, the treatment of whom by the Catholic Church provided both a powerful cultural myth and a cause for contention that was a key 'history war' in the field of relations between reason and religion. In 1613, Galileo's astronomical ideas were attacked on scriptural grounds, and in 1633 the Inquisition sought to settle the matter by condemning him for holding that the Earth moves and that the Bible is not a scientific authority. The role of the Inquisition was subsequently significant and symbolic in debate, and the subject registered intellectual and cultural trends. Symbolism was much in evidence in 1887 when a marble column commemorating Galileo was inaugurated in Rome to the applause of the anti-clerical press, only to be sharply criticised by the official Vatican newspaper. This was connected with the standing controversy between the Italian state and the Vatican, which was resolved only with the Concordat of 1929.

More recently, the general trend towards rehabilitation encompassed Pope John Paul II who in 1979 admitted in a speech that an injustice had been committed to Galileo. This led to the Vatican Study Commission and, in 1992, to another papal speech in which the attempt by senior clerics in effect to retry Galileo was closed with the implication that a key lesson of the affair was the harmony between science and religion.[9]

The relationship between religions and reconciliation is problematic because religions rely on a deep time of inherent truths that is not to be effaced by history. Thus, a secular notion of reconciliation, of sharing memories, coming to terms with the burden of the past and commemorating together so as to establish a collective memory and shared future, is inherently outwith religious themes of distinctive truth.

This can be seen in Sri Lanka where the powerful Buddhist clergy have played, and continue to play, a key role in Sinhalese assertion, a process that has contributed to the division with (Hindu) Tamils that took a violent form from 1956. That year, Sinhalese replaced English as the official language while the celebrations of the 2,500th anniversary of Buddha's attainment of nirvana provided an occasion for a heightening of tension, with criticism of the governing United National Party for allegedly insufficient care for Buddhism. This helped lead to the party's defeat in the polls. The new prime minister was to be assassinated in 1959 by a Buddhist monk, in part in response to the modest concessions granted in the Tamil Language Act, which permitted Tamil as an official language. An attack on Tamil cultural memory was seen in 1981 when Sinhalese nationalists destroyed Jaffna's public library, a repository of key documents.[10]

Empowerment through historic myth and grievance is a source not only of division but also of a reluctance to search for the compromises necessary if life is to continue both within and between communities. It focuses on 'been', and not 'becoming', on where one comes from, and not what one can do, on an incapacity, and not an active potential. Indeed, in place of national interests being presented in terms of 'We are strongest and thus should get' comes an alternative, 'We have been mistreated and thus should receive'. Empowerment through grievance thus focuses on the vindication of victimhood rather than any *real* commitment to a way forward.

On the other hand, much of history does deal with conflict, and with identification through difference, and to ignore this is foolish. Historical processes have also framed the environment, both the natural environment (with change and degradation being readily observable in recent time) and the human environment. For example, aside from the transformation of the built environment, it is also possible that the use of chemicals, in war and economy, have changed the genome.

Moreover, there is a sense that a consideration of the past can provide lessons.[11] However, there is a widespread determination to search not for complex lessons but for those that apparently offer obvious guidance. In short, the public treatment of history frequently takes on a demagogic form and also a quasi-religious character, with episodes providing homilies about what will happen if wrong choices are made. The emphasis thus is on sin, rather than redemption, with the curse being that of fundamental error, whether in the shape of supposedly malevolent racial, religious, social or political groups or that of malign and self-indulgent human will. In contrast, notions about learning from the past in an incremental fashion assume not a millenarian perfectability of mankind or ending of history but, rather, a notion of improvability. That, however, still poses a danger, that, in pursuit of an exemplary lesson, the past may be jettisoned if it does not contribute to, or correspond with, the lesson.

The most accurate history, one that notes the ambiguities of the past, the diversities of motives and the complexities of causation, is not one that corresponds with political and religious strategies, with utopian futures or with public needs for clarity, heroes and villains. Such a history is one that tells us most about the past and about ourselves. It is one that repays examination, but it can leave one with the stigma of Cassandra. For the individual, as for the nation, experience must be clearly and fully understood and built upon to ensure a better future. If we delude ourselves about the lessons of past events, we will not avoid the pitfalls of the past, or secure its successes, in the future. Indeed, an intelligent scepticism in predicting the future is the most pertinent lesson from the consideration of the past. As such, the informed study of history is a useful antidote to the all-too-often glib assumptions and predictions of politicians and journalists. Those who care nothing for the past will look sightlessly to the future.

SELECTED FURTHER READING

There is an extensive literature on this subject, and this brief list restricts itself to books published since 2000. Earlier works should be approached through the bibliographies and footnotes in these books.

Black, J., *Using History* (London, 2005).

De Baets, A., *Censorship of Historical Thought: A World Guide, 1945–2000* (Westport, Conn., 2002).

Bucur, M. and N. Wingfield (eds), *Staging the Past: The Politics of Commemoration in Habsburg Central Europe, 1848 to the Present* (West Lafayette, Ind., 2001).

Burrow, J., *A History of Histories: Epics, Chronicles, Romances and Inquiries from Herodotus and Thucydides to the Twentieth Century* (London, 2007).

Eriksonas, L., *National Heroes and National Identities: Scotland, Norway and Lithuania* (Brussels, 2004).

Fuchs, E. and B. Stuchtey (eds), *Across Cultural Borders: Historiography in Global Perspective* (Lanham, Md., 2002).

Gaddis, J.L., *The Landscape of History: How Historians Map the Past* (Oxford, 2003).

Grimsted, P., *Trophies of War and Empire: The Archival Heritage of Ukraine, World War II, and the International Politics of Restitution* (Cambridge, Mass., 2001).

Hobsbawm, E., *On History* (London, 2002).

Jager, S.M. and R. Mitter (eds), *Ruptured Histories: War, Memory, and the Post-Cold War in Asia* (Cambridge, Mass., 2007).

Mandler, P., *History and National Life* (London, 2002).

Powers, J., *History as Propaganda: Tibetan Exiles versus The People's Republic of China* (Oxford, 2004).

Restall, M., *Seven Myths of the Spanish Conquest* (Oxford, 2003).

Revel, J. and G. Levi (eds), *Political Uses of the Past: The Recent Mediterranean Experience* (London, 2002).

Rüsen, J. (ed.), *Western Historical Thinking: An Intercultural Debate* (Oxford, 2002).

Schivelbiesch, W., *The Culture of Defeat: On National Trauma, Mourning, and Recovery* (London, 2003).

Snyder, T., *The Reconstruction of Nations: Poland, Ukraine, Lithuania, Belarus, 1569–1999* (New Haven, Conn., 2003).

Stuchtey, B. and E. Fuchs (eds), *Writing World History 1800–2000* (Oxford, 2003).

NOTES

PREFACE

1 J. Black, *Convergence or Divergence? Britain and the Continent* (Basingstoke, 1994), p. 270.

1 INTRODUCTION: ACADEMIC AND PUBLIC HISTORIES

1 P. Lenihan, *The Battle of the Boyne* (Stroud, 2003).

2 G. Maurer, *Spanish Paintings* (Stockholm, 2001), catalogue, raisonné of paintings in the Nationalmuseum, cat. no. 6, pp. 54–9, NM. 5593. There is an earlier oil sketch in the Boston Museum of Fine Art, entitled *Time, Truth and History*, with the figures undraped, which dates from 1797 to 1800.

3 C.A. Whatley, *The Scots and the Union* (Edinburgh, 2006), pp. xiv–xv.

4 P.J. Corfield, *Time and the Shape of History* (New Haven, Conn., 2007).

5 J.E. Lendon, *Soldiers and Ghosts: A History of Battle in Classical Antiquity* (New Haven, Conn., 2005).

6 P. Conisbee, *Painting in Eighteenth-Century France* (London, 1981).

7 G. Dawson, *Soldier Heroes: British Adventure, Empire and the Imagining of Masculinities* (London, 1994).

8 K.E. Hendrickson, 'The Big Problem with History: Christianity and the Crisis of Meaning', *Historically Speaking*, 7 (2006), pp. 25–7.

9 S. Fitzpatrick, 'The Soviet Union in the Twenty-First Century', *Journal of European Studies*, 37 (2007), p. 53. For the tendency to draw on appeasement and the Munich Agreement for lessons, *Munich 1938: mythes et réalités* (Paris, 1979); D. Chuter, 'Munich, or the Blood of Others', in C. Buffet and B. Heuser (eds), *Haunted by History: Myths in International Relations* (Oxford, 1998), pp. 65–79.

10 M. Bentley, *Modernizing England's Past: English Historiography in the Age of Modernism 1870–1970* (Cambridge, 2006);

E. Breisach, *On the Future of History: The Postmodernist Challenge and Its Aftermath* (Chicago, Ill., 2003).

11 B. Klein, *On the Uses of History in Recent Irish Writing* (Manchester, 2007), pp. 6–7.

12 A. Curthoys and J. Docker, *Is History Fiction?* (Sydney, 2006), pp. 232, 234.

13 See <http://www.mala.bc.ca/history/letters>.

14 R. Samuel, *Theatres of Memory I: Past and Present in Contemporary Culture* (London, 1994).

15 J. Winter, 'The Generation of Memory: Reflections on the "Memory Boom" in Contemporary Historical Studies', *Bulletin of the German Historical Institute, Washington*, 27 (2006), pp. 69–92.

16 G. Beiner, *Remembering the Year of the French: Irish Folk History and Social Memory* (Madison, Wisc., 2007). For the recent situation, see pp. 325–34.

17 Stadial theories propound historical development through distinct stages.

18 E. Fox-Genovese and E. Lasch-Quinn (eds), *Reconstructing History: The Emergence of a New Historical Society* (London, 1999).

19 M. Lyons and P. Russell (eds), *Australia's History: Themes and Debates* (Sydney, 2005).

20 R.J. Aldrich, 'Never-Never Land and Wonderland? British and American Policy on Intelligence Archives', *Contemporary Record*, 8 (summer 1994), p. 143; S. Ellis, 'US Presidential Libraries: the Culture and Reality of the Freedom of Information Act', *Archives*, 25 (2000), p. 149.

21 C.U. Uche, 'A Threat to Historical Research', *Archives*, 25 (2000), pp. 136–40.

2 NATIONALISM AND THE CURSE OF HISTORY

1 A. Roshwald, *The Endurance of Nationalism: Ancient Roots and Modern Dilemmas* (Cambridge, 2006).

2 T. Turville-Petre, *England the Nation: Language, Literature and National Identity, 1290–1340* (Oxford, 1996).

3 A. Smith, *Chosen Peoples: Sacred Sources of National Identity* (Oxford, 2003).

4 W.B. Smith, 'Germanic Pagan Antiquity in Lutheran Historical Thought', *Journal of the Historical Society*, 4 (2004), p. 357.

5 P.M. Soergel, *Wondrous in his Saints: Counter-Reformation Propaganda in Bavaria* (Berkeley, Calif., 1993).

6 D.R. Woolf, *Reading History in Early Modern England* (Cambridge, 2000).

7 B.T. Whitehead, *Braggs and Boasts: Propaganda in the Year of the Armada* (Stroud, 1994).

8 G. Dipple, *'Just as in the Time of the Apostles': Uses of History in the Radical Reformation* (Kitchener, Ontario, 2005).

9 I. Fenlon, *The Ceremonial City: History, Memory and Myth in Renaissance Venice* (New Haven, Conn., 2007).

10 D.A. Bell, *The Cult of the Nation in France: Inventing Nationalism, 1680–1800* (Cambridge, Mass., 2001).

11 V. Lange, *The Classical Age of German Literature* (London, 1982), p. 50.

12 D. Blackbourn, 'New Legislatures: Germany, 1871–1914', *Historical Research*, 65 (1992), pp. 201–14.

13 T. Baycroft and M. Hewitson (eds), *What Is a Nation? Europe, 1789–1914* (Oxford, 2006).

14 P. Alter, 'Symbols of Irish Nationalism', *Studia Hibernica*, 14 (1974), pp. 104–23; C. Jelavich, 'Nationalism as Reflected in the Textbooks of the South Slavs in the Nineteenth Century', *Canadian Review of Studies in Nationalism*, 16 (1989), pp. 15–34.

15 L. Riall, *Garibaldi: Invention of a Hero* (New Haven, Conn., 2007).

16 K. Cramer, *The Thirty Years' War and German Memory in the Nineteenth Century* (Lawrence, Nebr., 2007); C. Clark, *The Iron Kingdom: The Rise and Downfall of Prussia, 1600–1947* (London, 2006).

17 D. Deletant and H. Hanak (eds), *Historians as Nation Builders: Central and South-East Europe* (Basingstoke, 1988); M. Branch (ed.), *National History and Identity: Approaches to the Writing of National History in the North East Baltic Region. Nineteenth and Twentieth Centuries* (Helsinki, 1999); D. Fewster, *Visions of Past Glory: Nationalism and the Construction of Early Finnish History* (Helsinki, 2006).

18 M. Fulbrook (ed.), *National Histories and European History* (London, 1993).

19 P.M. Dabrowski, *Commemorations and the Shaping of Modern Poland* (Bloomington, Ind., 2004). For the academic dimension, P. Brock, J.D. Stanley and P.J. Wróbel (eds), *Nation and History: Polish Historians from the Enlightenment to the Second World War* (Toronto, 2006).

20 I. Porciani, 'Mapping Institutions, Comparing Historiographies: The Making of a European Atlas', *Storia della Storiografia*, 50 (2006), pp. 48, 52.

21 J. Tollebeek, 'Historical Representation and the Nation State in Romantic Belgium, 1830–50', *Journal of the History of Ideas*, 59 (1998), pp. 329–53; A. Liakos, 'The Construction of National Time: The Making of the Modern Greek Historical Imagination', *Mediterranean Historical Review*, 16 (2001), pp. 27–42; O. Zimmer, *A Contested Nation: History, Memory and Nationalism in Switzerland, 1761–1891* (Cambridge, 2003).

22 W. Clark, *Academic Charisma and the Origins of the Research University* (Chicago, Ill., 2006).

23 W. Laqueur and G.L. Mosse (eds), *Historians in Politics* (London, 1974).

24 P.J. Geary, *The Myth of Nations: The Medieval Origins of Europe* (Princeton, NJ, 2002).

25 T. Lang, *The Victorians and the Stuart Heritage: Interpretations of a Discordant Past* (Cambridge, 1995).

26 N.M. Heimann, *Joan of Arc in French Art and Culture (1700–1855): From Satire to Sanctity* (Aldershot, 2005).

27 E. Siberry, *The New Crusaders: Images of the Crusades in the Nineteenth and Early Twentieth Centuries* (Aldershot, 2000).

28 J. Parker, *'England's Darling': The Victorian Cult of Alfred the Great* (Manchester, 2007), pp. 1–18.

29 E. Weber, *Peasants into Frenchmen: The Modernization of Rural France, 1870–1914* (Stanford, Calif., 1976), though see T. Baycroft, 'Peasants into Frenchmen? The Case of the Flemish in the North of France, 1860–1914', *European Review of History*, 2 (1995), pp. 31–44; A. Green, *Fatherlands: State Building and Nationhood in Nineteenth-Century Germany* (Cambridge, 2001).

30 J.R. Fears (ed.), *Selected Writings of Lord Acton* (3 vols, Indianapolis, Ind., 1986) Vol. I, p. 432.

31 Fears, *Selected Writings of Lord Acton*, Vol. I, pp. 177–82.

32 E.M. Spiers, 'Army Organisation and Society in the Nineteenth Century', in T. Bartlett and K. Jeffery (eds), *A Military History of Ireland* (Cambridge, 1996), p. 335.

33 C. Kidd, *Subverting Scotland's Past: Scottish Whig Historians and the Creation of an Anglo-British Identity, 1689–c.1830* (Cambridge, 1993).

34 M. Alexander, *Medievalism: The Middle Ages in Modern England*

(New Haven, Conn., 2007); A.J. Frantzen, *Bloody Good: Chivalry, Sacrifice, and the Great War* (Chicago, Ill., 2004).

35 R.S. Wortman, '"Invisible Threads": The Historical Imagery of the Romanov Tercentenary', *Russian History*, 16 (1989), pp. 389–408.

36 For the changeable nature of national character, P. Mandler, *The English National Character: The History of an Idea from Edmund Burke to Tony Blair* (New Haven, Conn., 2006).

37 J.R. Collis, *The Celts: Origins, Myths and Inventions* (Stroud, 2003).

38 C. Clark, 'The Wars of Liberation in Prussian Memory: Reflections on the Memorialization of War in Early Nineteenth-Century Germany', *Journal of Modern History*, 68 (1996), pp. 550–76.

39 J. Vidmar, *English Catholic Historians and the English Reformation, 1585–1954* (Brighton, 2005).

40 L. Scales and O. Zimmer (eds), *Power and the Nation in European History* (Cambridge, 2005).

41 D. Goy-Blanquet (ed.), *Joan of Arc, a Saint for all Seasons: Studies in Myth and Politics* (Aldershot, 2003); B. Melman, *The Culture of History: English Uses of the Past 1800–1953* (Oxford, 2006), especially pp. 10–12.

42 A. Mombauer, *Helmuth von Moltke and the Origins of the First World War* (Cambridge, 2001).

43 B. Bond, *The Unquiet Western Front: Britain's Role in Literature and History* (Cambridge, 2002).

44 J.S.K. Watson, *Fighting Different Wars: Experience, Memory, and the First World War in Britain* (Cambridge, 2004), e.g., p. 311.

45 J. Winter, *Remembering War: The Great War between Memory and History in the Twentieth Century* (New Haven, Conn., 2006).

46 S. Howe, *Ireland and Empire: Colonial Legacies in Irish History and Culture* (Oxford, 2000).

47 A. Dolan, *Commemorating the Irish Civil War: History and Memory, 1923–2000* (Cambridge, 2003).

48 T. Denman, *Ireland's Unknown Soldiers: The 16th (Irish) Division in the Great War* (Blackrock, 1992).

49 J. Black, *The Slave Trade* (London, 2006).

50 D. Fewster, *Visions of Past Glory: Nationalism and the Construction of Early Finnish History* (Helsinki, 2006).

51 M. Lasansky, *The Renaissance Perfected: Architecture, Spectacle and Tourism in Fascist Italy* (College Park, 2005).

52 C. Fogu, *The Historic Imaginary: Politics of History in Fascist Italy* (Toronto, 2003).

53 P. Palumbo (ed.), *A Place in the Sun: Africa in Italian Colonial Culture from Post-Unification to the Present* (Berkeley, Calif., 2003).

54 D. Welch, *Propaganda and the German Cinema, 1933–45* (London, 2001).

55 A. McClellan, *Inventing the Louvre: Art, Politics, and the Origins of the Modern Museum in Eighteenth-Century Paris* (Cambridge, 1994).

56 The Jagiellonian dynasty ruled Poland from 1386 to 1572 as part of a federation including Lithuania.

57 S. Plokhy, *Unmasking Imperial Russia: Mykhailo Hrushevsky and the Writing of Ukrainian History* (Toronto, 2005).

58 J. Marozzi, *Tamerlane* (London, 2004), p. 172.

59 For the wider perspective, M. Poe, *The Russian Moment in World History* (Princeton, NJ, 2004).

60 E. Katz, 'Memory at the Front: The Struggle over Revolutionary Commemoration in Occupied France, 1940–44', *Journal of European Studies*, 35 (2005), pp. 153–68.

61 M. Perrie, *The Cult of Ivan the Terrible in Stalin's Russia* (Basingstoke, 2001).

62 S. Yekelchyk, *Stalin's Empire of Memory: Russian–Ukrainian Relations in the Soviet Historical Imagination* (Toronto, 2004).

63 P.R. Magocsi and I. Pop (eds), *The Encyclopaedia of Rusyn History and Culture* (Toronto, 2002).

64 P. Kenney, 'After the Blank Spots Are Filled: Recent Perspectives on Modern Poland', *Journal of Modern History*, 79 (2007), pp. 753–4.

65 D. Bodde, *China's First Unifier* (Leiden, 1938).

3   HISTORY WARS AND MULTIPLE PASTS

1 H.R. Southworth, *Guernica! Guernica! A Study of Journalism, Propaganda and History* (Berkeley, Calif., 1977); N. Rankin, *Telegram from Guernica: The Extraordinary Life of George Steer, War Correspondent* (London, 2003).

2 R. Stradling, 'Moaist Revolution and the Spanish Civil War: "Revisionist" History and Historical Politics', *English Historical Review*, 122 (2007), pp. 422–57. I have also benefited from hearing a paper by Tim Rees delivered to the Exeter branch of the Historical Association.

3 For an attack on what is claimed to be a Republican bias in the historiography, R. Stradling, *Your Children Will Be Next: Bombing and Propaganda in the Spanish Civil War, 1936–9* (Cardiff, 2008).

4 G. Orwell, 'Looking Back on the Spanish War', in *England Your England and Other Essays* (London, 1953).

5 T. Akçam, *A Shameful Act: The Armenian Genocide and the Question of Turkish Responsibility* (London, 2007), p. xxi.

6 New York, 2006, London 2007, translation of Turkish work of 1999.

7 The naming of the region is itself a matter of contention.

8 For a recent guide to the extensive literature, T. Yoshida, *The Making of the 'Rape of Nanking': History and Memory in Japan, China, and the United States* (Oxford, 2006).

9 G. Hicks, *The Comfort Women: Japan's Brutal Regime of Enforced Prostitution in the Second World War* (New York, 1994); Y. Tanaka, *Japan's Comfort Women: Sexual Slavery and Prostitution during World War II and the US Occupation* (London, 2002).

10 F.R. Dickinson, 'Crumbling Pillars of the U.S.–Japan Security Alliance', *Orbis*, 45 (2001), pp. 637–42.

11 For a recent example, JapanFocus newletter, <http://www. japanfocus.org> for 16 July 2007, article by David McNeill.

12 F. Seraphim, *War Memory and Social Politics in Japan, 1945–2005* (Cambridge, Mass., 2006).

13 S.M. Jager and R. Mitter, 'Introduction' to their (as editors), *Ruptured Histories: War, Memory, and the Post-Cold War in Asia* (Cambridge, Mass., 2007), p. 2. See also G.W. Gong (ed.), *Memory and History in East and Southeast Asia: Issues of Identity in International Relations* (Washington, DC, 2001).

14 B. Coward and J. Swann (eds), *Conspiracies and Conspiracy Theory in Early Modern Europe: From the Waldensians to the French Revolution* (Aldershot, 2004).

4   NEW STATES AND THE POSSIBILITIES OF LINEAGE

1 The Jabhat al-Tahrir al-Watani (National Liberation Front) is known by its French acronym FLN, from Front de Libération Nationale.

2 H.T.H. Tai (ed.), *The Country of Memory: Remaking the Past in Late Socialist Vietnam* (Berkeley, Calif., 2001); C. Giebel, 'Revolution, War, and Memory in Contemporary Vietnam',

in S.M. Jager and R. Mitter (eds), *Ruptured Histories: War, Memory, and the Post-Cold War in Asia* (Cambridge, Mass., 2007), pp. 307–21.

3 Contrast P. Chatterjee, *The Nation and Its Fragments: Colonial and Postcolonial Histories* (Princeton, NJ, 1993) with V. Chaturvedi (ed.), *Mapping Subaltern Studies and the Postcolonial* (London, 2000).

4 A.T. Embree (ed.), *1857 in India: Mutiny or War of Independence?* (Boston, Mass., 1963). Among the important recent works that throw light on the social dynamics, T. Roy, *A Countryside in Revolt: Bulandshahr District, 1857* (Delhi, 1996).

5 K.A. Wagner, *Thuggee: Banditry and the British in Early Nineteenth-Century India* (Basingstoke, 2007), p. 228.

6 P. Chatterjee, 'History and the Nationalization of Hinduism', in V. Dalmia and H. von Stietencron (eds), *Representing Hinduism: The Construction of Religious Traditions and National Identity* (New Delhi, 1995); M. Misra, *Vishnu's Crowded Temple: India since the Great Rebellion* (London, 2007), p. 424.

7 C. Crow, 'Duel in the Crown', *History Today*, 57/12 (2007), p. 18.

8 A. Reid and D. Marr (eds), *Perceptions of the Past in Southeast Asia* (Singapore, 1979).

9 J. Black, *The Holocaust* (London, 2008).

10 M. Benvenisti, *Sacred Landscape: The Buried History of the Holy Land since 1948* (London, 2006).

11 E. Sivan, *Interpretations of Islam: Past and Present* (Princeton, NJ, 1985) cites, among other works, J. Yusuf, *Louis IX in the Middle East: The Palestine Problem in the Middle Ages* (Cairo, 1956), a work written in Arabic.

12 G.W. Rudd, 'The Israeli Revisionist Historians and the Arab–Israeli Conflict', *Journal of Military History*, 67 (2003), pp. 1263–70, 68 (2004), pp. 225–31.

13 P. Nobile (ed.), *Judgment at the Smithsonian* (New York, 1995); K. Bird and L. Lifschultz (eds), *Hiroshima's Shadow: Writings on the Denial of History and the Smithsonian Controversy* (Stony Creek, Conn., 1997); E.T. Linenthal and T Engelhardt (eds), *History Wars: The Enola Gay and Other Battles for the American Past* (New York, 1996); R.D. Newman, *Enola Gay and the Court of History* (New York, 2004).

14 S. Howe, 'The Politics of Historical "Revisionism": Comparing Ireland and Israel/Palestine', *Past and Present*, 168 (2000), pp. 225–53.

15 A. Groiss (ed.), *The West, Christians and Jews in Saudi Arabian Schoolbooks* (Jerusalem, 2003).

16 A. Lufti Al-Sayyid Marsot, *A History of Egypt* (2nd edn, Cambridge, 2007), p. ix.

17 G. Krüger, 'Coming to Terms with the Past', *German Historical Institute, Washington. Bulletin*, 37 (2005), p. 49.

18 L. Thompson, *The Political Mythology of Apartheid* (New Haven, Conn., 1985).

19 L.S. Graybill, *Truth and Reconciliation in South Africa: Miracle or Model?* (London, 2002); J.L. Gibson, *Overcoming Apartheid: Can Truth Reconcile a Divided Nation?* (Cape Town, 2004).

20 J. Bam and P. Visser, *A New History for a New South Africa* (Cape Town, 1996); A.E. Coombes, *History after Apartheid: Visual Culture and Public Memory in a Democratic South Africa* (Durham, Md., 2003); S. Jeppie (ed.), *Toward New Histories for South Africa: On the Place of the Past in Our Present* (Lansdowne, 2005).

21 For example, W. Nasson, *The South African War, 1899–1902* (London, 1999).

22 J.M. Gore, 'New Histories in a Post-Colonial Society: Transformation in South African Museums since 1994', *Historia*, 50 (2005), pp. 75–102; S. Marschall, 'Making Money with Memories: The Fusion of Heritage, Tourism and Identity Formation in South Africa', *Historia*, 50 (2005), pp. 103–22.

23 G. Verbeeck, 'Anachronism and the Rewriting of History: The South African Case', *Storia della Storiografia*, 49 (2006), pp. 88–9.

24 M. Monmonier, *From Squaw Tit to Whorehouse Meadow: How Maps Name, Claim, and Inflame* (Chicago, Ill., 2006).

25 M.K. Asante, *The History of Africa* (London, 2007), pp. 325–6.

26 D. Gavish, 'The British Efforts at Safeguarding the Land Records of Palestine in 1948', *Archives*, 22 (1996), pp. 107–20.

27 G. MacKenzie, 'Archives: The Global Picture', *Archives*, 24 (1999), p. 9.

28 J. Record, *Making War, Thinking History: Munich, Vietnam and Presidential Uses of Force from Korea to Kosovo* (Annapolis, Md., 2002).

29 A. Cinar, 'National History as a Contested Site: The Conquest of Istanbul and Islamist Negotiations of the Nations', *Comparative Studies in Society and History*, 43 (2001), pp. 364–91.

5 POST-COMMUNISM AND THE NEW HISTORY

1 'Identifying Histories: Eastern Europe before and after 1989', Special issue, *Representations*, 49 (1995); R.G. Suny, 'Constructing Primordialism: Old Histories for New Nations', *Journal of Modern History*, 73 (2001), pp. 862–96; U. Brunnbauer (ed.), *(Re-)Writing History: Historiography in Southeast Europe after Socialism* (Münster, 2004).

2 K. Brown, *The Past in Question: Modern Macedonia and the Uncertainties of Nation* (Princeton, NJ, 2003).

3 R. Ostow (ed.), *(Re)Visualizing National History: Museums and National Identities in Europe in the New Millennium* (Toronto, 2007).

4 J. Marozzi, *Tamerlane* (London, 2004), pp. 169–73, 421.

5 P.B. Henze, 'Dagestan in October 1997: Imam Shamil Lives!', *Caspian Crossroads* (winter–spring 2000), pp. 16–31.

6 R.J. Crampton, *Bulgaria* (Oxford, 2007), p. 411.

7 'German Institutes of Contemporary History: Interviews with the Directors', *German Historical Institute, Washington*, 38 (2006), pp. 69–70.

8 K. Pätzold, 'What New Start? The End of Historical Study in the GDR', *German History*, 10 (1992), pp. 392–404; G.A. Ritter, 'The Reconstruction of History at the Humboldt University: A Reply', *German History*, 11 (1993), pp. 339–45; A.S. Ernst, 'A Survey of Institutional Research on the GDR: Between "Investigative History" and Solid Research: The Reorganization of Historical Studies about the Former German Democratic Republic', *Central European History*, 28 (1995), pp. 373–95.

9 A.J. McAdams, *Judging the Past in Unified Germany* (Cambridge, 2001).

10 C. Gati, *Failed Illusions: Moscow, Washington, Budapest, and the 1956 Hungarian Revolt* (Stanford, Calif., 2006).

11 T. Judt, *Postwar: A History of Europe since 1945* (London, 2005), pp. 827–8.

12 P. Hatos, 'Kossuth and the Images of Hungarian Identity after 1989', *Hungarian Studies*, 16 (2002), pp. 225–36.

13 C.W. Hedrick, *History and Silence: Purge and Rehabilitation of Memory in Late Antiquity* (Austin, Tex., 2000); A.S. Marks, 'The Statue of King George III in New York and the Iconology of Regicide', *American Art Journal*, 13 (1981), pp. 61–82.

14 R. Brubaker, *Nationalism Reframed: Nationhood and the National Question in the New Europe* (Cambridge, 1996).

15 M. Todorova, 'The Mausoleum of Georgi Dimitrov as *Lieu de Mémoire*', *Journal of Modern History*, 78 (2006), pp. 377, 388, 401.

16 W. Bracewell, 'The End of Yugoslavia and New National Histories', *European History Quarterly*, 29 (1999), pp. 149–56; S.K. Pavlowitch, *Serbia: The History behind the Name* (London, 2002).

17 A. Solzhenitsyn, *Dvesti let vmeste, 1795–1995* (*Two Hundred Years Together, 1795–1995*) (Moscow, 2002).

18 L.A. Kirschenbaum, *The Legacy of the Siege of Leningrad, 1941–1995: Myth, Memories, and Monuments* (Cambridge, 2006), p. 284.

19 *Times Higher Education Supplement*, 18 November 2004, p. 11.

20 G. Sanford, *Katyn and the Soviet Massacre of 1940: Truth, Justice and Memory* (London, 2005).

21 R.W. Davies, *Soviet History in the Yeltsin Era* (Basingstoke, 1997). For an example of edited documents, O.V. Khlevniuk, *The History of the Gulag: From Collectivization to the Great Terror* (New Haven, Conn., 2004).

22 See also H. Kuromiya, *The Voices of the Dead: Stalin's Great Terror in the 1930s* (New Haven, Conn., 2007) and O. Figes, *The Whisperers: Private Life in Stalin's Russia* (London, 2007).

23 A. McEwen and E. Jocelyn, *The Long March: The True Story Behind the Legendary Journey that Made Mao's China* (London, 2006); S. Shuyun, *The Long March* (London, 2006).

24 J. Portal, *Art under Control in North Korea* (London, 2005).

25 T. Frank and F. Hadler, 'Overlapping National Histories: Confrontations and (Re-)Conciliations', *Storia della Storiografia*, 50 (2006), p. 130; K. Kazuhiko, 'The Continuing Legacy of Japanese Colonialism: The Japan-South Korea Joint Study Group on History Textbooks', in L. Hein and M. Selden (eds), *Censoring History: Citizenship and Memory in Japan, Germany, and the United States* (Armonk, NY, 2000).

26 T. Snyder, *The Reconstruction of Nations: Poland, Ukraine, Lithuania, Belarus, 1569–1999* (New Haven, Conn., 2003).

27 J. Horne and A. Kramer, *German Atrocities, 1914: A History of Denial* (New Haven, Conn., 2001).

28 L. Wolff, *Inventing Eastern Europe: The Map of Civilisation on the Mind of the Enlightenment* (Stanford, Calif., 1994).

29 D. Chirot (ed.), *The Origins of Backwardness in Eastern Europe: Economics and Politics from the Middle Ages until the Early Twentieth Century* (Berkeley, Calif., 1989).

30 J. Keane (ed.), *Civil Society and the State: New European Perspectives* (London, 1988), pp. 291–331; P. Hanák, 'Central Europe: A Historical Region in Modern Times: A Contribution to the Debate about the Regions of Europe', in G. Schöpflin and N. Wood (eds), *In Search of Central Europe* (Cambridge, 1989), pp. 57–69.

31 R.H. Wiebe, *Who We Are: A History of Popular Nationalism* (Princeton, NJ, 2002).

32 D. Northrup, 'Globalization and the Great Convergence: Rethinking World History in the Long Term', *Journal of World History*, 16 (2005), p. 266.

33 A.D. Smith, *The Nation in History: Historiographical Debates about Ethnicity and Nationalism* (Oxford, 2000).

6 BRITAIN, EUROPE AND THE FASHIONING OF MYTHS

1 I. Kershaw, *Hitler, 1936–1945: Nemesis* (London, 2000), pp. 821–2.

2 H. Schafer (ed.), *Zeit-Fragen: The Culture of European History in the 21st Century* (Bonn, 1999).

3 I have benefited from hearing a speech on this subject by the Patriarch of Constantinople.

4 N.A. Sørenson, 'Narrating the Second World War in Denmark since 1945', *Contemporary European History*, 14 (2005), pp. 295–315, and 'The Second World War and Continuity and Change in Danish History', in C.B. Christensen and A. Warring (eds), *Finland og Danmark: Krig og besaettelse 1939–45* (Roskilde, 2007), pp. 143–54.

5 P. Birnbaum, *The Idea of France* (New York, 2001).

6 D. Reid, 'Resistance and Its Discontents: Affairs, Archives, Avowals and the Aubracs', *Journal of Modern History*, 77 (2005), pp. 97–137.

7 See, for example, P. de Froment, *Un volontaire de la nuit dans l'enfer des camps Nazis* (Paris, 2005); O. Lalieu, *La Zone grise? La Résistance française à Buchenwald* (Paris, 2005).

8 C. Flood, 'The Politics of Counter-Memory on the French Extreme Right', *Journal of European Studies*, 35 (2005), pp. 221–36.

9 *Le Monde*, 23 November 2000.

10 J. Revel and L. Hunt (eds), *Histories: French Constructions of the Past* (New York, 1995); P. Nora, *Les Lieux de mémoire* (7 vols, Paris, 1984–92); N. Wood, 'Memory's Remains: *Les Lieux de mémoire*', *History and Memory*, 6 (1994), pp. 123–49.

11 F. Furet, *Interpreting the French Revolution* (Cambridge, 1981); S. Kaplan, *Farewell Revolution: The Historians' Feud, France 1789/1989* (London, 1995).

12 J. Klaits and M. Haltzel (eds), *The Global Ramifications of the French Revolution* (Cambridge, 1994).

13 J. Black, *The Holocaust* (London, 2008). The treatment of the Holocaust in post-war Germany is discussed in that book and not repeated here.

14 S. Berger, *Representations of the Past: The Making, Unmaking and Remaking of National Histories in Western Europe after 1945* (Pontypridd, 2002), pp. 5–6.

15 R.G. Moeller, *War Stories: The Search for a Usable Past in the Federal Republic of Germany* (Berkeley, Calif., 2001).

16 A. Schildt, 'The Long Shadows of the Second World War: The Impact of Experiences and Memories of War on West German Society', *German Historical Institute, London, Bulletin*, 29 (2007), pp. 29–31.

17 H. Heer, 'The Difficulty of Ending a War: Reactions to the Exhibition War of Extermination: Crimes of the Wehrmacht 1941 to 1944', *History Workshop Journal*, 46 (1998), pp. 187–203.

18 W. Kansteiner, *In Pursuit of German Memory: History, Television and Politics after Auschwitz* (Athens, Ohio, 2006).

19 F. Taylor, *Dresden: Tuesday, 13 February 1945* (London, 2004).

20 G. Schwan, 'Bridging the Oder', *Bulletin of the German Historical Institute, Washington*, 40 (2007), p. 46.

21 D. Barnouw, *The War in the Empty Air: Victims, Perpetrators, and Postwar Germans* (Bloomington, Ind., 2005).

22 S. Taberner and F. Finlay (eds), *Recasting German Identity: Culture, Politics and Literature in the Berlin Republic* (Woodbridge, 2002).

23 R. De Felice, *Fascism: An Informal Introduction to its Theory and Practice* (New Brunswick, NJ, 1977); B. Painter, 'Renzo De Felice and the Historiography of Italian Fascism', *American Historical Review*, 95 (1990), pp. 391–405; N. Zapponi, 'Fascism in Italian Historiography, 1986–93: A Fading National Identity', *Journal of Contemporary History*, 29 (1994), pp. 547–68.

24 A.M. Torriglia, *Broken Time, Fragmented Space: A Cultural Map for Postwar Italy* (Toronto, 2002).

25 P. Ballinger, *History in Exile: Memory and Identity at the Borders of the Balkans* (Princeton, NJ, 2003).

26 For a balanced recent account, P. Morgan, *The Fall of Mussolini:*

Italy, the Italians, and the Second World War (Oxford, 2007). On the treatment of Italy's Jews, M. Sarfatti, *The Jews in Mussolini's Italy: From Equality to Persecution* (Madison, Wisc., 2006).

27 R. Collins, *Visigothic Spain, 409–711* (Oxford, 2004), pp. 1–3.

28 R. Fletcher, *The Quest for El Cid* (New York, 1990).

29 J.M. Regan, 'Michael Collins, General Commander-in-Chief, as a Historiographical Problem', *History*, 92 (2007), pp. 318–46. For a recent Republican view, M. Ryan, 'The Kilmichael Ambush, 1920: Exploring the "Provocative Chapters"', *History*, 92 (2007), pp. 235–49.

30 C. Brady (ed.), *Interpreting Irish History: The Debate on Historical Revisionism* (Dublin, 1994); D. Ferriter, *The Transformation of Ireland, 1900–2000* (London, 2004), pp. 22–3, 531, 747–51.

31 For the strength of public myths, T.W. Moody, 'Irish History and Irish Mythology', *Hermathena* (1978–9), pp. 7–25, and R. Foster, *The Irish Story: Telling Tales and Making It Up in Ireland* (Oxford, 2002). For the failure to note IRA outrages, T.P. Coogan, *Wherever Green Is Worn: The Story of the Irish Diaspora* (London, 2001).

32 A. Jackson, 'Unionist Myths, 1912–85', *Past and Present*, 136 (1992), pp. 164–85; A. O'Day and N. Fleming, *The Palgrave Companion to Northern Irish History* (Basingstoke, 2005).

33 T.M. Devine, *The Scottish Nation, 1700–2000* (London, 1999).

34 M. Fry, *The Union: England, Scotland and the Treaty of 1707* (Edinburgh, 2007).

35 G.K. Behlmer and F.M. Leventhal (eds), *Singular Continuities: Tradition, Nostalgia, and Identity in Modern British Culture* (Stanford, Calif., 2000).

36 K. Robbins, *History, Religion and Identity in Modern Britain* (London, 1993).

37 For example, M. Houlbrook, *Queer London: Perils and Pleasures in the Sexual Metropolis, 1918–57* (Chicago, Ill., 2005).

38 M. Fisher, 'The Nation's Archives: Promoting an Understanding of Our Cultural Heritage', Maurice Bond Memorial Lecture, 2 December 1997, published in *Archives*, 24 (1999), p. 5.

39 T. Hunt, 'Elgar and Empire', Radio 3, 3 June 2007. Elgar (1857–1934) was Catholic and his sister was a prominent religious leader, which throws interesting light on the relationship between Catholicism and imperialism by this period.

40 For a critical account that received wide attention, P. Brendon, *The Decline and Fall of the British Empire* (London, 2007). Much of

the criticism has lacked adequate contextualisation.

41 J.C.D. Clark, *Our Shadowed Present: Modernism, Postmodernism and History* (London, 2003), pp. 89–109.

42 For a far from complete list, K. Robbins, *Great Britain: Identities, Institutions and the Idea of Britishness* (London, 1998); R. Colls, *The Identity of England* (Oxford, 2002).

43 *Today* programme, 12 May 2007.

44 P. Mandler, report for Royal Historical Society on Historical Association A-Level Forum, 10 September 1999, *History and National Life* (London, 2002), p. 133, 'La responsabilidad del historiador', *Alcores: Revista de Historia Contemporanea*, 1 (2006), pp. 47–61, and 'The Responsibility of the Historian', in H. Jones, K. Östberg and N. Randeraad (eds), *History on Trial: The Public Use of Contemporary History in Europe since 1989* (Manchester, 2007), pp. 12–26.

7 THE HISTORICAL DIMENSION OF MANIFEST DESTINY

1 J. Lepore, 'Our Town', *New Yorker*, 2 April 2007, p. 45.

2 T. Gitlin, *The Twilight of Common Dreams: Why America is Wracked by Culture Wars* (New York, 1995).

3 W.F. Brundage, *The Southern Past: A Clash of Race and Memory* (Cambridge, Mass., 2005).

4 P. Jenkins, *A History of the United States* (3rd edn, 2007), pp. x, 302–6.

5 G. Himmelfarb, 'Some Reflections on the New History', *American Historical Review*, 94 (1989), pp. 663–4; A.M. Schlesinger, *The Disunity of America* (New York, 1992); R. Lerner, A.K. Nagai and S. Rothman, *Molding the Good Citizen: The Politics of High School History Texts* (Westport, Conn., 1995); S.P. Huntington, *Who Are We? The Challenges to America's National Identity* (New York, 2004), pp. 174–7.

6 C. Crabtree and G.B. Nash, National Center for History in the Schools, *National Standards for World History: Exploring Paths in the Present* and *National Standards for United States History: Exploring the American Experience* (Los Angeles, Calif., 1994); G.B. Nash, C. Crabtree and R.E. Dunn, *History on Trial: Culture Wars and the Teaching of the Past* (New York, 1997), see also the perceptive review by S. Wilentz in the *New York Times*, 30 November 1997. For a critical view, J.P. Diggins, 'The National History Standards', in E. Fox-Genovese and E. Lasch-Quinn (eds), *Reconstructing History: The Emergence of a New*

Historical Society (London, 1999), pp. 253–75.

7 P.C. Hoffer, *Past Imperfect: Factions, Fictions, Fraud – American History from Bancroft and Parkman to Ambrose, Bellesiles, Ellis and Goodwin* (New York, 2004); J. Wiener, *Historians in Trouble: Plagiarism, Fraud and Politics in the Ivory Tower* (New York, 2004). For a regional example of bellicosity, W.E. Lee, *Crowds and Soldiers in Revolutionary North Carolina: The Culture of Violence in Riot and War* (Gainesville, Fla., 2001).

8 For a critique by Bellesiles, in line with academic scholarship, of the 'fabulous fables' and 'useful lies' central to the memorialisation of the War of 1812, 'Experiencing the War of 1812', in J. Flavell and S. Conway (eds), *Britain and America Go to War: The Impact of War and Warfare in Anglo-America, 1754–1815* (Gainesville, Fla., 2004), p. 230.

9 J.E. Haynes and H. Klehr, *In Denial* (2005).

10 J. Carter, *The Hornet's Nest* (New York, 2003), p. 465.

11 C.L. Bushman, *America Discovers Columbus: How an Italian Explorer Became an American Hero* (Hanover, NH, 1992); F. Fernández-Armesto, 'Columbus: Hero or Villain?', *History Today* (May, 1992). Reprinted in D. Snowman (ed.), *PastMasters* (London, 2001), pp. 366–74.

12 For blaming genocide, without evidence, on nineteenth-century capitalism, A. Trahtenberg, *Shades of Hiawatha: Staging Indians, Making Americans, 1880–1930* (New York, 2004).

13 M.L. Anderson, '"Down in Turkey, Far Away": Human Rights, the Armenian Massacres, and Orientalism in Wilhelmine Germany', *Journal of Modern History*, 79 (2007), p. 109.

14 For a German perspective, P. Bender, 'America: The New Roman Empire?', *Orbis*, 47 (2003), pp. 145–59.

15 A.J. Bacevich, *American Empire: The Realities and Consequences of US Diplomacy* (Cambridge, Mass., 2002); C. Johnson, *Blowback: The Costs and Consequences of American Empire* (New York, 2004); C.S. Maier, *Among Empires: American Ascendancy and its Predecessors* (Cambridge, Mass., 2006).

16 Interview in *Emel* (2007), available at <http://www.timesonline. co.uk/faith>.

17 E.S. Rosenberg, 'Bursting America's Imperial Bubble', *The Chronicle of Higher Education*, 3 November 2006, Section B, p. 12.

18 B. Atwood, *Telling the Truth about Aboriginal History* (London, 2005).

19 L. Ryan, 'Risdon Cove and the Massacre of 3 May 1804: Their

Place in Tasmanian History', *Tasmanian Historical Studies*, 9 (2004), pp. 107–23.

20 K. Windschuttle, 'How Not to Run a Museum: People's History at the Postmodern Museum', *Quadrant*, September 2001.

21 N. Levi, '"No Sensible Comparison"? The Place of the Holocaust in Australia's History Wars', *History and Memory*, 19 (2007), p. 132.

22 L. Ryan, *Aboriginal Tasmanians* (Sydney, 1996); H. Reynolds, *An Indelible Stain?* (Melbourne, 2001).

23 S. Macintyre and A. Clark, *The History Wars* (Melbourne, 2003).

24 M. McKinnon with B. Bradley and R. Kirkpatrick (eds), *New Zealand Historical Atlas: Visualising New Zealand [Ko Papatuanuku e Takoto Nei]* (Auckland, 1997), pp. 12-13.

25 See <http://www.teara.govt.nz>.

26 The *Dictionary of New Zealand Biography* is available on-line at <http://www.dnzb.govt.nz>.

27 A. Sharp and P. McHugh, *Histories of Power and Loss* (Wellington, 2001); G. Byrnes, *Waitangi Tribunal and New Zealand History* (Oxford, 2004); M. Belgrave, *Historical Frictions* (Auckland, 2004).

28 McKinnon, *New Zealand Historical Atlas*, p. 13.

29 However, there is extensive coverage in many museums such as the city one in Vancouver.

30 M.B. Taylor and D. Outram (eds), *Canadian History: A Reader's Guide* (2 vols, Toronto, 1994).

31 For example, P.A. Buckner and J.G. Reid (eds), *The Atlantic Region to Confederation* (Toronto, 1994).

32 J. Fonte, 'Liberal Democracy vs. Transnational Progressivism: The Ideological War Within the West', *Orbis*, 46 (2002), pp. 449–67, esp. 465–7.

8 CONCLUSION: THE WEIGHT OF HISTORY

1 F. Nietzsche, 'On the Uses and Disadvantages of History for Life,' in F. Nietzsche, *Untimely Meditations*, trans. R.J. Hollingdale (Cambridge, 1983), pp. 57–123.

2 F. Nietzsche, *On the Genealogy of Morals*, trans. W. Kaufmann and Hollingdale (New York, 1969), pp. 57–8.

3 H. White, 'The Burden of History,' in H. White, *Tropics of Discourse: Essays in Cultural Criticism* (Baltimore, Md., 1978), pp. 27–50.

4 Hawthorne to Henry Addington, Viscount Sidmouth, former

Prime Minister, 17 July 1807, Exeter, Devon Record Office, 152 M/C 1807/OI8.

5 E. Peters, 'The *Firanj* Are Coming – Again,' *Orbis*, 48 (2004), p. 4.

6 J. Black, *The Slave Trade* (London, 2006).

7 D. Mattingly, *An Imperial Possession: Britain in the Roman Empire* (London, 2006). For the more benign Victorian view, V. Hoselitz, *Imagining Roman Britain: Victorian Responses to a Roman Past* (Woodbridge, 2007).

8 R.J. Granieri, 'Telling It Like It Isn't', *Alternate History and International History*, 29 (2007), p. 343. For the value of such history, R. Lebow, P. Tetlock and G. Parker (eds), *Unmaking the West: Alternative Histories of Counterfactual Worlds* (Ann Arbor, Mich., 2005), and for a different view, R.J. Evans, 'Telling It Like It Wasn't', *Historically Speaking*, 5 (4), March 2004, pp. 11–14, criticising N. Ferguson (ed.), *Virtual History: Alternatives and Counterfactuals* (London, 1997).

9 M.A. Finocchiaro, *Retrying Galileo, 1633–1992* (Berkeley, Calif., 2005).

10 J. Spencer, *Sri Lanka: History and the Roots of Conflict* (London, 1990).

11 For an argument that the history of genocide provides an opportunity for prediction and, thus, prevention, B. Kiernan, *Blood and Soil: A World History of Genocide and Extermination from Sparta to Darfur* (New Haven, Conn., 2007).